CONTENTS

PART I
MY ESCAPE FROM AN ARAB MARRIAGE

PART II
OTHER WOMEN'S STORIES

PART III
RECOMMENDATIONS

DEDICATION

To My Mother

Who was my Rock of Gibraltar when it counted,

To every woman fortunate enough

To have escaped marriage to an Arab/Muslim,

and

To all women and girls everywhere who have yet

To escape the living hell

Of Arab/Muslim male dominance, oppression, and torture

ACKNOWLEDGEMENTS

A S MUCH AS I would like to acknowledge the following individuals by name, I have chosen not to do so in order to protect their personal safety, anonymity, and privacy. It would be unconscionable to risk their being subjected to possible pursuit and injury or death by militant Islamists who do not want knowledge about their dangerous intentions and behavior patterns to become available to the general public in the United States.

* * *

First, I would like acknowledge the constant interest and support of my roommate during the entire process of creating and publishing this book. It was not always easy when the content of my research haunted my days.

Second, I would like to acknowledge a very close associate of mine whose journalistic and editing skills were irreplaceable in the preparation of my manuscript and cutting down of extraneous verbiage so that it would be presentable to prospective publishers. Also invaluable were her consistent queries about how I was proceeding with finishing this project which kept me on track and focused. I am very grateful for her warm and genuine enthusiasm for the completion of this book.

Third, I could not have accomplished anything without the indispensable assistance of a wonderful librarian, CH, who almost invariably was able to locate and secure reference material I needed. Over time, we have become wonderful friends.

Fourth, a brilliant and talented friend, VT, whose skills with graphics were invaluable for the design of the dust cover. I am very grateful for his assistance.

Fifth, my publisher of wonderful supportiveness and patience I would like to acknowledge as being a mainstay as we worked together to forge my long manuscript into several books instead of just the one I originally envisaged.

PART I

MY ESCAPE FROM
AN ARAB MARRIAGE

CHAPTER 1

HEAR MY WORDS AND
THINK AGAIN

P ERHAPS YOU HAVE met a
dark-eyed, handsome, charming
student or business man from one of the Middle Eastern countries.
He is fun, sexy, spends money (perhaps a lot of money) on you,
he is very attentive, and makes you feel like a queen. Perhaps
you are beginning to think how wonderful a husband he would
make and what a nice life you would have together. Maybe he
has said that if you did get married, his family would love to meet
you and you are thinking how interesting it might be to visit the
country of his birth.

Or maybe one or two of your friends have been dating an
interesting Muslim male from Saudi Arabia, Iraq, Iran, Lebanon,
Morocco, Tunisia, India, Pakistan, the United Arab Emirates, Egypt,
Syria, Palestine, Kuwait, Sudan, Indonesia or any of the other
countries in the region. Perhaps one of the relationships has become
serious enough that discussions about marriage have taken place.

Perhaps they have talked about going to his country to meet his family after they are married.

*   *   *

I was married to an Arab national and soon found out that there is a dark side to Middle Eastern male friends where women are concerned which is a product of their upbringing and a deep-seated, integral part of their character. The entire Middle East has a documented history of secrecy, deception, and manipulation concerning women that no amount of Westernization will change. None of your Arab/Muslim acquaintances will ever tell you about this or allow you to see or experience it before you marry one of them. If you do marry a Muslim/Arab male, your life will change forever, especially if you have children. You will soon learn what it means to be terrified of your husband, especially if he is a Saudi who comes from the most radically conservative Islamic society in the Middle East. "Living happily ever after" will not occur for you and your children unless you are very, very careful to take every protective precaution possible.

*   *   *

If you are the parent or grandparent of a young woman on her way to college, and if you wish to protect her and her potential children from years of years of misery and danger in an Arab/ Muslim country where Westerners are hated, for the sake of that young woman you hold dear, *make sure she reads this book so that she knows how to protect herself.*

If you and/or any of your friends are not already involved with a man from the Middle East, the information in the following pages will help you draw informed conclusions about whether you wish to become acquainted with any Arab/Muslim man.

If you are dating a man from *any* Middle Eastern country, especially a Saudi male*, this book will help you learn what you need to watch out for. It is safer not to date any of them, but to be just friends you see at parties, in class, at work, or in group situations. As long as you are friends only, you will see the best side of them.

If you are have been dating an Arab/Muslim male, especially one from Saudi Arabia*, and you have become pregnant, *do not tell him you are pregnant.* You will learn in this book why you should not tell him you are pregnant and how you can prevent him from trying to take the child from you if you decide to keep it.

If you are considering marriage, especially to a Saudi male*, *delay the proceedings* until you have read through this book and know what you will surely encounter if you do become the wife of a Muslim/Arab.

If you or any of your friends have already married a Middle Eastern male, especially one from Saudi Arabia*, and if you value your personal safety and your freedom, *it is essential that you do not leave the United States or any other Western country where you are protected by laws and attitudes which are woman friendly.* This book will tell you what awaits you the instant you set foot inside a Middle Eastern country as the wife of a male from any society in this part of the world.

Relationships with Arab/Muslim males, especially from Saudi Arabia, are dangerous in the extreme.* An increasing number of these individuals come to the United States to find gullible American women to marry and to use to get a Green Card and/or citizenship so they can use their marriages as fronts while they work with terrorist groups.

*   **For your safety, stay as far away from Saudis as possible.** Women who married Saudi nationals and went with them to Saudi Arabia and took the children along are still trapped in Saudi Arabia, being subjected to total domination, torture, rape, slavery, and abuse from which they cannot escape because the Saudi government will not let them leave. Because of centuries of tradition, Saudis believe that they still have the right to enslave anyone. And they act out this belief daily by luring gullible young women into marriage as well as abducting women and children onto planes for Saudi Arabia, taking them to their country, never to escape.

There is much documentation that, during the last decade, a great many students from the Kingdom have been heavily involved in al-Saud funded Islamist terrorist activities with the undermining of American society as we know it and the Islamization of the United States as their ultimate goal.

For those women thinking about becoming involved with Arab/Muslim males, there is a wonderful website called "Loving a Muslim" (www.domini.org) which has been formed to be a support group for women who are involved with Muslim men and who need moral support, answers to questions, advice about how to cope, or more information about the complexities of life with Muslim males. If you cannot access it directly for some reason, go to www.faithfreedom.org, click on "Links" in the side panel, scroll until you find the "Loving a Muslim" link, and click on it.

What follows is the story of my marriage to an Arab and those of other women who made the same mistake in good faith, believing that their husbands would continue to treat them as intelligent, well educated, beautiful, and valued individuals in their own right.

*   *   *

Chapter 2

Beginnings

(The family names in this narrative have been changed
to protect the privacy of the individuals mentioned.)

I CANNOT REMEMBER the first time I met Jamal abu Ahmed. The first day he registered himself on my consciousness was on a summer afternoon when he showed up, unannounced, at the front door of the boarding house in the University District where I was staying.

I was alone in the boarding house when I heard the doorbell ring. When I answered it, I opened the door to find standing in front of me a short, dark man with straight black hair cut very short, butch haircut style. He had on a light brown corduroy jacket which fell to mid thigh, making him look even shorter.

"Can I help you?" I asked carefully. "If you are looking for someone in particular, I am the only one here at the moment. However, I can take a message and make sure the right person gets it."

"Hi there. I came to see you," he replied. "Don't you remember? We met on campus a week or so ago."

I looked at him blankly because he was, as far as I could remember, a total stranger.

"I'm sorry," I said. "I don't remember meeting you, but it is possible that I ran into you for a second in the student lounge. What is your name?"

"It was only a couple of weeks ago." he insisted. "My name is Jamal. What is yours?" he asked flashing me a large, electric smile.

Against my better judgment, I answered. I couldn't see any real harm in at least being polite. However, I did not ask him to step inside.

"Well," I said after a couple of minutes of small talk, "I've got to leave because I need to study. It has been nice talking to you." I started to close the door.

"Wait," he interposed before the door closed. "Could I have your phone number? Maybe we can get together for coffee sometime."

I gave it to him, figuring he would lose it. I exchanged numbers with students because we mingled in and out of class so often. All of us collected phone numbers on a regular basis, usually scribbled on napkins. Because there was so much going on, everyone wanted to be able to contact as many of their acquaintances as possible in order to keep up.

After he left, I wondered for a couple of minutes where we might have met and then forgot about him since he did not interest me much. In fact, I thought he was kind of pushy.

About a week later, the phone rang. I picked it up, expecting it to be for one of the other girls in the boarding house.

"Hello," I said.

"Hi! Is this Cassandra?" asked a voice I did not recognize.

"Yes it is. May I ask who is calling?"

"This is Jamal. Remember? I came over the other day for a couple of minutes."

"I think I do. How are you?" I asked, trying to be polite.

"Fine. Say, would you like to go out for coffee?

"Sorry. I can't. I'm already going somewhere. Maybe another time, okay? Maybe I'll run into you in the student lounge." I said in response, in a hurry to get off the phone and get on with my day because there were some friends I wanted to find on campus. I left shortly after the phone call because there was in international coffee hour in the student lounge and I wanted to go listen to the political discussions.

Jamal was, however, persistent, so at one point or another, we started meeting for coffee.

The wonderful thing about coffeehouses is that they are a wonderfully relaxed and informal environment that is conducive to a natural flow of conversation about anything of interest. This is the perfect setting in which to develop friendships. I preferred meeting friends in such a setting because it was neutral territory in which one could meet and talk to a dozen people in the space of an afternoon absolutely free of commitment of any kind to any particular individual. It was no different where Jamal was concerned.

During one of the early coffeehouse conversations, I asked him the questions one normally asks of a foreign student.

"It's obvious from your accent that you weren't born in this country, Jamal. Where are you from?" I asked him during the course of the conversation about classes and life in general.

I was not quite able to place him since as yet I knew no Arabs. I had become friends with students from India, Japan, China,

Dominican Republic, Spain, England, and myriad other countries. The male Arab students were just beginning to arrive on campus and not many people knew them. The Arab women students would not start coming over until later, after their brothers and cousins had settled in and knew their way around and even then, not many were to be found.

"I am from the Middle East," he replied.

"Oh, are you Jewish?" I asked. It was a logical assumption, after all. Israel was considered to be in the Middle East and I knew there were quite a few Israelis on campus.

"No. I am Arab." he stated proudly.

"Is your family still back there? Do you have any brothers and sisters? What does your father do?"

"Yes, my family is still in the Middle East. I am the oldest and I have three brothers and two sisters. My father is a policeman."

"Oh, really! Do any of them want to come here to go to school or to live?"

"Most of them do, but it's really expensive and they can't afford it." he admitted to me a little ruefully.

"How did you manage to get here then?" I asked since I had tumbled to the fact that his family was not well off.

"I went to school and worked very hard for many years to get very high grades so I could get a scholarship to study in this country." he answered, very seriously and straightforwardly.

"Well, I think that is a real accomplishment. How long did it take you to get to the United States?" I asked since it was obvious that here was a person who had a lot of persistence and was willing to work hard to achieve his goals.

"It took me seven years."

"Seven years! Why so long?"

"Because I had to keep trying to get on the list to come and the list of people who wanted to come was always very long. The quota filled up very fast every year and you just have to keep putting your name in and hoping that it will be your turn next."

"Well, I think you deserve congratulations for having succeeded! Where did you go to school before coming here?" I asked.

"I went to school in Redlands, California, and got my degree there. I loved every minute of it! We had great parties!"

"Are you in graduate school here, or what?" I asked him.

"I'm just beginning graduate school in Engineering," he replied. "It's a tremendous amount of work. I study all the time."

"What do you want to do after you get your Masters?" I asked since I figured he had some sort of general plan mapped out for his life after all the effort he had put in to even get to this country to go to school.

"I want to marry an American girl, get my citizenship, and bring my family over here so they can become citizens," he stated in tones of dead seriousness.

At this point in my life, I did not think too much about what Jamal's goals might mean for other people besides himself. While I had studied a great deal about the religio-philosophies, art, literature, and historical characteristics of everyday life of ancient India, Greece, Egypt, Iran, Celtic Britain, and India and had become acquainted with a lot of foreign students, I really knew nothing to speak of about Middle Eastern societies of today. And I did not know any students from the Middle East because they had not been here until just recently. Neither did I know anything about foreign students obtaining American citizenship.

Jamal's goals seemed reasonable and admirable to me at the time since I was too naïve to discern the implications of his being part of a double minority (an Arab from Israel?!), his personal history, and his goals where any American woman was concerned.

Neither did I realize until much later that in Middle Eastern cultures everywhere, being a policeman is considered to be a humble, low class job. I also learned that all Middle Eastern men are instantly insulted if anyone implies that they are of the lower classes whether or not it is true (the more so if it is true) because every Arab male is taught from birth to considers himself a superior individual and that money and power are necessary to be considered a man with prestige among his male family members and friends.

Since moving up the social/economic ladder is virtually impossible in Arab cultures, one of the best ways to achieve this is to come to the United States as a university student, educate oneself into a higher socioeconomic profession, and become a citizen of this country.

Had I known as much about Arab societal characteristics as I do now, I would have refused absolutely to have anything with him for any reason because I would have been aware of the way women, especially wives, are thought of and treated by Middle Eastern men whether or not they claim to be Westernized . . . .

For over fourteen centuries in the Middle East, to be born a girl has been and still is to a source of shame and embarrassment to her family. There are no celebrations of joy at her birth; instead a silence and sadness descend over the household. The father of the new daughter feels as though his manhood has been undermined and blames his wife for not having given him a son.

If she is not killed at birth, a girl child is made to feel ashamed of her body, inferior, and subservient because she is not male. If there is a boy in the house, he gets all the attention, all the best food (the girl child gets the leftovers from the meals after the boy and his father have finished), all the freedom to come and go as he pleases, the chance to get educated, and most of the attention from his parents. The girl child is taught to work and serve the males in the house as humbly as a slave from the time she can walk.

From the moment a girl child is born, the parents begin searching for an advantageous alliance with a family which has a son to marry off. Or there will be an older male nearby who may have one or more wives and who is looking to acquire a new, young female to marry. In any case, an agreement is made and when the girl reaches marriageable age, which can be as young as nine years of age, the prospective husband pays the agreed upon dowry (he is in effect buying the girl), the ceremony is performed, and the poor girl is shipped off to her new husband's household, there to be abruptly and painfully introduced to her new life as the unwilling recipient of his lust whenever he is in the mood, to wait on him and on his other wives, and to become pregnant with one child after another before she is barely out of childhood. She is, in effect, his slave. She must obey him without question and do whatever he wants because he is her master—he owns her, body and soul. If he says she cannot eat, she does not eat. If he tells her to sleep in the shed out back, that is where she will sleep. If he wants to have sex with her in front of his friends, she must do it. She can do *nothing* on her own without his permission. If she does not produce sons for him, he can discard her without giving a reason, he can take other wives, and if he chooses to kill her, no one will interfere with him. He is absolute ruler of what goes on in his own household and the authorities will not interfere. This is characteristic of *every* Arab/Muslim country, especially of Saudi Arabia.

Wives are considered property. It is not important whether they think, whether they are educated, or whether they have needs or wants of their own to be addressed. As far as the Arab/Muslim male is concerned, she is there to take care of his sexual desires, serve him, and to produce children, preferably boys. The ideal wife is completely submissive to his every desire and she is breeding children as often as possible. Wives under control and children are a form of wealth and prestige for every Arab/Muslin male. This is equally true for Western wives if they are trapped in the country of the husband's birth where all the laws are on the side of the male.

CHAPTER 3

DEVELOPMENTS

JAMAL AND I were dating fairly regularly and the relationship seemed to be progressing on a positive basis. One afternoon, he had a bright idea.

"Let's have a party!" he exclaimed. "I will ask all my friends over so they can meet you! It'll be great!"

"Why not? I replied. "I am always interested in meeting more foreign students. When shall we have it? I need some time to organize food and drinks."

"Let's have it this coming Saturday. Finals end on Friday. It will be perfect timing!"

"Okay. Do you want snackies or some hot food? Do you want just beer or do shall we have some additional drinks? We have to have coffee so everybody can sober up before they drive anywhere after the party."

"Good idea! If I know these guys, they will need it."

And with that conversation, Jamal began spreading the word among his friends and I began getting the food and drinks organized. We ended up with everything imaginable ready for his friends to eat and drink all they wanted!

The party, if I do say so myself, was a great success! While Jamal schmoozed with his friends, I kept the mechanics of the party going smoothly. As glasses were used and set down, I scooped them up, washed them, and set them out for the next wave of demand for drinks. This went on for hours since our party attendees were determined to make every minute count where partying was concerned. I kept the food coming. Every few minutes, I made the rounds with a tray of goodies since I was determined that no one would do without their fair share of food. This went over very well since Jamal's friends, being mostly from the Middle East, loved being waited on and catered to. I even wore a head scarf (*de rigeur* for women in the Middle East) to make them feel more at home. This went over well also. As I was cleaning everything up after everyone left, Jamal raved about how well the party went and about the fact that his friends liked me.

We began giving parties on a regular basis. The formula we had used with the first party ensured success every time. I overheard Jamal on more than one occasion bragging about how I worked so hard to keep everything clean.

Our parties always went beautifully smoothly and everyone thought we made a great couple. We worked so well together it was easy to assume that our personalities meshed well enough to consider the possibility of a permanent arrangement.

As the relationship progressed, I began considering that it was time to introduce Jamal to my mother to see what she thought of him. At this point in time, the relationship was fun and interesting and very much the typical college pairing of mutual friends.

I called my mother one bright and sunny morning and asked her if I might bring a friend over from college so she could meet him. After the usual statements about how "the house wasn't clean enough because of sewing all over the place," she gave in and said we could come the following weekend.

Saturday came. The weather was beautiful, especially about 5:00 am, as we set out to drive about 300 miles to Mother's house with as much dispatch as possible since we wanted to be back on campus by late Saturday night or early Sunday morning, if possible, to get ready for classes on Monday.

The visit went over pretty well, considering that my mother had never in her life before met anyone from a foreign country, let alone from the Middle East. She lived a very quiet life, working as a bookkeeper during the week and working on her gardening or sewing on the weekends and in her spare time. While she was not yet widowed, she and my father had been separated for most of my life, so she was very much the mistress of her own domain. Visitors were not always welcome—especially if they were unexpected.

I was somewhat on tenterhooks about this first meeting because, by now, I knew Jamal to be en extremely intense personality—fun, but intense and sometimes difficult to deal with. I was also clearly aware that Mother had more than enough backbone to withstand him and that her intuitive and analytical powers were extremely sharp. I did not mention this to Jamal because I wanted him to act normally so that Mother could size up his character and whether he was as he presented himself to me and others.

At the time, I had no inkling that these two people were destined to be matching wits in deadly earnest and that Jamal would make the horrendous mistake of underestimating my mother's battle prowess and her ability to win where the welfare of her children was concerned.

I was to learn later that Arabs are a terribly intuitive people and that, unless one was very careful to keep one's thoughts shielded from showing on the surface, they would be read the instant you came into the group, especially if they already knew you.

On several subsequent weekends between classes and more or less on impulse, we drove across the state to my mother's home for a few hours each time so she and Jamal could get better acquainted. While she did not always appreciate our drop in visits, they seemed to be on cordial terms and she did not object to our relationship becoming serious enough to consider marriage. Jamal could be quite charming when he chose to and he did his best to ensure that his possible future mother-in-law liked him.

Even though the relationship between us was positive on the whole, situations came up which revealed personality characteristics in Jamal which gave hints that he was quite accustomed to getting his own way in every little detail when it affected his perception of his public image. For example, the birthday of one of his friends who regularly attended our parties fell on the same day we had a big get together planned and Jamal wanted a perfectly decorated birthday cake, complete with a birthday greetings on it, at the party for this friend.

"Hey Babe, Leah's birthday is Saturday!" Jamal exclaimed delightedly. "Let's have a birthday cake for her with Happy Birthday on it!"

"That's a great idea. She will love it. Let's make it a surprise for her", I responded. "Where are we going to get the cake? There isn't much time."

"I think I know somebody who can do it cheap", he said musingly. "If she's not available, we'll have to find a bakery even though it will be expensive."

The rest of the week passed quickly. By Friday afternoon, we were getting concerned that the cake would not be done in time. Jamal's friend had agreed to bake the cake and do the lettering even though she had short notice. We were able to pick it up on Saturday morning and bring it over to his apartment. We carefully unwrapped it.

"Doesn't it look great?!" Jamal exclaimed. "She did a beautiful job!"

"Absolutely! Leah will be so surprised." I said, giving his arm a little hug.

We put the cake on a table about an hour after we had brought it home. Someone somehow touched the lettering on the cake by mistake.

"What happened to the cake! Look at it! It is ruined!" Jamal screamed out of the blue. "It's no good! Throw it away! It's not perfect!" he continued at the top of his voice.

We rushed over to look at it. The atmosphere was tumultuous and thick with his anger.

"Jamal", I said to him. "It's not that obvious. We can fix it."

"Well! Do it!" He yelled at me. "It's got to be perfect or it's no good!"

Between two or three of us women, we managed to salvage the lettering to Jamal's satisfaction. Even though none of us said anything, all of us were still stunned by the ferociously menacing nature of his tantrum and sulking over what was actually a trivial matter, easily fixed.

Had I been as informed about the characteristics of Arab/Muslim societies as I was about the various other cultures I had studied, such a display on Jamal's part would have signaled the end of the relationship because I would have realized that here was a person who had been allowed from birth to get his own way and consider himself the center of the universe as he saw it, with everyone else's wants and needs taking last place.

All of us have had to deal with a spoiled child caught up in so much anger and/or frustration that a screaming fit or temper tantrum ensues, no matter from what culture we come. But how many of us are faced with an adult male exhibiting the degree of lack of control and menace over such a relatively minor matter as Jamal had shown? In Western cultures, we are taught by parents, school, and society at large that such displays are childish and inappropriate as we become adults. We learn how to redirect such impulses into more constructive directions.

In traditional cultures such as the Mediterranean cultures and the Arab/ Muslim societies, there is nothing the adult male in a family won't do to ensure the birth of as many male children as possible. Sons are proof of his manhood and are a source of pride and prestige for him in society.

All male children, especially the firstborn son, are treasured from the moment of their birth when the fingers of the midwife separates "one thigh away from the other as if they are the legs of a chicken, eager to reveal whatever good or evil lies hidden between them, to be the first one to let out a screaming 'Yoo-yoo' if her eyes fall on a penis ('May the name of the Prophet protect and guard it'), if she glimpses the sacred organ bestowed by Allah on males alone."[1] All boy children, especially the firstborn, are spoiled and cosseted constantly simply because they are male. They are also made aware as babies of the pleasure associated with their sexual organs because Arab/Muslim mothers consistently massage the penis with love and gentleness because they believes that such stimulus will help the penis to grow larger and stronger. Also, when any boy child is being fractious or irritable, his mother massages his genital area to soothe and lull him into peaceful contentment.

A boy is given everything he wants, even at the expense of his mother or sisters. If a sister, for instance, has something he wants, she is forced to give it to him. It could some an object as minor as an apple given to a sister that her brother has decided that he wanted as was the case with Sultana, a Saudi princess, when she was a little girl. "Ali slapped me to the ground, but I declined to hand over the shiny red apple just given me by the Pakistani cook. Ali's face began to swell with anger as I hovered over the apple and quickly began to take huge bites and swallow them whole. Refusing to give in to his male prerogative of superiority, I had committed a grave act and knew that I would soon suffer the consequences. Ali gave me two swift kicks and went running for our father's driver, Omar, an Egyptian. My sisters feared Omar almost as much as they feared Ali or my father. They disappeared into the villa, leaving me alone to face the combined wrath of the men of the house."[2]

Because she stood up to her brother and refused to give in to him, Ali was given all of her toys and complete control over what Sultana was allowed to eat at mealtimes—if he allowed her to eat at all. He gave her only the smallest amounts of food to eat so that she was hungry all the time. In addition, he would wave plates of hot rice and chicken in front of her at night before she went to sleep to add to the torture. Ali was only nine years old and Sultana only seven.[3]

As the boys, especially the firstborn sons, in a family grow up, they are included in family councils, they have first choice of everything after their father, and they can order around their mother and sisters as much as they wish since women and girls are considered inferior and subservient to men and boys. Boys are taught from the beginning that the role of the male is to control and be in charge of the women in the house and that the role of the women and girls is to be docile, as nearly invisible as possible, and to be obedient at all times to every male in the family. The males have the right to treat the women and girls in the family in any manner they choose since they have the power of life and death over every female family member—literally.

Jamal's vicious, childish, screaming display of temper and display of a controller mentality over such a trivial incident as the lettering on a cake was a very clear symptom of how he had been raised and of his expectations from the women in his life. I did not have the knowledge to realize the long-term significance of what I had witnessed so I gave him the benefit of the doubt, much later to my sorrow.

CHAPTER 4

COMPLICATIONS

BOTH JAMAL AND I were in classes with heavy workloads so we finally had to cut down on the parties we gave and concentrate on classroom assignments or pay the penalty at the end of the quarter. He was in graduate school in the Department of Engineering and going after his Master's Degree. I was pursuing a double major in Comparative Literature and in Political Science and expected to earn Bachelor's Degrees in both. I was also minoring in Middle Eastern Literature.

At one point or another, the subject of marriage came up and, for the life of me, I cannot remember the occasion on which we decided to go ahead and take the plunge. I know that he had the idea in mind, but had not made an issue of it. I was seeking stability in my personal life and getting married to Jamal seemed like a good idea at the time, based on how well our personalities and academic goals appeared to mesh. We decided to set the date for sometime in the fall which was several months in the future. Since we both wanted a church wedding, and since we had both attended

Episcopalian churches in the past, we decided on the church of that denomination near the campus.

I telephoned Mother to give her the news and asked her if she would help me plan it. Of course she said, "Yes," even though I think that she must have had reservations on the one hand and hopes on the other that, in spite of the cultural differences, the marriage would work out.

The first thing I did was set out to find my engagement and wedding rings. I knew I did not want a diamond set because they bored me. I loved colored stones and favored especially rubies and emeralds as I still do today. After looking all over downtown, I found the most beautiful emerald cut dark green emerald wedding ring set. The stone was slightly flawed, but the color was wonderful! I fell in love with the set immediately and arranged for Jamal to see the set the next day. He liked them well enough, but the price was $450.00—very high when one is a student in graduate school and on a tight budget. However, he did consent to buy them and I was the proud wearer of a gorgeous engagement ring.

Because I was in school and not about to drop classes, the wedding had to take place near the University rather than in my hometown. So Mother gave me the green light in planning the wedding.

Since Jamal and I had managed to secure a church date, that at least was taken care of which made it possible for me to concentrate on finding The Dress. It seemed to take forever since I had to sandwich the search in between classes and on weekends. I finally found one at what was considered the best department store in town. It was a classic design and the veil was simple and uncluttered to go along with the dress. The bridesmaids' dresses were elegantly simple.

Floral decoration and the bouquets were taken care of and, finally, all the details of food for the reception and the guest list were under control.

Mother came to stay with me the last week before the wedding to provide family support and a helping hand when I thought I was going to be overwhelmed.

About five months from the day I first met Jamal, I married him. The day of the wedding came and the weather was blessedly beautiful—not too hot, not too cold. I do not remember the ceremony at all—just vague recollections of walking down the aisle and well wishes from the guests and of changing into my suit after the ceremony so that we could leave in traditional style even though we were not going on a honeymoon as such since school was in session. Most of all, I remember my mother being there for me, my Rock of Gibraltar, through thick and thin.

Jamal was in a navy blue suit, looking quite well groomed and like a happy bridegroom should look. To the casual observer, we looked like the typical newlyweds starting out life as a happily married couple.

After we mingled with everyone at the reception and thanked everyone for coming, it was finally time for us to leave. Someone had decorated Jamal 's car with "Just Married" banners, cans had been tied to the back fender, the presents had been loaded into the trunk, and the best man had duly made sure that it was ready for us whenever we chose to leave.

The time finally came when it was time to leave and return to Jamal's apartment to change clothes and to settle in as man and wife. It was only a temporary arrangement since we needed to find a place which could accommodate two people comfortably.

CHAPTER 5

REVELATIONS

I WILL NEVER forget the first ten minutes after we arrived at Jamal's apartment. The whole building was very quiet since everyone was gone. I put down the corsage and, as I was standing there, a feeling of doom came over me. I looked at the man I had just married and I knew in the marrow of my bones that I had made a horrible mistake. I also knew that my life had taken a turn which I absolutely did not want and that it was too late to back out. All I could do was to try to make the best of it.

During the next couple of weeks, we searched the neighborhood looking for an apartment that we could stand to live in and that we could afford. I was working at the campus library part time only and Jamal was living off a scholarship which had to last him all year, so to say that we would be living on a limited income is putting it kindly.

We finally found what was the equivalent of a basement apartment within walking distance of campus. It was somewhat decent and it was affordable so we took it.

I called Mother to let her know we had found something so she would be assured that disaster was not imminent. I tried to sound positive, but I am sure that her intuition was in good working order because she showed up a couple of weeks later to see for herself where we were living and if I was all right. I was very glad to see her because I was definitely out of my depth and I really needed her supportive, experienced presence—someone I knew was on my side and wanted the best for me.

One afternoon, about two weeks later, Jamal came into the room where I was trying to study.

"I think you should quit school and find a full-time job," Jamal said suddenly. I looked up, unpleasantly surprised.

"Why?" I asked. "I thought we had talked about this and agreed that both of us would stay in school and get our degrees."

"We need the money, babe." he replied.

"Well, why don't both of us get part-time jobs so that we can survive without dropping out of school?"

"I can't. I have to get my Master's Degree."

"Well, I have to get my Bachelor's Degrees. I am not going to quit school. I will look around for a part-time job, but it will have to work around my classes." I had to say something to get him to ease off. His constantly intense approach to everything was beginning to get to me.

I started looking around and found a good possibility. The hours I would work would be from the afternoon until about 6:00 or 7:00 pm. I was very pleased and went home to share the good news. I thought Jamal would be very pleased that I had found a possibility.

"Guess what! I found a job!" I told him, expectantly.

"What are the hours?" he asked.

"From 3:00 in the afternoon until 7:00," I replied.

"No," he said emphatically. "You have to be home to cook my dinner."

"What?" I asked incredulously. "Why can't you cook your own? We need the money!"

"No, no," he said. "I am your husband and you are supposed to cook my meals for me. I don't want you to take it."

This put me in an impossible situation. Here he was, insisting that I get a job as soon as possible in one sentence and in the next, telling me that I had to be home to cook his meals. That would work only if I quit school, which I was not about to do. He was trying to take control of my life and I was not going to let him do it.

I went to my new employer, as I recall, and told them that I could not work the hours they wanted me to so I had to quit. I did not have the courage to tell Jamal that I had quit because I knew he would lose his temper, so I made up a stupid lie to tell him when I got home—exactly the wrong kind of lie, which I was to learn very shortly.

"Why are you home early?" Jamal asked when I walked in the door.

"I quit the job." I said.

He looked at me in an angry manner and asked, "Why?"

"Because," I said, "The boss was bothering me."

"WHAT!!!" exclaimed he, instantly in a rage. "Who was it? What is his name? I am going to go out there and talk to him!"

I began to realize what I had done it by saying that so I backed off. "I don't know. Let's just let it go."

Jamal stomped around the apartment in a towering rage, but after a while, he began to calm down.

Pretty soon, he put on his coat and said, "I have to go to the library to study. I am getting behind in my assignments."

"Okay, I will see you later." I replied, looking forward to the peace and quiet.

I eventually found a part-time job as a waitress which allowed me to make some money and to get away from Jamal for several hours a day.

But I always had to come home, sooner or later. And every night when we went to bed, he never let me just go to sleep. He was insistent on having sexual relations before the need for sleep was allowed to play its part. And after every single session, he arose immediately, went into the bathroom and washed himself off assiduously. I had the feeling that once he had climaxed he could not wait to remove all traces of his interaction with me. It was almost as though he felt compelled to remove all traces of womanhood from his body to get rid of the contamination.

My impression was absolutely correct though I could not have said why at the time. I learned later that, traditionally, "in every Arab society, the sexual act is considered polluting and is surrounded by rituals and ceremonies designed to destroy any potential closeness between husband and wife so that the act itself occurs only for the purpose of procreation. The possibility that the couple will melt into total identification with each other and possibly grow to love one another is anathema to the Muslim god, Allah, who is extremely possessive and does not want anything interfering with worship and devotion to him. Arabs from every Muslim society have grown up with the attitude that intimacy with women is essentially contaminating and, once the act is finished, to remove all traces of the sexual encounter as speedily as possible. In yet another setting, women are made to feel inferior and unworthy once the man has gotten what he wants.[1]

A few weeks later, I missed my period and suspected, with a sinking heart, that I was pregnant. Yes, I wanted children, but not now, and not with him.

When I was sure, I knew I could not keep it a secret forever. I had to tell him. I hoped he would be nicer to me since it was his child that I was carrying.

In the evening, a few days later, I worked up the courage to open a conversation with him.

"Jamal," I said experimentally, trying to ascertain whether or not he was in a civil mood.

"Yes, what is it?" he asked.

"I have something to tell you I think you will be pleased about." I said.

"I am pregnant."

"Really? That is great!" he exclaimed, delighted. "How are you? Are you feeling okay?"

"I feel fine. Just queasy, that's all. It will be nice when I don't get morning sickness anymore."

He looked at me for a minute and then made a disturbing announcement. "I know it's going to be a boy." He was so pleased he could hardly contain himself.

I didn't respond, but something told me that he was absolutely correct. It was then that I began to realize that Arabs were extremely intuitive and something told me I was going to have to very, very careful where Jamal was concerned. I understood the implications of this because I grew up in a household where the ability to read people and to develop intuitive knowledge was exhibited on an everyday basis. My mother was very much this way and she had taught me to read and analyze underneath the surface of people and happenings from the time I was small.

After that announcement, his sexual attentions became even more focused on me. His attitude about this activity is expressed very well in the Qu'ranic sura (2:222): "Women are your fields; go, then, into your fields whence you please." In other words, I was to be at his disposal whenever the urge, night or day, hit him.

After my announcement, he even more greedily watched me undress and could not wait to handle me whether or not I wished it, especially after I became quite pregnant. It was not long before I began to realize that his thinking began and ended below the beltline and always at his convenience. I began to hate him and to loathe being anywhere near him because I could not help thinking of him as one huge, overgrown, repulsive penis.

My classes and time on campus was beginning to be a real godsend because I would temporarily forget that I was anything other than a student. I loved my classes and never let anything prevent me from attending every one of them. Every exam brought me one step closer to graduation.

One morning after Jamal had gone to school, I called Mother.

"Mother?" I asked after she answered the phone. "Have you got a minute?"

"Sure," she answered. "Is everything all right?"

I paused for a moment before answering.

"Well, not really. We aren't getting along all that well. Jamal wants me to quit school and get a full time job, but I absolutely refuse to do it. I am going to get my BA, no matter what."

"I am really glad to hear that," Mother said. "Stick to your guns."

"There is another reason I called, Mother." At this point I was reluctant to have to tell her. "I am pregnant. And Jamal is sure it is going to be a boy. I hope he is wrong, but I don't think so."

"I think it is wonderful that you are going to have a baby, even though you aren't getting along with Jamal!" She exclaimed in a quietly enthusiastic voice. "Never think otherwise. You need to think positive about this so that your baby will be born healthy and strong."

"That is pretty close to impossible right now, Mother," I responded. "The only thing positive is being in school."

"I know, dear," she said. "But you need to try hard to be positive. Also, you need to be smart and careful about what you do and say around him until we can figure out the best way to cope with him and with this marriage."

"Okay. I am sure glad you were home when I called!" As I said that, I looked out the window to make sure Jamal was not coming up the walk. "I will continue going to school and try to get along with him as I have been doing so far."

"Don't worry," she said. "We will figure something out. Just give me some time to think about the best way to handle everything."

"All right," I said in relief. I'll be interested to know what you figure out. I should go now because I need to go to class. Thank you for the moral support! Love you, Mother."

"Love you too. I will talk to you later," Mother said as she hung up.

I felt a lot better after talking to her. Always had I known my mother to be infinitely resourceful, especially in difficult situations. I had very confidence that, sooner or later, she and I would come up with a solution. I was willing to bet a divorce was going to happen sooner or later, but the circumstances had to be better than they were at present.

After he learned that I was pregnant, Jamal escalated his insistence that I quit school. I categorically refused and began spending as much time on campus as possible so as to avoid him. One morning, I told him I was going to the school library to study. On the way, on impulse, I stopped off at a mutual acquaintance's apartment for a minute to socialize and distract myself since it was on the way to the library.

"Hi, Mehdi!" I said as he opened the door to his apartment. "How are you?"

Medhi Shah, an Iranian student, was one of my favorite people. He was one of those young men who had led a sheltered life and was quite an innocent, and it was an endearing quality which characterized his relationships with everyone. Jamal also knew him.

"Hi! How are you? Please come in," he answered as we both paused in the foyer. "I haven't seen you for a while. How are things going for you?"

"They are okay, I guess, Mehdi." I responded. "I just thought I would drop in for a minute. I am on my way to the library to study and just wanted to see how you were."

At that moment, Jamal walked in unexpectedly. Both Mehdi and I looked at him in surprise since there had been no knock at the door first. As I observed the expression on his face, I could see that he was going to go off in a fit of temper.

He looked at me as though I was dirt and asked, "What are you doing here!? I thought you were going to the library!"

"I am. I just stopped in here for a second to say to Mehdi. I am not doing anything wrong."

From the expression on his face, you would have thought he had caught us in an awkward moment when in reality, all we were doing was passing the time of day—and in the morning, yet.

"Were you following me?" I asked him. "You were, weren't you!? You thought I was up to something!" I said as it began to dawn on me this was exactly what he was doing!

We started arguing. Then he delivered a bombshell which I have not forgotten to this day.

"I have had as good sex with you as I have had with anyone," he said, right in front of Mehdi! Poor Mehdi was terribly embarrassed for two reasons. First, he knew absolutely nothing about sexual intimacy and two, for someone to make a statement of such a personal nature in front of him violated every rule of privacy and decorum with which he had been raised. I think I was as embarrassed for him as I was mortified for myself at being part of such a conversation in front of a third party, especially a friend. I never forgave Jamal for such a crude and misplaced display of possessiveness.

"Mehdi, I have got to go to the library now," I said in an effort to end this confrontation before it got any worse. "I will see you later." I pointedly said nothing to Jamal as I left in total psychological disarray. He may not have realized it at the time, but what he had just done caused me to hold him in total, utter, permanent contempt with all my body and soul.

Had the above scenario taken place in any Arab/Muslim country, I would have been very badly beaten and maimed, or killed outright by him.

In Arab/Muslim countries, once you marry an Arab male, you lose control of your fate because he owns you. You are considered a citizen of the country you husband comes from simply because you married him and you are residing in that country. His word is law and he is your absolute master. You and any children you have are his property to do with as he wishes. You are not allowed to pursue even the smallest of activities without his permission. Because your husband's prestige and male status depends directly on your sexual behavior and purity, he will go to any length to make sure your every action is under his control, that you are obedient to his every wish. For these reasons, he does not want you to go anywhere without him as the 'guardian of your virtue'. For you, as his property, to be caught with a man who is not a relative results in an instant assumption by your husband that you are, or are about to, commit adultery and thereby sully his family honor. He will almost surely beat you senseless to make you properly obedient and submissive or he will kill you outright simply to save face with the rest of his family and his friends.

A third alternative, if your husband is feeling generous, is that he will throw you out of the house with only the clothes on your back. If you have children, you will lose them. For example, I know of an American woman who married an Egyptian and moved to Egypt with him to live. He pursued the normal activities of every Egyptian male which included seeing other women whenever he chose. He expected her to stay at home as befitted a good wife in the Middle East, doing housewifely things such as cooking, sewing, and making babies. After a long period of time, she began to resent bitterly her husband's freedom to do whatever he chose with whomever he wished to it with. She determined to start doing the same for herself and began to go out for coffee with friends, some of them male. Inevitably, she was seen with one of her male friends in one of these coffee shops by someone who knew her husband. It was irrelevant that she and her friend were doing nothing but drinking coffee. She was a married woman and the man with her was neither her husband nor a relative, so she was committing adultery by the Middle Eastern definition of the word. She was summarily thrown out of his house onto the street with nothing but the clothes on her back. Her two little boys were kept by their father and she was never allowed access to them again. The only reason she survived was because she was able to contact her parents in the United States so they could wire her money to come home.

Your husband will get away with anything he chooses to do to you because the authorities in Arab countries will not intervene in private family matters between a man and his wife, a centuries old custom. Furthermore, he will be well thought of in society because he asserted his domination over a disobedient, adulterous female in his household and saved his honor. You will have no recourse because women have no rights in the tribal patriarchies which are characteristic of these countries. The men rule and they rule absolutely in all matters as they have in the Middle East for over fourteen centuries.

While there has been some progress where women's rights in some Arab societies are concerned in the last few years, every time the power structure in any of the Middle Eastern countries is threatened, the members of that power structure issue new edicts further dominating and limiting every aspect of women's behavior to indicate that the men in charge of government are still strong enough to maintain their rule.[2]

Women are always the first target for this kind of abuse because they are least able to fight back. While the definition of "manhood" in Arab/Muslim societies includes domination, abuse, cruelty, and callous lack of regard and decent treatment for women as human beings on the part of the males in each household, based on my experience and on those of other unfortunate women, this is a far more accurate definition of a premeditatively abusive Arab /Muslim male.

CHAPTER 6

CONFRONTATION

A FTER WE WERE married, Jamal brought up more than once that he wanted me to sign papers for him so that he could get his citizenship. With an American citizen sponsoring him, the waiting period would shorten by several years.

One afternoon when Mother was in town, the subject of sending for Jamal's birth certificate came up. He was in a quandary where to have it sent and had been quietly stewing about it to himself for several months, at least.

"I need to send for my birth certificate home, but I need to have an address here which I know will be a safe one so the birth certificate doesn't get lost." he said, almost to himself. "I don't want to send it to our address because we might move or the mail might get lost by somebody else living here."

"What about one of your friends?" I asked. I'm sure they would be careful with it."

"Maybe so, but I don't want to take the chance." he said in reply.

Everybody brainstormed about possibilities of where to have the certificate sent for a few minutes. We did not seem to be making any progress.

"Well, you could have it sent to my address," Mother said. "I won't be going anywhere and there is no one else in the house to pick up the mail but me. It would be about the safest address I can think of."

"That would be great!" he said with relief. "Where I come from, birth certificates are very hard to get and even harder to replace, especially from overseas. Thank you very much. What a perfect solution!"

I didn't say anything. I had never actually committed to signing his papers. I let him assume that I would because it avoided another scene in which he tried to bully me into doing what he wanted me to do. Furthermore, I was still somewhat afraid of him and did not know whether he would lose his temper completely and take it out on me physically. With my being pregnant, I really did not want to take any chances on getting roughed up.

Jamal was concerned that I stay in good shape so the baby would be born healthy, especially since he was sure it would be a boy. This was certainly the normal thing for an expectant father to worry about, but there was an odd element to his focus on my pregnancy, something I could not quite put my finger on which did not feel right. I kept getting the feeling that the only reason he wanted me to be sure to do take care of myself was because he wanted the baby to be absolutely perfect. More than once, I caught him looking at me and the growing baby as though I was purely and simply breeding stock he had mated with to produce the finest offspring possible for his own purposes. Once the baby was born, it occurred to me that he might decide I was superfluous.

He accompanied me to a couple of the doctor's visits, but after the first time or two, I started going by myself which was more than fine with me. However, he did start making remarks to me about my being mentally unstable. I ignored them because there was no point in responding to them I knew that I was under a great deal of stress and that I was handling it as well as could be expected under the circumstances.

I continued my normal activities with one addition—that of visiting the Christian Science Reading Room on University Avenue on a regular basis. Several years before I transferred to the University, my mother started going to the Christian Science Church because it was such a positive, healing faith. She brought home several of the texts which all the church members read. I had looked through them on more than one occasion, one in particular, *The Footsteps of Truth,* by Mary Baker Eddy of which I had a copy. I had read through it before beginning college. It was not so much a biblical type of work as a text containing wonderfully uplifting, inspiring, commonsense truths one could apply in everyday living . . . . The idea came to me one afternoon when I happened to be walking by it and really noticed its existence. Something told me that here was a place absolutely right for me to be visiting at this time in my life. The strain of my deteriorating marriage was a constant factor. I had the feeling that I was being watched by him and his friends whenever they could manage it. When I paused in front the Reading Room, I had the strongest feeling that here was a place in which I would be completely safe. So I went inside that first afternoon, found a copy of *The Footsteps of Truth*, and sat down to read. I stayed for an hour or so that first day, reading, and a feeling of blessed peace and deep happiness came over me. It was such balm to my beleagured soul! After that, I went inside every day and read of concepts in words which helped me so much gather strength to continue with what I had to do. No one ever bothered me and I was never intruded upon by anyone. It was wonderful! My time there was an interlude of peace and love in the midst of the most harrowing period in my life.

*   *   *

The school year progressed It was not a far distance to walk to and from campus for which I was grateful because the weather not only turned cold, it snowed! I remember how ultrasensitive I was to everything because of my misery—the snow, the rain, the beauty of the stars and the campus landscaping which had been one hundred plus years in the making, my classes, and my time with friends who never exhibited undue curiosity about my situation.

I was packing a small lunch everyday—there was not much food in the apartment so everything I packed had to count in terms of nutrition. I ate a lot of cheese sandwiches as I recall. Fortunately, I have always been blessed with good health which I never abused with the usual vices and this stood me in good stead during the nine months of my pregnancy. So, while I did not eat much, I ate sensibly and it sufficed.

At some point during the school year (all the days seemed to meld into a long continuous span of time) Mother was in town to make sure I was all right. One morning, she and Jamal and I were in the bedroom when he asked her a question.

"I am glad you are here because I have been wanting to ask you—have you received my birth certificate in the mail yet?" he asked anxiously.

I waited to see what Mother would say. I hoped that she had not yet gotten it because if she had, it meant that I was going to have to commit myself one way or the other. I had not brought the subject up at all at any time since Mother said he could have the certificate sent to her home. I did not want to stir up a hornet's nest or take the chance that Jamal would ask me directly if I was going to sign his citizenship papers.

"No," said Mother in a considering tone of voice. "I haven't. I wonder why it is taking so long?" From the tone of her voice, one could swear that she was as much at a loss as Jamal as to why the document had not yet arrived.

After a minute or so, he left the room and went into the bathroom for a few minutes.

After the door to the bathroom had closed, Mother leaned toward me in a careful fashion because she did not want what she had to say next to be overheard.

"Jamal's birth certificate did arrive a couple of weeks ago, but I burned it up." she said in a very quiet tone of voice. "Do not tell him. It has to remain a secret because you don't know what he will do if he finds out."

I just looked at her in sheer gratitude and relief.

"Thank god, I said just as quietly." I didn't want to sign his papers, but I didn't know how I was going to get out of it I am so glad I can't stand it."

My estimation of my mother's ability to outflank Jamal went up about ten notches. I knew that we were going to be in a survival situation for a very long time and that we were going to need every tactic we could devise in order to come out of it with some semblance of victory, especially if the baby did turn out to be a boy.

Neither of us ever told Jamal what she had done though I am sure he eventually figured out that she had destroyed it. I was already learning the wisdom of silence where informing him of anything was concerned.

The relationship went from bad to worse. I spent as little time at home as I could manage which was easy enough because of classes and friends I could meet at campus events and in the student lounge. The conversations invariably ranged around politics in the international area and what we thought the United States should be doing to make the world a better place. We also shared opinions on our classes and what careers we were considering once we graduated.

One friend in particular, David Leslie, was wonderful with his sideways sense of humor and general sense of conviviality and tact. He would offer to buy me a Coke occasionally and I always accepted with total gratitude at his kindness. Kindness became more precious than gold to me during the long months while I was in school and trying to maintain some sort of equilibrium. Being able to laugh at the jokes of my friends saved my sanity, I believe. It was during that period in my life that I discovered the ability to laugh in spite of hellish circumstances to be a precious gift from the gods. Because of my extreme situation, every detail of my surroundings, the nuances of conversations with my friends, and the fact that I was fighting for my psychological survival magnified everything into ultra high detail of color, texture, and sound.

Even though the pregnancy, which I was very self-conscious about, was progressing and becoming more apparent, I never brought it up in conversations because I did not want to burden my friends with my problems when I knew they had their own to deal with. My friends were wonderfully tactful. No one mentioned it for which I was terribly grateful because getting through this pregnancy was a living nightmare for me under the circumstances.

They will never know how much I loved them for the way they were when I needed so much to be around them.

One of the courses I was taking, I believe it was during Winter Quarter, was Russian Literature. A friend of mine who knew Jamal was taking it also. She and I tended to sit together as we were on good terms. The one thing we did not discuss was what was going on between Jamal and me. One morning, before the beginning of class, I was already sitting in my place when this friend came in and sat down. She quietly walked over to where I was sitting and handed me an envelope in a subdued manner, as though she was uncomfortable about her action. Since the professor was not yet beginning his lecture, I went ahead and opened it. What I had before me was a petition for divorce from Jamal. I read it over and put it away and directed my attention to the professor who had begun talking. I was surprised that he had initiated it because, in this country, it is the woman who customarily initiates such proceedings. I knew he was asking advice of his father, who was in Israel, and who knew nothing about American lifeways. It was obvious to me that, again, he had followed his father's advice to his own detriment. While I knew that a divorce was brewing, I had not been in a particular hurry about initiating it because it would cost me money I did not have. So, looking at the picture as a whole, I came to the conclusion that Jamal probably did me a favor, even though he had intended to humiliate me further by persuading a friend to serve the papers instead of having it done by a court official.

I called Mother and told her. She reacted in much the same way I had upon receiving the petition. However, we quickly moved to the practicalities and discussed the necessity of obtaining a lawyer.

"Why don't you let me find the lawyer?" she suggested. "It is much better for you to concentrate on taking care of yourself and going to classes."

"That's fine with me," I said. "I have no idea about which one would be the best. It needs to be someone here in town since that is where the papers were served."

"All right." she responded. "Let me think on this so I can find the best person. I will call you back in a couple of days."

"Okay, Mother. Thanks. What would I do without you?" As I hung up, my mind was more at rest. With my mother in the picture, I very much doubted that Jamal would stand much of a chance, even though we were being very careful not to say anything which he could use against us.

Sure enough, about a week later, Mother called back.

"Honey, I think I have found the perfect lawyer," Mother said with enthusiasm. "His name is Henry Soderlund and he is from the best law office in town."

"That is great!" I said. "What do we do now?"

"Leave that to me," she said. "I will call him and ask him to take on your case. Then we will need for you to go see him. I will let you know."

When she called back a few days later to let me know when the appointment was, she had some interesting information to relay to me.

"I have the appointment set for around 1:00 next Wednesday," she said. "When I talked to him after he had contacted Jamal's lawyer, he told me that Jamal told his lawyer that you are really unstable and very nervous all the time."

"Is that so?" I replied. "We both know I am not mentally unstable even though Jamal has done his best to tip me over the edge with his continual harassment. I think both lawyers will be for a surprise, don't you?"

"Yes, I think so too. It will be interesting to watch Mr. Soderlund the first time he meets you. I will come to your place on Wednesday so we can go see him together. See you then. Bye bye."

I hung up also, gladness in my heart. We were finally taking positive steps to begin the laborious process of getting me extricated from this disastrous marriage.

The week passed uneventfully and Mother showed up a day or so before the scheduled appointment on Wednesday.

Mother and I showed up at Mr. Soderlund's office suite; neither of us had met him before and we were curious as to what he was like. After a few minutes, the secretary showed us into his office.

When we walked in and sat down, waiting calmly until he was ready to begin the conversation.

"Good afternoon," he said cordially, "You must be Mrs. Ahmed." he said. "And you must be her mother," he said to Mother as he looked in her direction.

"Yes to both questions, "I said. "I am pleased to meet you."

"I was told that you were very mentally unstable and very nervous," said Mr. Soderlund as he looked at me. "You certainly don't seem that way to me. You walked in here very calmly and quietly and you are very self-possessed for someone in your situation."

"Thank you, Mr. Soderlund. I appreciate that very much."

"Jamal is trying to make her look bad so he can have things his way in the divorce proceedings," Mother said to him.

"We are going to do our best to prevent that," Mr. Soderlund replied to her.

"I am sure you will." Mother rejoined.

Confidence in each other had been established so we were able to get down to the details of our divorce petition. All were agreed that the most important point, custody of the baby when it was born, was the number one priority. I had no intention of allowing Jamal to have anything to do with it, let alone gain custody. Everything else such as division of any property was minor since we really had nothing worth fighting over.

After the appointment was over and the game plan established, Mother and I left Mr. Soderlund's office, relieved to be in capable hands.

"The important thing now," said Mother, "is to say nothing to anyone. We don't want either Jamal or his lawyer to know what we are thinking or what we might do."

"I totally agree," I said. "He is very sneaky and will do anything to get what he wants. Forewarned is forearmed and I don't intend to let him know anything at all!"

Agreed on what we would and would not do, we then went our separate ways—she went home and I went back to school.

CHAPTER 7

STALKED

I KNEW THAT Jamal was stalking me day and night, either directly or through his friends. I was careful always to be with a group of friends because I knew that he wanted to catch me in what he could label a compromising situation and show during divorce proceedings that I was immoral and an unfit mother.

Then one afternoon, when I walked in the door of the apartment, Jamal was waiting for me with a smirk on his face.

"I am going to take you to the University Hospital to have you tested because you are mentally unstable. I think you have had a mental breakdown," he said in a menacing tone of voice. "Get your things together."

I just looked at him with a flat, hostile stare. I wasn't surprised because I had figured that it was a matter of time before he would try this.

"I'm not going," I said, and continued to stare at him.

"Either you go or I will call the police and have you taken there," he said.

"Oh, all right. I'll go," I said. I knew that unless I went of my own free will, I might not be able to control what happened next. I got my purse in hand and went out to the car with him.

I knew perfectly well why he wanted to have me tested. He hoped that I would be declared unstable so that he could take the baby away from me when he or she was born. I also knew that I was in great mental health, considering that fact that I was pregnant, we had virtually no money to live on, and that the hate between us was growing by leaps and bounds. I also knew how the tests worked because I had grown up with a mother from whom I had learned how to use psychological analysis on an everyday basis since childhood. I had also taken some basic courses in psychology and knew exactly what to expect in the interview. Jamal did not know that I was quite comfortable with the actual interview process and I was not about to tell him.

Sure enough, at the University Hospital, I got the usual "how are the fruits similar" question. The interviewer was not quite happy with my answer so he suggested to Jamal that I be taken to the County Hospital psych ward for further examination. He did so gladly and left, probably assuming that he had won this round. I was there for a few hours before an interviewer came to see me.

After I was admitted to the ward itself, I was required to take off my clothes and put on a ward gown. All of my personal effects were taken from me and put in a container to be put somewhere safe. It is amazing how quickly you begin to feel as though you have no identity when everything you are accustomed to carrying is taken from you. This, on top of being pregnant.

While I was waiting to be interviewed, I made the acquaintance of a woman who looked very unhappy and withdrawn. After we had talked for a minute or two, I asked her why she was in the ward.

"Because I tried to commit suicide," she said, showing the razor cuts on her arm. "I have tried to commit suicide more than once."

"Why?" I asked.

"Because I don't want to live." she responded.

At that point a nurse came out and called my name. She took me to a small office and seated me by the doctor who was waiting for me.

"How are you Mrs. Ahmed?" the doctor asked. His manner was quite kind and reasonable. "Your husband tells me that you are mentally unstable and need treatment. What do you think about what he says?"

Well," I replied after a few seconds, "Considering that I am taking classes at the university, working toward my degree, I am pregnant, Jamal has sued me for divorce, and we barely have enough money to live on, I am definitely up tight, but I am not mentally unstable."

"I can certainly understand why," the doctor said after a second of observing me sitting quietly, waiting for his response. "I don't think you need to stay overnight. Normally it is required, but I am going to let you go home. Why don't you call your husband and have him come and get you?"

After I called him, I was allowed to get dressed and retrieve my belongings.

When Jamal arrived about twenty minutes later, I was ready to go and conversing quietly with the doctor.

When he walked in, I could see that he was a bit puzzled and off balance because he had not expected to be called back to come and get me the same afternoon. A quiet instinct told me to do something that seemed entirely contradictory under the circumstances. Because I had learned years ago the wisdom of following quiet urges that did not always make sense like this one didn't, I paid attention. I walked over to Jamal, put my head on his shoulder, and cried a little bit.

"She seems quite normal to me", the doctor said, after observing my action. "You can take her home. She is fine."

We walked out, got into the car, and left the hospital. Neither of us said a word all the way home. As we walked in the door to the apartment, I turned to him, gave him a look of utter contempt, and just laughed. Jamal did not say a word. What could he say? He had played his trump card and lost badly. From the expression his face, I knew that he knew he had forever lost the war psychologically and that I was as clearly aware of this as he was. I was not the least bit afraid of him anymore—I hated him with every last breath in my body and he knew it.

A few days later, I made arrangements to stay with a friend, Joanne, for a few days so I could relax and put my problems behind me as much as possible for a while. It was wonderful being away from Jamal! There was a huge party planned at Dario's the following evening and I wanted to be in good frame of mind so I could escape my troubles for a while and enjoy it.

Jamal persisted in tracking me. He called Joanne's house several times to talk to me. When I heard his voice on the phone, I hung up. I wanted nothing to do with him.

I went off to class with Joanne the following morning and spent most of the day on campus. That afternoon when I returned to Joanne's home, her mother, a well-meaning but utterly traditional person, asked if she could talk to me for a minute, so we sat down on the couch.

Mrs. Crawford said in her kind way, "Your husband came over to see me this afternoon while you were at school. He was so unhappy and concerned about the baby. He told me all about your personal situation and how he would like to make the marriage work. He wants you to come back to him as his wife. This isn't right. You are married to him and you should go back to your husband."

As she talked, I was so stunned I could not say anything to her statements about how I "should go back to my husband". How could she possibly know what he was really like underneath his façade of charm and likeableness? Was I ever going to be free from him? What could I say that she would have understood? She was the wife of a missionary and had lived a traditional, happily married lifestyle. She knew absolutely nothing about Arabs or about Jamal. I could tell from her words that he had pulled out all the stops to make her feel sorry for him. It was obvious to me that he had succeeded brilliantly in his powers of persuasion.

I could not believe that even he would be so pushy and intrusive as to actually go to a complete stranger and talk about a sensitive personal situation which involved other people besides himself. Had he no sense of what was appropriate to burden outsiders with? There was no other conclusion to draw except that he was so self-absorbed and egocentric that he assumed he had the perfect right to trample on anyone's personal space and desire for privacy to whatever extent it took to help him succeed in getting what he wanted. He had certainly decimated what little peace of mind I had been able to create for myself while at Joanne's home.

This was equivalent to another nail in his coffin, put there by himself in an irretrievable fashion. Actions such as the attempt to have me committed and talking to Joanne's mother doomed him to abysmal failure to obtain what he wanted. No woman with any backbone and self respect would tolerate this kind of individual in her life once she learned what she was dealing with. Additionally, I grew up fiercely independent. Jamal did not know this because I had never told him.

A few hours later, Joanne and I went to the party, but any sense of joy and anticipation was utterly lost to me. The party was doing beautifully; I watched some of my friends dancing to Chubby Checker's rendition of "Peppermint Twist". I had to smile to myself quietly as I watched them, thinking that here I was watching my foreign student friends, who had come from the upper class in their respective countries, frenziedly involved in such a wonderfully frivolous activity such as the harebrained, teen-aged dance called "The Twist." What an anomaly, considering that most of them would eventually return home and play a part in governing their respective countries!

Other than the brief distraction of watching my friends dance, all I could do was stand against the wall, psychologically shattered, and try to recover some semblance of equinamity. After a few minutes, a close friend of mine from India, Deb Das, walked in the door. I had confidence that he would sense my presence because our mutually intuitive communication lines were quite strong. Sure enough, his antennae were up and almost immediately, with his unerring instincts, he saw me almost immediately. I was so glad to see him! Here was a person I could trust and let my shields down with and not have to worry about being betrayed to Jamal! He walked over to me in that almost distracted manner of his and asked me what was wrong. He and I had become acquainted over several months since we knew so many of the same foreign students and, in turn, the Americans who knew them.

Deb was of the Kshattriya caste and had family in Calcutta and Bombay. All of them were Westernized and quite well off.

Deb had attended Cambridge University and claimed to have received a First at graduation. He wrote wonderful poetry and stories. In short, he was a superb example of the type of brilliant, artistic, upper class intellectual who most women found irresistible. He was the one individual I trusted enough to confide in about my situation when we would be sitting alone at a table on many occasions in the student union building. He was a wonderful listener and was always quietly, tactfully supportive. I knew for a fact that he held Jamal in contempt and that he would never say a word about me or about anything I told him to anyone. Deb was a wonderful friend and a wonderful psychological refuge during all those long months. I owe him a debt I can never repay.

So when Deb asked me what was wrong, I told him that Jamal had taken it upon himself to appear at Joanne's house and tell her mother the whole story behind my back. Deb just looked at me for a moment.

"The swine," was all Deb said. He understood. I loved him for the wealth of compassion and support expressed in those two small words. I think he saved me that night, just by being there in the same room as a staunch and understanding friend. And I am sure that Jamal hated him for being what he could never be—pure class and my trusted friend.

I knew Jamal was having his friends spy on me. I could feel it. Every once in a while, he would call me from somewhere and try to get me to come back in between threats. While I refused and stayed with friends, those phone calls took their toll. On many occasions after one of these calls, I phoned my attorney because I did not know what else to do.

"Mr. Soderlund!" I screamed at him every time after he got to the phone. "Make Jamal stop calling me! He is driving me over the edge because he won't leave me alone" He stops for a while and I start calming down, and then he starts it up all over again!"

"I will try to see what I can do. I will contact his lawyer," Mr. Soderlund said to me on every occasion. To his credit, he never treated my outbursts as if they came from a person who was losing mental control.

This scenario occurred periodically. Now that I think back on it, I would not be surprised to learn that Jamal was, in fact, intentionally trying to make me go over the edge psychologically by making these calls. What he was doing, without realizing it, was far different. Rather than causing me to lose possession of my soul and self-confidence, he was creating in me a tactically skilled, implacable enemy, knowledgeable about the worst characteristics of Arab males the awareness of which would be used against him in every future encounter which he invariably initiated. Always, he would lose; always, he would lose face. To this day, he has undying hatred for my mother and me because we always outsmarted him.

In early spring of that year, there was an international conference on campus which all of us, Americans and foreign students alike, looked forward to attending because we were all into politics and global understanding. It was a forum of speakers on a variety of politically oriented subjects, all of whom were well-known in their fields of endeavor.

I went in and sat down, and was waiting in anticipation for the proceedings to commence when Jamal walked in and sat down at the far end of the long conference table. He wanted me to know that he knew where I was and what I as doing. I simply ignored him and after a while, he left because he could not get a reaction out of me. He really, really hated the fact that I continued to go to school, maintain good grades, and cope as best I could.

Just before the conference, I asked a favor of a classmate and friend, Patsy Smith, who lived just across the street from the main campus.

"Patsy," I asked hesitantly, "Would it be possible to stay with you for a couple of days? Jamal has sued me for divorce and he and his friends have been following me around for several weeks. He spies on me all the time, hoping to catch me in a compromising situation so he can get custody of the baby. I would love to get away from him for a few days so I can relax and pull myself together. I promise it won't be for any more that a couple of nights."

"That would be fine," she said. "Would you like to come and stay over tonight and tomorrow?"

"That would be wonderful! I'll get my basic stuff and come over after the conference going on today!"

As I walked to her apartment building later after class, I noticed Jamal and friends following me. While I certainly did not want them to think I was afraid of them, I hurried enough so that I reached the door before they did and slipped in, locking the door just before they had a chance to get in. Jamal motioned to me, indicating that he wanted to talk to me, but I shook my head "No." and went on inside.

The next day, Patsy and I were talking.

"Jamal called me on the phone today."

"Oh, really." I responded. "What did he have to say?"

"He asked me why I was letting you stay with me. I told him that it was none of his business. Then he hung up."

I reached over and gave her a big hug. "Thank you so much! I don't want him to be bothering you. I should go," I said in remorse.

"That's okay. You can stay. It's no problem. He doesn't bother me." Patsy said. firmly. What a joy it was to have such a staunch friend! Jamal had the ability to scare people when he wanted to, but it was obvious that Patsy was not one of them.

It finally became clear to Jamal that he would never be able to repair the damage done to the marriage and that I hated him with all my soul. Looking back on those months before I went home to my mother's to have the baby, I believe it never occurred to him that he could not wear me down and force me to move back in with him where he would have easy access to the baby after it was born.

Having been born in a Middle Eastern family as the firstborn son was of no advantage to Jamal after he moved to the United States. Had we moved back to any country in the Middle East, I would never have had a chance. He would have had control of every single aspect of my life and no one would have interfered.

He would have forced me to quit school if, indeed, he allowed me to go in the first place. If I had not quit school willingly, he would probably have beaten me, starved me, or otherwise deprived me of basic living needs until I finally gave in just to stay alive. He would have almost certainly have threatened to take the baby away from me and turn me out on the street after the baby was born if I did not comply with his wishes.

I would have been forced to stay at home all the time. There would be no freedom to go anywhere unless he was with me. There would certainly be no opportunity to socialize with friends, especially males, on my own in any public place. To do so would be to invite immediate, life-threatening retribution the instant the baby was born because to be seen with a man other than your husband or a relative is considered adultery in the Middle East. The usual punishment is death by one means or another. Stoning is one of the most common methods. Being burned alive is another method. Whatever the method, it would be arranged and carried out by a male member of Jamal's family once the care of the baby was safely arranged.

He would have watched me day and night to make sure that I did not somehow escape from him because I was carrying his baby and he wanted that child, no matter what happened to me, after the birth. He might have let the baby stay with me as long as it was nursing because that was the simplest solution for the care of the baby. However, after the nursing period was over, my status would be problematical. If I was very, very obedient and very, very submissive, he might let me stay with the child. However, I would live in constant fear of being thrown out with nothing but the clothes on my back. How I survived if that happened would no longer be of any concern to him and it would not have mattered because he would have the child firmly in his grasp and women, after all, were expendable.

CHAPTER 8

UNDER SIEGE

DAYS CRAWLED BY. I kept going to school, doggedly determined not to let my personal misery stop me from missing classes or finishing the quarter. (To this day, one recurring nightmare for me consists of variations on the themes of being late to classes, not be able to find the classroom, not being able find my locker, or forgetting what classes I am taking.)

When I wasn't in class, I was in the library studying or in the student union building talking to my friends who continued to diplomatically ignore my developing pregnancy. I was very careful never to talk about anything that was going on in my personal life. And I was extremely careful never to be seen alone or with any one person, especially male. By this time, I was well acquainted with how vengeful Jamal could be, and I wanted to protect my friends and supporters from him. The best way I could do that was to make sure none of them could possibly be accused of being alone with me at any time.

I received a call from Mother one afternoon in the middle of the week.

"Guess what? Jamal had me served with subpoena to appear in court for the divorce!" she said in a surprised tone of voice.

"What in the world for?!" I exclaimed in disbelief. "Surely he knows you would be there in any case!"

"Maybe he thinks I will be a witness in his defense," she rejoined. "He can't be that naïve. Just because we got along at one time doesn't mean a darn thing. He can't be dumb enough to think I would not be on the side of my own daughter!"

"It was an unnecessary expense on his part since he did not need to have it issued. Oh well, that is money we did not have to spend."

"It will be interesting to see what happens. The court date is pretty soon. I will sure be glad to get this over with. Then I am free to get through this quarter and come home."

There were a few casual acquaintances I saw talking to Jamal or to one of his friends. When that occurred, I avoided those people from that instant because I had to assume that he was trying to recruit watchers from whom he might be able to gather information detrimental to me.

Deb and I met fairly regularly in the student lounge. The best time to meet seemed to be in the afternoon when the room empty was virtually because everyone was either in class or had other things to do. I would be sitting there, reading one of my textbooks. He would come wandering in, casting his eyes around the room to see who might be present, as he always did no matter where he was. Then, as though it was an afterthought, he would plunk his books down on the same table and go get coffee. After he returned and sat down, we would have a lovely, quiet conversation. He invariably asked after my well-being which was the signal to discuss any recent difficulties caused by Jamal and how to cope with them in the best way. I believe he found our friendship as rewarding as I did because he did not have to pretend to be anything special— just himself as he chose to be that day.

CHAPTER 9

RESPITE AND ESCAPE

T HE END OF Spring Quarter came at last. I got through my final exams with aplomb and knew that I would be able to return in the fall, which I looked forward to since I had yet to earn my degree.

I sought out Deb and said, "Goodbye." It was bittersweet because, while I was desperate to escape Jamal and go home, I knew I would miss Deb's quiet, ongoing intuitive understanding and support. Then I left campus and went to the apartment still shared with Jamal to pack.

Fortunately he was not there. Even so, I was extremely nervous—the last thing I wanted was to run into him while I was trying to make my escape. I believe I took all my clothes and personal items—I cannot remember for sure because I was in such a hurry. I knew Jamal could likely intuit what I was doing and show up to stop me. I had to move quickly enough to be out of the University District before he realized I was leaving.

Several days previously, I had called ahead to the Greyhound bus station to ascertain the departure time home, and I had the price of the ticket in hand, stashed safely in my purse.

It was a beautiful sunny afternoon in June when I took my suitcases in hand and headed for the nearest bus stop to head downtown where the bus station was located. It was difficult carrying those cases because I was pretty heavily pregnant and due to deliver in July. As I was waiting for the bus, I kept looking around to make sure Jamal was not around.

The bus came and someone helped me get my suitcases on board, thank goodness! I relaxed because, so far, I was succeeding in my desire to leave town without difficulty. When the bus reached the stop across the street from the Greyhound station, and almost the instant I got off the city bus and began walking over to the bus station, I began coughing. There was no discernible reason for the problem because I did not have a cold or sore throat. I went into the bus station and waited in line to purchase my ticket. My timing was good, and I knew I would not have long to wait before my bus left for the eastern part of the state. But as I waited, the coughing got worse and I couldn't stop. As I waited in line, I kept looking around to see if Jamal had somehow figured out where I was and had come to make one of the huge, horribly embarrassing scenes he was so good at. I didn't see him.

I finally was able to purchase the ticket, take my suitcases out to the bus, and have them stowed onboard. I was in terrible shape because I was so strung out with nerves.

All the past months, I had managed to keep my psychological system in balance and my emotional reactions damped down to concentrated objectivity by focusing only on getting through school until the end of the quarter. I had succeeded very well, but now that the pressure of school was off, the months of strain were beginning to show on the surface.

I simply could not stop coughing. I kept looking around, paralyzed with fear that the awful person I had married was going to somehow show up and prevent my escape. I knew he would do anything he could to embarrass me to death and to stop me from leaving.

I climbed onto the bus, coughing nonstop, and found a seat. I could not wait for the bus to leave the station! After a few minutes, the bus driver did indeed start up the motor and begin our journey. I kept a sharp eye out in case Jamal came careening into the bus station at the last minute, but, blessedly, he did not. For about the next ten minutes (it seemed like hours!), I continued to cough, but, gradually, the compulsion to do so left me. As I thought about how I had been afflicted with the coughing for at least fifteen minutes, which I had never been afflicted with before, I finally figured out that was a reaction to my almost paralyzing fear that he would find out where I was and come and get me as he did once before when I tried to escape him by going across the state to an old boyfriend's house at Christmas—he showed up at the doorstep the next day, and I had to go with him to avoid a scene at my old friend's parents' home. This time I succeeded in eluding him, even if only temporarily, and I thanked every god I knew of that I had done so.

CHAPTER 10

REFUGE

NEVER HAVE I enjoyed an eight-hour bus ride across the state as much as I relished every minute of this one! I was content to sit by the window and look out at the sunny landscape. When I tired of that, I took out my book and read. I didn't mind the rest stops along the way—I was free and felt like my own person again.

Away from Jamal, I savored the peace of mind I took for granted before I had found out, too late, that spending a few years in the United States had not changed his lifetime of conditioning that males, especially first born sons, always get their way and that wives are property, to be molded into the way their husbands want them to be.

Mother knew what time the bus was to arrive, so she was there to give me a warm hug before we scooped up my luggage and put it in the car.

There is no place, and there never will be any place, like the home where you were nurtured, loved for yourself, and protected as you grew up. My mother's house was no exception. As I looked around my childhood home when I first stepped in the door, the shields I had kept so impenetrable and erect the past few months quietly began to dissipate. I was safe at last and had no need to look over my shoulder every five minutes or so.

One of the very first things I did (I remember it to this day, oddly) after unpacking was to go over by the heater where I and my siblings had spent so many hours keeping warm in the wintertime and sit down by it on a little stool as I used to do. I recall looking around the living room and at the cork tiles my brother and I had helped Mother put on the hardwood floor underneath. I looked at the living room walls, painted green, which my brother had painted for her. Then I looked in the kitchen at the long ceramic counter which Mother had so laboriously installed herself because she was so particular about how she wanted the kitchen to look, and the cupboards which she had refinished several years ago. All of her hard work was a labor of love for her home, and one could feel the regard for her personal surroundings in every room in the house. Such contentment I found that day, sitting there, being home!

Had I had been able to do so, I would have erased the last year and a half and begun again, a wiser person who was more careful about who she chose to associate with on more than a casual basis. I would have chosen to associate with no one on other than a casual basis and followed the example of my friend, Patsy Smith, who wisely focused on her education. And, certainly not less important, I would have spared my mother so much grief and worry!

However, that was impossible. I had a baby on the way and I was to be a mother very soon. This child had to be protected at all costs. I had a husband not to be trusted to tell me the correct time, let alone demonstrate decent, ethical behavior where the baby and I were concerned.

While I planned to return to school sometime after the baby was born because it was necessary to have at least an undergraduate degree in order to hope to obtain a decent job and, eventually, develop a career, I was going to have to wait until the baby was born and the divorce was final, at the very least.

Jamal called several times after I got home, wanting to know when the baby was going to be born. Mother and I refused to tell him or give the least clue because we knew he would show up, whether or not he was welcome, and insinuate himself on everyone. We also knew he would be watching the newspaper so we determined to keep the announcement out of the paper.

I was able to find an obstetrician, a Dr. Graham, who was a wonderful doctor. His behavior and attitude toward his patients was so gentlemanly and diplomatic that you could not help but like and appreciate him. How often does one actually enjoy visiting a doctor on a regular basis?

As the final couple of weeks passed, Dr. Graham decided that inducing the baby might be an alternative to consider if it looked like I was going to go much over the nine months before the birth took place.

As it turned out, that is exactly what happened. My doctor decided that it was time and decided that we would jumpstart the birth process. I went into the hospital the next day to be introduced to the world of giving birth. When I went to sign in at the desk, Mother and I asked firmly that the announcement not be put in the local paper. We also stressed that no visitors were to be allowed, except for my mother, just in case that Jamal somehow found out when the baby was born.

After being prepped, which was a drafty process, I was given a shot to make the contractions begin. And they did. I remember being asked what type of anesthesia I wanted when it was time. I asked for the local since I saw no sense in being completely unconscious. When the last contraction finally came, it seemed like it was going to go on forever as first the baby's head came out of the birth canal, and then the rest of body followed, smooth as silk. A couple of seconds later, I heard my newborn's first cry as he sucked air into his lungs for the first time. I was the proud parent of a baby boy, 6 pounds, 2 ounces, and 21 inches long—healthy and whole and perfect. After Mother had seen the baby in the nursery, she came to tell me that he was a beautiful baby. The first time I got a really good look at him, he was sleeping. All of a sudden he woke up and opened his eyes. I saw these huge dark orbs looking at me intently as though he knew I was his mother, and I believe we bonded at that moment. It was love at first sight for both of us. This love and bonding would have been equally true if my new baby had been a girl.

In any country in the Middle East, the wife of an Arab being pregnant and giving birth faces a much different set of attitudes than in a Western country. To begin with, boys are much more valued from the day they are born than are girl children and there is nothing an Arab male won't do to ensure the birth of sons. When a boy is born, everyone celebrates. There are screams of joy from the midwife announcing that a boy is born, parties, congratulations, and sometimes bursts of gunfire take their place in the celebrations. The new father, whose status and prestige have just increased, shows off his new son to his fiends and neighbors. The relieved mother is inside, thanking Allah for having given her a son.

If a girl is born, there usually is no joy and happiness. It is a time for mourning and silence. The midwife mutters that a girl is born, if she hasn't abandoned delivery the instant she realizes that she has helped deliver a child of the 'wrong' sex. It even happens that, before the umbilical cord is cut, the mother is slapped for having given birth to a girl! The family is offered condolences instead of sweets and the husband is ashamed.

"It is God's will," he might say, trying to save face. "Maybe next time it will be a boy."

The mother of the new baby girl will be under intense pressure to produce a boy child next time—in fact, her very survival may depend on it. A woman's status in Arab/Muslim societies depends on whether she has sons. A wife who does not bear sons is considered deficient and of low status in society.

"My wife is worthless; she has only given me girls." is a common complaint.

If the wife of an Arab male does not bear boy children, her husband will either divorce her and take another wife, or he will marry a second wife in the hopes that she will bear sons.

When an Arab male is asked how many children he has, he will reply, "Four children" meaning that he has four sons. If he is pushed, he may add, reluctantly that he has daughters also.[1]

His sons will be the light of his life. They will be treated like young princes and given the best of everything, an education, and freedom to come and go as they please. His daughters will be treated like servants. Their place is to be submissive, obedient, and at home. They will not be allowed to receive education outside the home since they will be married off as soon as possible for a good price and will contribute to another household.

Thank god I am an American living in the United States and have borne my child here where both sexes are equally wanted, loved, and valued!

*　　*　　*

I was lying in my hospital bed the next day, thinking about things. It was peaceful and quiet with the sunshine coming in the window. I dreadingly half expected Jamal to come pushing his way in, having somehow talked the hospital into allowing him into the maternity ward. As I thought about this possibility, I realized at that moment, that if he did get into the maternity ward and show up in my room, I was going to throw myself out the window to get away from him forever. Fortunately, he never found out until sometime later that the birth had taken place and by that time, I was at home and better able to cope with the fact that he existed.

The rest of the summer was spent in caring for my newly born son whose name I had spent many weeks working out. I wanted him to have strong, masculine names which were beautiful to the ear as well. I looked up the meanings of names in several books and finally decided on two. The one I chose for his first name is German in origin and means "ruler". His chosen middle name is Latin and means "priceless". Altogether, a worthy combination of names for a darling little boy with great big brown eyes, a warm wonderful laugh, and an indomitable spirit!

A couple of weeks after Damien was born, Jamal called. He said he was in town and wanted to come and see the baby. He also wanted to know what I had named him. I refused to tell him and told him also that he would be turned away if he came to the house. He was so angry! But I had long ago gotten over any fear I had of him. I had found out by now that I had backbone and plenty of it. No low class, loud mouth, dominating male from the Middle East was ever going to push me around again. I simply kept quiet while he uttered his threats until he finally ran down.

I'll see you in divorce court," I said. "Bye." And hung up.

He called a couple more times after that, hoping that I would give in, but with no success. However, we were very careful to keep all the doors and windows locked at all times and to NEVER leave the baby alone.

When it was no longer necessary to nurse Damien, I began looking for a job. We needed the extra money coming into the household account. I was also hoping to save some money toward the day when I could return and finish getting my degree. I eventually found one down at a neighborhood restaurant that served the type of country meals truckers and laborers like to eat because there was plenty of good food on the plate. The local sheriff ate there on occasion also, which was to prove a providential coincidence.

One afternoon when I was working, the sheriff came in. I needed to ask him a question because Jamal had been calling again, saying he had a perfect right to come whenever he wanted to see the baby before anything was settled in divorce court. So, when the Sheriff came in, I decided to see what he had to say.

"Sheriff, could I ask you a question?" I asked him as I served him lunch.

"Sure", he replied

"I am in the middle of a divorce. I am living at my mother's house until it is settled. My husband says he has a perfect right to come and see the baby even before the divorce takes place. He even got a policeman to call once, trying to talk me into letting him come over. Can he do this legally?"

"You say it is your mother's house?"

"Yes," I replied.

"All you have to say the next time he calls is that you cannot let him in because it is not your house, it is your mother's and you cannot let in anyone without her permission." the Sheriff said thoughtfully. "If he comes here and tries to get in, you just call me and I will take care of him."

"Thank you so much," I aid, said with relief. "He has given my mother and me such a hard time! He doesn't care about anyone but himself and tries to scare everybody into doing what he wants them to do. I will be glad to call you!"

Sure enough, a few days later, Jamal had someone in the police department call again. I told that person exactly what the Sheriff had told me to say and there was nothing either the caller or Jamal could do about it. The calls finally stopped.

CHAPTER 11

DIVORCE AT LAST

THE COURT DATE set for the divorce came at last.

My divorce attorney had seen Mother and I a couple of times so that we could make sure all of us knew what to expect in court and how to respond with the cross-questioning by Jamal's attorney.

The day before we were due in court he asked us to come in one last time.

"Be sure to answer only the questions put to you. Don't add anything extra. It could work against you," Mr. Soderlund cautioned us.

"What should I wear?" I asked.

"Just wear something sensible and conservative. You should be fine with something like you are wearing now."

The next morning we were at the courthouse just before 9:00. Mother and I arrived before Jamal and his lawyer. As they walked in, I was interested to observe that Jamal seemed somewhat cocky and that his attorney looked a little seedy around the edges.

The case started out pretty much as divorce cases do with Jamal and I presenting personal perceptions of what had been transpiring up to now. Some of what Jamal had his attorney say was obviously motivated by his Middle Eastern background because of the emphasis on my not cooking his meals, of not quitting school to get a job, and of my refusal to live in the apartment with him no matter what our relationship was. He also mentioned the fact that he thought I was mentally unstable.

When it was my turn, I brought up the fact that Jamal had sued me for divorce while I was pregnant with his child.

We then moved on to the issue of custody. Jamal's attorney put him on the stand for a startling line of questioning that went something like the following:

"Mr. Ahmed, your wife has just had the baby. Is this correct?"

"Yes."

"Mr. Ahmed, who do you think should have custody of the child?"

"I should. I believe that my wife is unstable and should not have custody."

"How would you take care of the child, Mr. Ahmed. You are still in school as a full-time student."

"Two friends of mine who recently got married have said they would be willing to look after it while I was in class."

"Are they here today, Mr. Ahmed?"

"Yes, they are. Right over there."

At this point, I looked over to where Jamal had indicated. He was referring to the woman he had had serve me with my divorce papers and her boyfriend. When they were called to the stand, they looked uncomfortable at being brought into the middle of something that was really none of their business. This was typical of what Jamal did to his friends.

Jamal's attorney asked them, "Are you willing to take care of the child?"

"Yes, we are." They then left the stand.

Then I was called to the stand. I was a little numb at this development. I was sitting there and I think Jamal's lawyer had just spoken to me.

"Do you know this couple, Mrs. Ahmed?"

"Yes."

I think he asked me a question about whether I thought they would be able to care of the baby properly. I did not say anything. At this point, the judge intervened. I think he must have realized that the months of psychological bludgeoning that Jamal had subjected me to had resulted in a momentary standstill of my thinking processes at this point in the proceedings.

"Do you want them to take care of the child?" he asked me.

"No." I said.

He then dismissed me from the stand. I went and sat down. I believe it was at this point that he gathered his papers together and began to outline to the court his synopsis of the proceedings and what his decisions were.

For the next ten or fifteen minutes, I sat spellbound as the judge outlined the proceedings which had just taken place. His choice of language and terminology was impeccably professional, but the nuances of his voice, as he outlined the conclusions he had come to while observing and listening to all that had been said, revealed how outraged he felt about the underhanded tactics Jamal had used from the beginning of our marriage to the present in his premeditated, long-term strategy to take custody of my son from me by making me look like an unstable and unfit mother.

Then the judge arrived at the stage of his presentation where he stated his determination of the terms of custody, visitation, and child support payments: Custody was unreservedly awarded to me. Jamal was to be allowed to come to see the child once a month for two hours on one weekend day a month *in Mother's house*, supervised, for the next two years. At that point, he would be allowed to take my son with him to his house for the weekend only once a month. He was required to pay $100 a month as child support, which was quite a lot at that time for a graduate student going to school full-time.

I could not believe what I was hearing! The judge had basically told Jamal what an abusive, deceitful, self-centered, low-class individual he was in such a way as to leave Jamal no room for any kind of rebuttal. The judge also had said things about Jamal to his face that, had I said them, I could have been sued for slander. I wished so much that I had instant recall because that presentation by the judge was a masterpiece of verbal retribution for the nightmare I had been through in my attempts to protect myself from his machinations. I was so grateful to the judge, I could have cried right there in the courtroom.

Jamal just sat there throughout the entire dressing down he received. There was nothing else he could do. I am sure that he sincerely regretting bringing his friends along in anticipation of victory. Instead, they were witnesses to his humiliation.

As the judge concluded the proceedings, and as I got up to leave, Jamal hurried over to me and said something about "staying in contact." I simply said, "We'll see." and walked off, free at last!

I have never been more grateful, than at that point in my life, to have been born in the United States, the best Western country in the world for a woman to be born in because of the plethora of gender equal law-based rights we have here.

Had I been living anywhere in the Middle East as Jamal's wife, I would not have had a chance of obtaining a divorce. I would have had to stay with him, obedient to his every wish, no matter what he did to me, in order to survive.

There is a tragically common mistake many Western women who have married Arab/Muslim men make. They assume that because they are citizens of the Western country in which they were born, and that because they got married in their own country, they are still safe and free if and when they accompany their husbands back home to their respective countries. **This is not the case**.

The instant you step inside the border as the wife of one of that country's male citizens, you are considered a citizen of that country, bound by its laws and by your husband's wishes. It does not matter that you were born elsewhere and have no wish to change your citizenship. You are automatically Syrian, Saudi, Iranian, Egyptian, Iraqi, Lebanese, Sudanese, Moroccan, Yemeni, Kuwaiti, Tunisian, etc.—wherever your husband is from. And so are your children if you brought them with you. He has undisputed dominion over your every move and those of your children. The authorities will not interfere, no matter what he does to you, because it has been the custom for over a thousand years not to interfere with any Arab/Muslim male's domestic activities. You are his property and that is as it has been for over fourteen centuries. You are not allowed a future. You can only grow old and die.

If you are married to an Iranian citizen, there is an added piece of information you need to be aware of. Iranians are Shiite Muslims and there is a type of marriage which only the Shiites still practice *Mut'a* or *sigheh* are terms for temporary marriage. This type of marriage can last as a few minutes or for ninety-nine years. Both the initiation and the termination of this "marriage" are determined by the male; if the woman wants a divorce she must go before a judge and hope that he decided in her favor.

Most significantly for you, "*sigheh* is the only way a Shiite man can marry a non-Muslim woman. Unlike the Sunnis, who allow Muslim man to marry other monotheists [such as Christians], Shiites demand conversion from all non-Muslim women, as well and non-Muslim men, before a permanent marriage is valid."[1] What does that mean in plain language? If you are in Iran, should your Iranian husband want to, he can say your marriage is not valid, that you are not legally married to him since you are not a Muslim. If he does, though, you might be able to use that technicality to get out of the country on the grounds that, since you are not legally married to him, you are not an Iranian citizen and therefore free to leave the country. If you have children by him, he will probably keep them unless you can somehow get them out of the country as did Betty Mahmoody, author of *Not Without My Daughter*.

Every wife in the Middle East lives in fear—fear of being beaten, fear of not bearing at least one son, fear of losing her children, fear of growing older and less attractive, fear of being superseded or replaced by at least one additional wife, fear of divorce and being cast out with nothing, fear of being killed if her husband becomes angry enough—the list goes on.

Any Arab/Muslim husband living in the Middle East can divorce his wife at any time without stated cause. He doesn't even have to let his wife know he is divorcing her—he can do it secretly, just as he can take additional wives secretly. All he has to do is say, in front of two male witnesses, "I divorce you." three times and he is free of her. However, it is a far different matter for the wife to divorce her husband. She can get a divorce, a legal separation, or dissolution of the marriage, but she must show serious cause—impotence, insanity, extreme cruelty, presumed death, desertion, lack of maintenance, or dangerous, contagious or repulsive disease, and, if anyone cares to risk harsh penalties, adultery. And even then, the final decision is up to male judges whose bias is almost always in favor of the husband.[2]

In the event of divorce, the wife is allowed to keep the children if they are still nursing. Generally, the mother has custody of daughters until puberty and sons until the age of seven when the father usually takes custody. If, for some reason, a boy stays longer with his mother, he *must* go with his father at the age of puberty, whether he wants to or not. Even though these provisions are by law, especially in the case of boys, the father often simply takes the children, no matter the ages, and there is no authority in place to force the father to return them to their mother.

No matter the actual circumstances, in every Arab/Muslim society the blame for the failure of the marriage will be laid at the feet of the woman. Every Muslim/ Arab country has been and still is predominantly a tribal patriarchy from pre-Biblical times and, in every case, especially since the advent of Islam, the males take no responsibility for any of their actions unless there might be retribution from other males. They make the female part of the population the scapegoats for every irresponsible, reprehensible, immoral act they themselves choose to commit. They simply say, in essence, "She made me do it," if there is a woman within sight anywhere on the horizon. Arab/Muslim males commit any number or combination of despicable atrocities on women whenever the opportunity arises because they know they can say, "She was flaunting herself." The poor innocent girl, sometimes still in childhood, is the one beaten to within an inch of her life, stoned, tortured, or killed outright even though she is the unwilling, brutalized, and hysterical victim while the real savages, the males in question, walk off scot free, laughing.

Many of the facts about what life is like for women in Middle Eastern countries, especially in Saudi Arabia because it is the most extreme, are difficult for women born and raised in Western countries to believe. For that reason, I encourage you to read as many of the reference materials in the Bibliography as you wish in order to set your doubts at rest. Much of the information is very disturbing.

Only by being informed about the differences in how women and girl children are thought of and treated in Arab/Muslim countries, can you take action to protect yourselves against being trapped and subjected to the same atrocities.

CHAPTER 12

AFTER THE DIVORCE

L IFE RETURNED To a semblance of normalcy—I was working full-time and had learned to appreciate the lack of turmoil in a 9 to 5 existence. For me, this period in my life was a time of healing and regrouping psychologically.

Mother was delighted to be taking care of Damien, who was the light of both our lives, when I was not home. I remember clearly how I used to watch him in his crib as he lay sleeping. I often hoped he would wake up long enough to raise his head and look through me with those huge brown eyes of his that you could see from across the room! It was easy, even as young as he was, that Damien had an extra measure of intelligence because of the vital mix of genetic inheritance.

The only disturbance in our lives was when Jamal was due to arrive for his monthly visitation. We knew that he would be very quick to complain to the court if he did not get his time and if everything did not appear to be just right. We made sure that Damien had on some of his cutest clothes and had been fed so there could be no complaints of any kind. We always scheduled the visit for the weekend day when I would be working because for us to be in the same location at the same time would have resulted in a disastrously explosive situation which would surely have led to legal complications.

Mother and I talked about my going back to school since I had not yet gotten my Bachelor's Degree. This goal was equally important to both of us. I believe that I was determined to succeed in reaching this goal as much for Mother as for myself because I knew that one of the sorrows in her life was that she had never been able to finish college and obtain a degree for herself. We were a team, working toward two common goals—taking care of Damien and keeping him safe and clearing the way so I could actually finish school and obtain my Bachelor's Degrees.

"I'll take care of the baby so you can go back to school and get your degree," Mother said one day when we were discussing future plans.

I gladly agreed. I did not say so, but I missed my international friends and globally oriented classes terribly. To take advantage of the international campus environment was, after all, why I had transferred to this particular university in the first place. I also was not going to give up on obtaining my degree.

I was able to get the paperwork filled out in time to return to school in January, contingent on an interview with Dr. Riley, Dean of Arts and Sciences. He was an older gentleman, kind and easy to talk to. When I told him about my personal situation with my pregnancy and divorce being the reason for not getting high enough grades to prevent my being put on probation, he understood completely. After we had discussed at some length about my determination to get my degree, he said in that quiet way of his that he thought I "should have another chance at school." I was so happy I almost flew! Never again did I slack off on preparation for classes and exams!

By now I had found out where the bulk of my academic interests lay and had switched my major declaration to Comparative Literature. A year or so later, after becoming acquainted with the fascinating intricacies of political science and international relations, I added the major of Political Science. There was a lot of trepidation which accompanied this decision because I was not at all sure I knew enough to do well in those classes. However, I took the jump. My first class was International Relations. I loved every second of it! The main textbook was *Politics Between Nations* by Henry Kissinger of Harvard University, a brilliant and eminently readable book which I virtually digested whole. The evening before the final exam, I stayed up all night and re-read the whole book at one sitting. As a result, I was wired the next morning and more than ready for the exam which, along with the class, I aced. What a boost to my self confidence where political science studies were concerned!

Sometime after I started back to school, Mother decided that she wanted to move to where I was attending school. With her usual efficient approach, she was able to find a very nice house with a back area totally inaccessible to anyone and it was close to the campus. She found work at an employment agency downtown, a completely new venture for her, which took a lot of courage. She became so skilled at her job that the owners found her indispensable to consistent office production of income!

We agreed that my baby and I should live with her while I was going to school. I worked part-time at the library to take care of the tuition, which I loved since I have lived in libraries ever since I could read.

Jamal came fairly regularly on visits to see Damien, scheduled by us so I would be out of the house, at school. A few times he brought his new wife, a woman he had met in school and, who, I understood at the time, came from a family in which the father figure was quite strong. This was significant because she sounded like the type of woman who Jamal could dominate and who would accept such treatment. I had seen her a few times in school; she struck me as someone easily intimidated since she backed off from me when I walked by her one day on the way to class.

The few visits on which she accompanied Jamal did not seem to go very well, according to what I heard later from Mother. She was not all that crazy about the fact that Jamal was paying child support and interested in a child who was not hers.

CHAPTER 13

ROUND TWO

ABOUT TWO years later, I received a summons from Jamal's attorney to appear in court for a hearing on child custody. This was an unpleasant bombshell, to say the least.

It seems that Jamal was having Mother's house watched periodically, apparently to ascertain whether or not I was actually living there and looking after Damien. On the basis of having not seen me coming and going whenever the watcher happened to be there, he made the assumption that I was indeed not there and being a mother. He further assumed that he had grounds for challenging custody and proceeded to contact his lawyer to begin the attempt to gain custody of Damien.

On the appointed day, Mother and I were in court right when the doors opened. This gave us a few minutes to settle in and take stock of the environment and to note those who came in after us. We were interested to observe that Jamal had brought his wife along, probably with the thought that she would be witness to his clever overturning of the custody ruling. We had gone over the probable testimony with my divorce lawyer and knew exactly what we were going to say.

The proceedings started out with, I believe, questioning about the environment in which Jamal had his visitations at Mother's house. Through his attorney, Jamal tried to establish that he had, in fact, not been able to have visitation with Damien alone in the living room, that Mother could come into the room at any time. When I was on the stand, the other attorney tried to browbeat me into acquiescing that, indeed, visitation conditions were interfered with simply because Mother was present in her own house. He kept hammering at me that she could have come into the room at any time to which I answered with increasing firmness, "But she didn't." The judge put a stop to this line of questioning because it was going nowhere.

Then came the crux and reason for these proceedings—that I had not been home to do my motherly duties by Damien.

Jamal wanted desperately to prove that I had not been home and he had coached his lawyer to bore in on the fact that I had not been seen coming or going within an undefined period of time.

To all questions put to both of us by both attorneys, our answers were the same—I had been at home, but I had not been outside in public view very often. Damien had been looked after as usual with no problems whatsoever.

There was one change in the visitation rights. Since Damien was three years old, Jamal was to be allowed to have him at his home for one week in the summer.

The testimony drew to a close and the judge prepared to present his findings.

Once again, I sat and listened in amazement at what the judge had to say. Again I would have given anything for instant recall.

This presentation, although by a different judge, was just as precisely couched in professional language and equally effective, by tone of voice and choice of wording, letting Jamal know the scorn and contempt in which he was held by the court for his vicious, stealthy attempts to destroy my credibility as a mother and take my son away from a loving and wholesome home environment where he was loved for himself alone.

Again, all Jamal could do was sit there and take one psychological blow after another to his ego, all of it brought on by himself. There was an added element of humiliation this time. His wife was sitting there, witnessing the dressing down.

I believe the judge had a very good idea of the kind of mentality Jamal was before any of us ever came to the courtroom. He would have had access to the previous court documents which set a precedent for these proceedings. He also could easily have had a word with Mr. Soderlund and the wonderful judge who had presided over the divorce itself. I will never know, of course.

It is impossible to appreciate enough the fact that our judicial system is impartial on the basis of gender when it comes to hearing and rendering decisions which affect the lives of American citizens. Neither is it possible to appreciate enough the fact that men and women alike act as judges, attorneys, and other officers of the court.

Such impartiality is impossible to come by in Middle Eastern countries. Most legal decisions are implacably biased against women. The Shari'a states unequivocally that men are a degree above women. Muslim jurists are unanimous in their view that men are superior to women in virtue of their reasoning abilities, their knowledge, and their supervisory powers. And since it is the man who assumes financial responsibility for the family, it is argued, it is natural that he should have total power over the woman. These same jurists, of course, totally neglect changing social conditions where a woman is able to earn contribute her salary to the upkeep of her family—power over women remains a divine command and 'natural' or 'in the nature of things.' Muslim thinkers continue to confine Muslim women to the house—to leave the house is against the will of God and against the principles of Islam. Confined to their houses, women are then often criticized for not having any experience of the outside world.

An Arab/Muslim woman rarely is allowed to present her own case. She is required to have a male relative represent her case. She is dependent entirely on whether her representative is sympathetic to her plight. Even when a male is presenting her position in the legal dispute, the judges rarely find in her favor unless the situation is so extreme, or her representative is so influential, that she is able to receive a higher degree of fairness exhibited in the decision handed down to her. That does not happen often and the likelihood is always very much problematical.

If it is a divorce case, she must prove impotence, lack of maintenance for her and the children, if there are any, or a horribly disfiguring disease. While the mother is lawfully supposed to have custody of the children until the age of seven, if the husband decides to take them immediately, there is no legal apparatus in place to get them back for her. Few Arab/Muslim governments will interfere on an Arab mother's behalf when her husband has custody of his own children.

It will never happen that the judge will be outraged at the behavior of the husband toward his wife. If there are problems with the marriage, the wife will be blamed. She will be told in no uncertain terms that she is a disobedient wife, and that her place is to provide for her husband's sexual pleasure, to serve him, and to bear his children without complaint.

CHAPTER 14

GRADUATION

L IFE WENT BACK to normal. I continued to take classes, quarter after quarter, slowly, slowly working my way through the requirements for my chosen disciplines and for area graduation requirements. The quarter came when everything was completed and it was possible for me to graduate Matriculation was in June, of course, and I would not have missed the graduation ceremony for all the gold in the world. It had taken me years and years to get to this point and I was going to enjoy it!

Of course, Mother came with me! She was not going to miss this either. In a very real sense of the word, the degree I received that night was not just mine, it was ours—we both had earned it by surviving harrowing months thrust upon us by an egotistical maniac and through unceasing effort on both our parts.

As I was walking down the aisle in the midst of about 300 other graduates, I was wondering where Mother was sitting and could she see? I looked up into the stands and caught her eye immediately—it was as though I had known where she was from the beginning. I looked and her, she looked at me, and we both smiled for each other alone. This was our accomplishment in the face of great odds. I told her after the ceremony that as far as I was concerned, the Bachelor's degree I had just been given was hers.

CHAPTER 15

AFTERMATH

M Y STORY IS one of many years of struggle which took place before finally achieving victory and freedom. I am one of the lucky ones.

The setting for my travails remained anchored in the United States where women can take their worth, intelligence, political participation, obtaining an education, mobility, and freedom of choice for granted without fear that these rights will disappear overnight. This is what saved me and my son.

I was lucky for another reason. The person I married had neither desire nor intent to return to his native country in the Middle East to live and so did not attempt to kidnap our son and leave the United States. He came here with the goal in mind to obtain citizenship for himself, bring his family over to this country, and help them become American citizens as well. He has accomplished these goals for which he must be given full credit for a job well done. To my knowledge, he has never looked back once he arrived on our soil.

Damien is today an accomplished professional in engineering. He has a lovely wife and three beautiful children who reflect the care, love, and training that is lavished upon them. Two harder working and more dedicated parents cannot be found anywhere.

Again, I was one of the lucky ones. Read on and weep.

PART II
OTHER WOMEN'S STORIES

CHAPTER 16

MARRIAGES MADE IN HELL

M OST RELATIONSHIPS BETWEEN Arab/Muslim foreign national males and American women begin in a similar manner: both individuals meet as students an American university and become acquainted with each other. She is intrigued by his dark looks and lively personality. The male, especially if he is Saudi, can be irresistibly charming and attentive—possibly more so than Arabs from any other country.

"Tender words are spoken, gifts are given, and promises are made. Usually [never], no mention is made of the potential problems of different cultures and religious backgrounds. But, once the woman has been lured into marriage, the man too often turns into a tyrant, becoming abusive and rude to his wife, or becoming too interested in other pretty women.

Differences in religion and culture soon begin to create serious marital problems. The woman's normal way of dressing, which was greeted with compliments during the courtship, is now declared too revealing. Loud, abusive accusations are thrown in her face if she should dare to speak to another man.

What few non-Arab women realize is that *every* Arab male is accustomed to getting his way in all family situations. There will be no peace at home until he is recognized as the undisputed ruler, a fact that many non-Arab wives do not realize until it is too late. When the couple begins to have children, the husband will invariably insist that the children be raised solely as Muslims. The mother's religious heritage is considered of no importance."[1]

The above scenario is just the beginning. It will be obvious from the following examples that while the most horrific examples of malignant and life-threatening marriages are between Saudi males and Western women, similar nightmare marriages to Arab/ Muslim nationals from other countries are just as endemic and perilous for American women and children.

*   *   *

Patricia Roush married Khalid al-Gheshayan from Saudi Arabia. Her daughters were kidnapped by their father and are still in Saudi Arabia.

One of the most famous examples of how marriage to an Arab/ Muslim male can quickly turn tragic and dangerous for a Western woman is Patricia Roush, author of the book, *At Any Price*. She met a Saudi, Khalid al-Gheshayan, when both were college students in California. After a few weeks, Pat tried to back out of the relationship, but he pursued her relentlessly, telling her how much he loved her, could not live without her, and manipulating her into doing favors for him because she felt sorry for him.

After she succumbed to his blandishments and married him, she found out she was pregnant. In her book she says, "I did not know at the time that I was pregnant. When I found out, it was too late. I should never have told him and just disappeared and raised my baby, but I didn't. I always felt I could handle anything. My false sense of control and confidence was to be my undoing."[2]

Her husband, Khalid, was basically a wastrel. He was out regularly, drinking, smoking, and pursuing women. He did not have to worry about staying in school because he received money on a regular basis from his sponsor, the Saudi Educational Mission in Houston, Texas, whether or not he attended classes. His father and other relatives sent him money as well.

"During the next few weeks [after the birth] I regained my strength, and one night while I was rocking and nursing Alia in the living room, the door opened. Khalid stumbled in, tripping over himself. I could smell the alcohol and cigarettes from across the room. He was accusatory and began cursing me. He had a gallon of wine in his hand. I got up with Alia in my arms and walked into the bedroom. He followed me.

'Don't think I don't know what you are going to do, you bitch. I'm sick of you, and I'll show you who's in charge here.'

He pushed me, with Alia still in my arms, against the wall. She was three weeks old.

'I'll fix you. You're not making any calls.'

Then he went to the telephone and pulled the cord out of the wall. After losing his balance a few times, he left the apartment with the gallon of wine in his hand."[3]

That was enough for Patricia. She made him move out.

Not only had Khalid Geshayan been drinking excessively, he had been arrested for vandalism and assault and battery. He had also been hospitalized with a diagnosis of paranoid schizophrenia, acute and chronic alcoholism, and alcoholic hepatitis.

Shortly afterward, he was deported back to Saudi Arabia and Patricia filed for divorce when Alia was two years old. Khalid, in true Arab style, threatened to make trouble for her if she did divorce him. When he was able to return to the United States and to San Francisco, his father came with him. Between them, she was talked into taking Khlid al-Gheshayan back on the pretext that he was in business with his father and that he had stopped drinking. Furthermore, she was still under the illusion that he could not do her any real harm. Agreeing to take him back was the biggest mistake of her life because it opened the door to heartbreak and pain that would never leave her.

She gave birth to a second daughter, Aisha, in 1982. Even though she had not carried through with the divorce, Khalid was never around, and her world centered completely on her little girls. She needed a profession that would afford her a living salary so she enrolled in a three-year nursing diploma program at St. Luke's School of Nursing in San Francisco.

Khalid talked her into taking a trip to Saudi Arabia with the girls so his Saudi family could meet them. They were gone for six weeks and returned to the United States just before her classes were to begin in the fall. However, she had to drop out a few months before graduation because she had contracted hepatitis in Saudi Arabia. Since she was not receiving any money from her husband who had been in Saudi Arabia for several years, her financial situation was getting desperate.

After months of pleading on Khalid's part, Pat decided to take the girls and join him in Saudi Arabia because she badly needed time to recover her health and to get her finances back under control. She also thought he had finally changed his lifestyle into that of a responsible, reasonable person and that the marriage might work, finally.

When she and her daughters arrived, they lived on an isolated piece of land owned by Khalid's father. They lived in isolation away from everyone and had no phone. Pat was not allowed to drive or to use taxis and the girls had no school that was safe for them to attend. Everyone wanted to come home very much.

Patricia's stark testimony before the Committee on Government Reform on June 12, 2002, tells her story in the plain unvarnished style that only comes with having to hoard one's psychological strength and courage every moment in order to cope with the reality of her horrendously difficult goal—that of getting her daughters back safe with her:

"One night I was talking to [Khaled] Gheshayan about coming home and he suddenly jumped up, ran after me and chased me into the bedroom. He closed the door and threw me on the floor and began to kick me in the chest with his feet. I was screaming for him to stop and Alia was screaming on the other side of the door, 'Mommy, Mommy.'

After what seemed an eternity, he finally stopped and I couldn't breathe. I had a pain in my chest and couldn't raise my arms up without severe pain. I asked him to take me to the hospital. I thought my lungs were punctured. He told me, 'I can kill you and throw you out into the desert and no one would even know.'

He was right. I was in the middle of the Arabian desert with a madman and he could do anything he wanted to me. There was no one to help me. Alia clung to me and was crying, 'Mommy, Mommy, are you all right? What did you do to my Mommy?' He told me he would take me to the hospital and, 'If you tell anyone what happened, I'll kill you.'

I had a cardiac contusion, fractured breastbone and several broken ribs. I told one of the German doctors working at the hospital that I had been beaten by my husband and the doctor pretended he didn't hear me. He couldn't do anything to help me. He was a foreigner and under Saudi law had no power. He probably saw Saudi women coming into that emergency department all the time with broken bones. In fact, I met an American doctor at the King Fahad hospital who told me he treated many Saudi women being beaten by their husbands is very common. Her husband has the right to beat her. It's the law. Gheshayan had right to beat me or kill me. As he told me, 'You are an American and I am a Saudi. Who are they going to believe?'

I went home with him and the children. I secretly called the American Embassy from a pay phone and they told me, 'If he doesn't sign your exit visa, you will never leave and your children certainly wouldn't be able to leave with you, even if by some chance you get out.' I was afraid for all of us. The girls and I huddled together. One night we were in the car with him in the downtown Riyadh. The girls were in the back seat and I was in the passenger seat covered in black. Alia made a sigh and Gheshayan suddenly turned around and slapped her right across the face. She was six years old. She screamed, 'Mommy, help.' I opened the car door, got out and pulled both girls out of the back seat. We started to walk down the dark, dirt streets with no sidewalks.

I had no money, no passports, no friends, and was in imminent danger of being killed at any time. He pulled up along side of us in the car and said, 'Get in. Where do you think you are going?' We got in the back seat and said to Alia, 'And she stays here.'

Alia screamed again and said, 'Oh no. No.' I held her and Aisha in my arms. We were terrified.

So for the next several months I did what he said and submitted to him. I convinced him to come back to the States and get the scholarship back. He liked that idea but he wouldn't give me the money to leave. I convinced him to take me to the American embassy and they gave me a repatriation loan to get out. They told me he must sign my exit visa and the exit visa for the girls or we wouldn't be able to get through airport security. They couldn't help us. The girls and I left Riyadh in May 1985.

We went to Chicago instead of San Francisco because I needed help from my family. We were so glad to get out of Saudi Arabia but were without any money or resources. I stayed with relatives, filed for divorce, and went back to nursing school. After I got on my feet again, I got an apartment and sent for our things from San Francisco. I was one semester from graduating from nursing school and we would be financially all right in just a few short months. I was planning on buying a house after graduation. We were free and started to be happy in our new lives together. Alia was attending the same school my mother and I attended. We felt safe at last.

My divorce was final, I was awarded custody of my daughters and Gheshayan was out of our lives forever. So we thought

Just as everything was looking so good, he showed up, hired a private detective to find us, paid an attorney to overturn my divorce and custody decree on the grounds that he had not been properly served papers. He followed me in a rented car, stalked me night and day, tried to get Alia out of school and called me constantly. I went to the police and tried to get a restraining order and they told me he hadn't broken any laws and there was nothing they could do.

He convinced me he was in Chicago to stay and only wanted to see the girls. He said, 'Pat, I only want to see my children. If I was going to take them, I would have never allowed you to leave Saudi Arabia with them. I just want to live here and go back to school. I would never do that to you.' After two months of this, I believed him and allowed him to see the girls on a weekend visit. He took them. It was Super Bowl Sunday—January 26, 1986. The Chicago Bears were at New Orleans. I knew how much he hated living in Saudi Arabia and I believed him. I don't know why. He never came back with my daughters.

I called the State Department and Office of Overseas Citizens Emergency and they told me, 'You will never see your children again. They are gone. There is nothing we can do.'

I called Gheshayan in Arabia and he told me, 'Come here and do exactly what I want or you will never see them again. The United States cannot help you now. The embassy cannot help you. Go ahead and get Reagan. Alia and Aisha are never allowed to leave Saudi Arabia again.'

If I had gone back to Saudi Arabia, he would have killed me, but first he would have broken every bone in my body and mutilated me. Or he would have locked me up in a room all alone with only enough to keep me barely alive before he finally beat me to death.

One of the punishments in Saudi Arabia for women who disobey is 'the woman's room.' They lock up a woman in a dark, isolated room and give her only enough food for a slim existence. She is kept there until she goes mad.

This was the beginning of my two decade nightmare."[4]

Patricia Roush has never succeeded in getting her daughters back safe. She has seen them once in ten years, surrounded by guards in a set up interview where it was obvious that they were being brainwashed to hate America and being forced to become Muslim. They were told by their father that Allah would kill their mother's family if they ever went back to the Unites States and they were told that they would never be allowed to see her again.

When they grew older, they were sold to husbands for money called a dowry in that country. Fairly recently, Patricia was told by indirect sources that her oldest daughter just gave birth and that Pat is now a grandmother. She does not think she will ever see her granddaughter. But she will never give up on getting her daughters back.

Gheshayan is still as deranged and cruel as ever. It is beyond horror to think about what he has probably done to his daughters over the years. The State Department has done nothing to help. In fact, it has hindered, along with the Saudi government, any strategies which might have been instrumental in bringing Alia and Aisha back home.

Patricia Roush is forced to live with the knowledge that her daughters have been and still are being manipulated, abused, and robbed of all joy of life by their utterly cruel, uncaring father and the men he sold his daughters to as "brides". I cannot imagine a worse hell on earth for any caring mother.

I have told her story in part but I urge you to read her book, *At Any Price*, to really understand how marrying a Middle Eastern male will change your life forever and not for the better.

Maureen married Mohamad Hisham Dabbagh from Syria. Her daughter was kidnapped by her father and may be in Saudi Arabia.

Maureen and Mohamad were married and settled down in Medina, Ohio. The relationship was in trouble from the start, wracked by fighting and arguments occurring because of cultural and personality differences. During one of the fights, Mohamed told her that he had only married her in order to obtain citizenship;

this was a cruel blow to Maureen because she loved him and thought he genuinely loved her.

The fighting eventually began to include physical abuse of both herself and her daughter and it had been getting harder and harder to protect her daughter from being the object of his violence and rage. Then her husband began sexually abusing Nadia, saying that this was how Arabs show affection for their daughters, and, when on their third wedding anniversary, Maureen actually caught him in the act, she walked out on him right then, taking Nadia with her to seek safety in a battered women's shelter. Maureen had not been able to take money, credit cards, or anything else that would help her survive because Mohamad had liquidated all of her assets or had everything put in his name. As she was leaving, Mohamad was laughing as he said, "'You'll be back . . . you have no money and nowhere to go.'"⁵ On top of everything else where he was concerned, she also found out that Mohamad was wanted for crimes in several countries and had begun the process of taking a second wife. She sued for divorce. It was finalized before Mohamad's application for citizenship went through so he knew he had to depend on his daughter to get his green card (his "green card" daughter, he called her).

While Mohamad was granted visitation rights, Maureen was very reluctant to let him have visitation without supervision. She pleaded with the courts not to allow him to take Nadia on unsupervised visits since he had threatened more than once to take their daughter with him to Syria and that Maureen would never be allowed to see Nadia again. The courts ignored her and ordered her to let him take their daughter out of state for one of the visitations. She obeyed, but with terrible premonitions about the outcome.

That was the opportunity Mohamad had been waiting for. He wanted to hurt Maureen in the cruelest way possible for leaving him and divorcing him, stopping his citizenship processing— through the abduction and abuse of the daughter she adored more than her own life. The effect on Nadia did not matter to him. He took his 3-year-old daughter, who did not want to be with him in the first place, to Syria without warning, without a thought of the effect on Nadia. He did not care about the child except as a tool through which to obtain his citizenship and to inflict continuous torture on Maureen.

Maureen has neither seen nor spoken to her daughter since the kidnapping in 1992. Maureen has moved heaven and earth in her efforts to get her daughter back:

"She has picketed, sued, cajoled. She has hired lawyers, bounty hunters, and charlatans. She has spent $2,000,000 that she didn't have by raising enormous sums of money and going into debt. She has been featured on the Voice of America radio network and Worldwide Web sites dedicated to solving international child abductions. She has gained the support of the U.S. Senate, which passed a resolution calling on the U.S. and Syrian governments to do all in their power to reunite Nadia with her mother.

Maureen has connected personally with people all over the planet by sending emails and internet postings from her kitchen laptop computer. One Web site operator claims 10 million people have expressed support for Dabbagh, as her updates ricochet through cyberspace via e-mail forwarding and subscription lists, creating a sort of perpetual motion messaging machine.

Still, no Nadia."[6]

Maureen went to Syria, trying to find her daughter but with no success. Ironically, she has been able to help other parents retrieve their children but she has not been able to make any progress on securing her own daughter safely in her arms to bring her back home. There have been promises to recover Nadia made by Syrians to whom she had paid huge amounts of money. Maureen even went to Lebanon, acting on the promise made by one of these individuals that he would bring her daughter to her from Syria. He disappeared with the money and left her waiting vainly in Lebanon for a month before realizing that he was never coming.

She and the State Department believe that Mohamad is now working in Saudi Arabia where he is safe from prosecution for getting into trouble in Syria and from the United States. However, there are international warrants out for his arrest so, if he is in Saudi Arabia, they are supposed to deport him. So far that has not happened.

It is entirely possible that Nadia is being raised by his parents in a secret location to prevent her being rescued. However, Maureen has received information that Mohamad gave Nadia to a terrorist group in Syria. This implies that he might have been involved with Saudi intelligence in some capacity, hence the job in the security hospital to keep him out of reach of the United States and Syria. Maureen is not giving up hope. She continually works on ways which will help her, she hopes, to find her little girl and bring her home.

Monica Stowers married Nizar Radwan from Saudi Arabia. She, her son, and her daughter are still in Saudi Arabia because she cannot take them out of the country.

Monica Stowers met Nizar Radwan at the University of Dallas. He courted her until she consented to marry him. She thought that he loved her. What he did not tell her was that he had a wife and family back home. Arab/Muslim males often have more than one wife since they can have up to four simultaneously. These additional wives are often kept secret from the first wife simply because the husbands wish to do so. Keeping secrets like this gives the males a sense of power and superiority which they value much more highly than their wives' feelings.

After Nizar finished his education in the United States, he and Monica went to Saudi Arabia. Upon their arrival, she was left at his mother's house and it was then that she discovered her husband's already existent wife and family. She also found out that his relatives did not like her and wanted her gone. Monica told Nizar that she wanted to return to the United States. It was at that point that she found out that, without her husband's written permission, she could not leave the country. Fortunately for her, he agreed to let her leave. She was relieved because the embassy had informed her of the need for his signature on the exit visas she had secured for herself and the children.

However, a few days later, when Nizar said he was taking the children to the park, Monica waited patiently at home for their return. After waiting for hours, it became clear that he had disappeared with them and was not bringing them back.

She went to the American embassy to obtain help finding a lawyer to represent her. All the embassy gave her was a list of attorneys which was useless since there are no divorce lawyers in Saudi Arabia. She then went to the Saudi courts which was just as useless since Saudi courts are Islamic Shari'a which have been against women's rights of any kind since the advent of Islam.

The court outlined the guidelines very clearly. "The court ruled that because I was a woman, a Christian, and I wanted to take my children to the U.S., Nizar got complete custody of them and could even determine when I could see them. The judge only asked him orally to let me see the children. My son was seven and my daughter was a year and a half. Nizar's family tried to get me into a home for indigent Saudi women.

I got threatening phone calls and had trouble sleeping at night. I decide I could get more accomplished in the U.S. I left Saudi Arabia, which turned out to be a big mistake."[7]

Upon her return to the United States, Monica went to Washington to see her state senators, the State Department, and the National Center for Missing and Exploited children. None of these visits helped her in the least because Saudi Arabia is not a signatore to the Hague Convention and so ignores such attempts. She went to the Saudi Embassy in Washington and was treated with ridicule. It was then that she realized that no government was going to help her retrieve her children. She was going to have to work alone.

In 1987, Monica was allowed to return to Saudi Arabia to see her children, but all the visits took place in a police station. While her son knew that Monica was his mother, her daughter had been told that her Palestinian stepmother was really her mother, that Monica was only Rasheed's mother.

In 1990, Nizar gave Monica a visa to revisit her children in exchange for a good reference for job he wanted. In spite of the fact that the interviewer did not want to hire Nizar, he did so to help Monica see her children.

When Monica arrived, she found that her son had been sodomized by his uncle and older stepbrother and was presently in the hospital to have his appendix removed. It was then that she decided to stay and try to get her children out of Saudi Arabia.

After Rasheed was out of the hospital, Maureen and he picked up her daughter, Amjad, up at school and went to the American Embassy. They were allowed entry, but, when the embassy personnel realized that she had come to seek sanctuary and was going to stay, various employees tried to make her leave even though she told them of her situation.

"Karla Reed's attitude was relentlessly cold and unfeeling. 'This is not a hotel. We have nowhere for you to stay,' she said in a not so pleasant tone.

'I'm claiming sanctuary on U.S. territory.'

I remembered from a civics class that invading an embassy is the same as invading that embassy's country.

'People are mistaken if they believe this is U.S. soil. This is Saudi soil and the Saudis can come in here whenever they please.'

Later I heard that the **U.S. government had to sign an agreement that it would not use the U.S. military stationed in Saudi Arabia to help mothers escape with their children.** [bolding mine]

'I've been in contact with Washington, and I can have you removed.' said Karla.

"I'm not going anywhere." I told her. She left in a huff."[8]

Monica went to make some extremely telling and important comments about embassy personnel:

"This is something I was to encounter over and over again as I had to deal with the embassy and its rotating personnel over the years: the arrogance of consuls and vice consuls I had to go to for help; their ignorance of the environment they were working in (all the ones I dealt with in the early and mid-1990s spoke no Arabic and Syrian clerks were doing any government business that had to be done in English for them);

and the utter lack of imagination on their part that something
really bad was happening. They were too busy schmoozing
with big shots and business interests, partying, traveling, and
doing whatever it took to make their CVs look good. Many
American expats I met over the years encountered the same
arrogance and lack of help. (I had to laugh as I was reading
an autobiography written by Kirk Douglas, . . . talking about
this same kind of arrogance and ignorance personnel at an
embassy in Europe displayed to him!) This is no coincidence.
Another American mother in the same situation as I, Debra
Sultan, told me she called up an embassy and told them her
Saudi husband had beaten and kicked her out of her house,
and she was told the embassy is not a hotel!" [bolding mine]

Several hours later, Karla Reed, miffed at Monica's
determination to stay in the embassy with her children where it
was safe, called security. Two Marines came in, accompanied by
one of the embassy employees, Frederick Pauleski, who felt brave
since he was in the company of the two military professionals. The
Marines had the decency to be apologetic about what they were
being asked to do—throw three desperate American citizens out
of their own embassy they had come to for protection! Monica
would not let Pauleski anywhere near her or the children because
she held him in much deserved contempt for his spinelessness at
not helping her.

The embassy van dropped Monica, Rasheed, and Amjad off at
her ex-mother-in-law's house at which point Nizar taook Amjad
and locked her up in his house. Monica and Rasheed went into
hiding in order to save themselves from being arrested.

About this time, the 1991 Gulf War started so the authorities
were preoccupied with handling the difficulties. Monica found out

that while the U.S. embassy arranged to have other American citizens evacuated, she was never called so she and Rasheed could be evacuated also.

After the Gulf War, Nizar used a lie about meeting her to celebrate Amjad's birthday to orchestrate her arrest by the religious police. As she was thrown into prison, she called to her son to contact a Saudi princess she knew so she would be able to get assistance from someone with influence. It worked beautifully because Princess Noura gave her a paper with her stamp on it so she was safe until her residency papers came through. From then on, her ex-husband could not touch her in any way because she was under the sponsorship of the daughter of the Crown Prince. This probably saved her life.

Monica's son was in terrible shape. He was being taught outright lies at school and finally had a nervous breakdown. He was admitted to the hospital where he was diagnosed as having "conversion reaction" which was not too surprising since the Saudis routinely force non-Muslims to practice Islam, no matter what their spiritual beliefs are, or they will be abused and possibly killed.

When Amjad was 12 years old, Nizar had married her off to a radical cleric in Dhahran. Amjad and her 'husband' came to visit, and when the cleric was ready to leave, she refused to go with him. When he left to find Nizar, Monica and Amjad left quickly and went into hiding. During this time, Monica learned from her daughter that the stepbrother had had intercourse with her from behind.

The American embassy was aware of what was happening with this family and did nothing.

When Monica's ex-husband was able to get Amjad back, he promptly beat her up. When Monica tried to get the police to do something before her daughter suffered severe injuries or was killed, the police chief said that Islam allowed a father to beat his children. When Amjad went to court with her father, she found an opportunity to escape. Then she found her mother and the two moved to another location. A gang of brothers hired by Nizar followed them around, waiting for a chance to grab Amjad. Fortunately, they were finally arrested.

Nizar went to the office of the governor of Riyadh and spoke to a Prince Ahmed about forcing Monica to hand over Amjad to her father or be deported. Monica refused to send her daughter back to an environment where she was beaten, sexually abused, not going to school, and married off to some stranger by her father. It was to no avail. Amjad was turned over to her father. She managed to escape a couple of time to Bahrain with friends, but she was always caught. She turned 19 without more than a 6th grade education. What has happened to her no one knows since her husband divorced her and married his cousin. Hopefully, she is living with her mother.

Monica's son, Rasheed, never really had a chance. He is now on drugs and involved in self-destructive behavior.

Monica was diagnosed with cervical cancer and had to have a radical hysterectomy. She and her children are still in Saudi Arabia. Her son can leave whenever he wants to, but she is still unable to take her daughter home to the United States because no one in the U.S. government will help her.

Monica has some observations to make about government support of its citizens that bears repeating and remembering:

"It [the World Trade Center bombing] could have been prevented. It made me recall the anger I felt in the past when I went to the visa section of the U.S. embassy in Riyadh and saw all those Saudis in line for visas—the line stretched around the building at the beginning of summer. They could easily go, but my children, American citizens both, were denied that right.

When an American comes to any U.S. embassy in dire straits, they should receive help getting out with their children. I can assure you that the Saudi government does not hesitate at all to help Saudis take their children away from foreign spouses. The Saudi government even issues passports under a different name to Saudis to enable them to enter the U.S. Why aren't we fingerprinting them and developing a database? It is very careless not to. I've been told by maids and drivers from the Philippines working for the royal family.

It is scandalous that American mothers are not allowed to travel to Saudi Arabia to see their children unless their kidnapping Saudi ex-husbands get them visas. The American government values their 'special relationship' with Saudi Arabia over the human rights of its own citizens.

It is disgraceful that even now American mothers are stuck in Saudi Arabia and cannot leave when they want to.

I am asking the American government to remember what it stands for, human rights, and they should not forget this in exchange for perks from countries which have abysmal human rights records."[9]

Kristine Uhlman married Mustafa Ukayli from Saudi Arabia. Her two children were taken by their father to Saudi Arabia where they still remain.

Kristine met Mustafa while they were graduate students at Ohio State University. He courted her with charm and attention to everything that would please her. He was successful in his suit and they were married. Within the next three years they had two children, a daughter, Maisoon, and a son, Hami.

As the marriage grew older, Mustafa became physically abusive. Kristine took action because she was one of the few American women who knew something about how Arab/Muslim men operate. She moved herself and her three children to an unknown location and changed their names because of her certainty that he could surely come after the children and kidnap them. Even her parents, who did not understand why she left such a "presentable husband," did not know where she was because she communicated with them through a third party. She finally was able to win temporary custody of both children from a court in Denver, Colorado.

Mustafa stayed at her parents house, playing on their ignorance of the Arab/ Muslim male mentality and made up stories about how Westernized he was. All the while he was sneaking out of the house, closing the joint bank accounts and getting the requisite paperwork ready in preparation for a quick getaway to Saudi Arabia after he had successfully snatched the children from their mother.

As every Saudi can do when he wants to because he has access to huge amounts of money on a regular basis, Mustafa hired thugs to find his children and kidnap them at the first opportunity. Money was no object and sure enough, Kristine and the children were located. The children were kidnapped suddenly and roughly right in front of their home. Mustafa and the children he had wrenched from their mother were back in Saudi Arabia almost immediately.

"'Within three days, Kristine told me [Betty Mahmoody], "Mustafa had divorced me in the Islamic court in Saudi Arabia and was given custody of the children and all our assets."'[10]

Kristine knew that neither government would help her recover her children, but she hoped that she would be allowed to at least contact them. The Saudi ambassador said he would see what he could do as long as she did not go to the press. She promised not to do so, hoping that this would help her cause. She was hoping to be allowed into the kingdom, establish residency, and then go before the Islamic court to present her case. She waited two years before she was granted a special residency permit to live and work in Saudi Arabia.

A week after Kristine arrived, she was arrested and put in a women's prison where most of the population were children and toddlers. There were no sheets or mattresses and no regular meals since food was brought by families of the inmates. Her parents were contacted and told to stay away from the press if they wanted help for their daughter. She was in prison for five days and she has never known why she was arrested in the first place.

Since she had established herself as a legal resident of Saudi Arabia, Kristine was hoping that she would be granted permission to appear before the Islamic court and have a chance to gain custody of her children before they turned seven years old.

She finally convinced the Islamic Court to hear her case. Her lawyer left her the second day, stranded in an all-Arabic speaking court environment, because he was not making enough money. She was denied custody because of a photograph of her and the children leaving church that was produced in evidence—she would affect their "religiousness".

During that year, Kristine was allowed to see her children only five times. She finally could not stand the strain any longer and returned to the United States. In 1986, she was allowed to see them, but only with his new wife in the room. They had been taught to hate the United States. They considered themselves Arabs and they had been fed racial bigotry. For example, that America gives passports to Jews and that this country has no mosques. Worst of all, their father had brainwashed into thinking their mother did not love them. All Kristine has are her memories and her dreams of them as her children. If they ever come to this country to study, perhaps she will have a chance to get to know them. She does not know.[11]

Beverly married Majid from Iran. Her daughter was taken by her father back to Tehran. Beverly was finally allowed to join them in Iran where she is today.

Beverly met and married Majid, a student from Iran, in Tuscon, Arizona The marriage was far from perfect and, as she later told Betty Mahmoody, she was afraid he would kidnap their daughter, Sabrina, and take her back to Iran. He did not want her to come to Iran because he wanted a divorce and he knew he would get a better deal under Islamic law.

Beverly pleaded for months with her husband to let her come and be with her daughter. She finally wore him down and he agreed to let her come. It took tremendous courage on her part to leave the United States, knowing she might never be allowed to see her family again. She also knew that Sabrina would never be allowed to leave Iran and she chose to be with her daughter, no matter what. They are there to this day.[12]

Meg met and married Hossein, a student from Iran. Her two children were taken by their father to Iran. She followed to be with her children and has been there ever since.

Meg had met Hossein, probably on a college campus somewhere in the Midwest. When they got married, Meg believed that they would be as successful a married couple as they were when they were dating. They had two children, a boy and a girl. However, as time went on, Meg's husband changed from the good natured boyfriend and companion she had grown to love into a demanding, suspicious person she hated being around.

She finally filed for divorce. This caused the onset of a chain of events she could not have predicted. Hossein kidnapped the two children and took them back home to Iran.

Meg was desperate to get back her children so she followed them to Tehran where she lived for eight years in a two-room house shared by her husband's large family. She was not allowed to talk to anyone from the West and she was not allowed to go anywhere by herself or without permission.

Sometime after they had their third child, Hossein gave her permission to take the baby to the United States to see Meg's aging parents. She was, however, not allowed to take the other two children with her.

While she was in the United States, she had an opportunity to talk to Betty Mahmoody. She told Betty that if her living situation in Tehran were half as good as Betty's had been she would "have it made." Meg was living in a part of town where two-room houses commonly housed as many as fifteen people, with no air conditioning or modern facilities.

Meg knew she had to return to Iran—she could not desert her two older children. Before she left, she received a letter from her daughter urging her to stay in America, but Meg could not do it. She could not leave them to fend on their own, not knowing what they were going through. I doubt that any mother could have after reading Betty Mahmoody's book, *Not Without My Daughter*.

She arrived safely back in Tehran because she is trying to give them some sort of a dream, some sort of a happy life. She has not been heard from since.[13]

Kit Bell married Sabri Hashim from Libya. Her two children were taken by their father back to Libya. She has never been allowed to have anything to do with them.

Kit Bell met Sabri Hashim when they were graduate students at Portland State College in Oregon. He was handsome, charming, and as attentive to her as anyone could wish. They were married amidst joy and high hopes for a happy future. A few months after their first child, a son, was born, Sabri talked Kit into making a trip to Libya with him, ostensibly for a short time only.

When she wanted to return to the United States with their son, Sabri refused to let them leave. She gave birth to a daughter while living there.

Kit and the children were in Libya for three years, unhappy and confined as are all women living in the Middle East. She could do nothing without permission and her every move was watched. Eventually, she was able to talk Sabri into letting her and the children go back to the United States for a vacation. Almost the instant after she was once more on American soil, she filed for divorce and went into hiding.

It was to no avail. Sabri promptly came back to this country to contest the divorce and to find where Kit was hiding with the children. The judge, who held the passports, ordered Kit to make her children available for supervised visitation. She was afraid to do so and told the judge she feared for her life and for the security of her two little ones. In spite of her fear, the judge told her that she would be jailed for contempt of court if she did not comply. She knew that if she were in jail, the children would be in even greater danger, so she came out of hiding.

The first visitation was uneventful. When it came time for the second one, Sabri talked the supervisor into letting him take the children into a toy store alone. That was all the opportunity he needed. He and the children vanished without a trace. He cabled his attorney three weeks later to say that he and the children were back in Libya.

Kit tried and tried to talk him into letting her come back to Libya to visit the children. She begged and pleaded. Sabri told her in no uncertain terms that, as far as they were concerned, she was no longer part of their lives and that she no longer existed for them.

He did relent long enough to send photos of them several years later to prove they were still alive after Qaddafi's Tripoli headquarters was bombed by the United States military. Her son, Ahmed, was six years old and her daughter, Camella, was four and the photographs tore Kit's heart out. She knew she would never be able to see them again.

Even so, she knows her mother-in-law loves the children very much and that she will take care of them with everything that is in her. Kit has still never been allowed to speak to them. She does not know whether they ever receive the letters and gifts she sends them She has learned, to her never ending sorrow, about the control Muslim/Arab males have over their children, their callous treatment of women, and about the severe cultural differences between the West and Arab/Muslim countries.

Kit will never be at peace with the fact that she and the children she would like so much to be with are half a world away from each other. Ahmed and Camella are growing up without her and without knowing her. Maybe someday, she hopes . . . . [14]

Mariann Smith married Khalid Saieed from Iraq. Her two children were taken by their father back to Iraq where they are today.

Mariann met Khalid when they were students at a community college near Detroit, Michigan. He had originally come to the United States to obtain an engineering degree. Mariann, who appreciated his lack of vices and undemanding ways, fell for him at first sight. They were married six months later.

Khalid went on a six-week visit back home to Iraq about six months after they were married. When he returned, and when Mariann told him she was pregnant with their first child, he was furious. They had agreed not to have children for five years so that he could finish his schooling

"'You did this on purpose," he said heatedly. 'You've ruined my life."[15]

Khalid was so angry, he moved into his own apartment, leaving Mariann stranded without money to live on. She lived from hand to mouth with virtually nothing to eat.

Khalid was not concerned about her predicament; in fact, he moved to Texas to go to school about three weeks before the baby was born. When he returned several months later, he ignored his new son as though he did not exist. He never helped to care for him in any way, leaving Marainn with full responsibility for both baby and household in addition to holding down a full-time job.

She now knew him to be untrustworthy, and this was brought home to her again when he disappeared again about eighteen months later. Even so, she ignored her mother's concern that Khalid might abduct Adam and go back to Iraq.

Mariann became pregnant a second time and Khalid was beside himself. He had been working toward his master's degree and he knew he would have to drop out of school and get a job, which was the last thing he wanted to do. He did not speak to Mariann for months. When three months had passed after the second baby, a girl, was born, Khalid took off to California to enroll in school.

She delivered an ultimatum to Khalid about coming back to take care of his responsibilities or he would lose his family which, to his credit, he did. She became a stay-at-home mother while her husband worked. However, the infighting continued, but with time, an added element. Khalid had transformed into as puritanical a father who ever lived where his daughter was concerned. For example, she was not allowed to bare her midriff in any fashion (she was three years old).

Khalid had suggested to Mariann on more than one occasion that they move back to Iraq for a year or so to see whether life might not be easier there and to let his family get to know their son's children. Mariann did not trust him enough to take the chance that he would not allow them to return to America. Furthermore, they had agreed to raise their family in the United States so she did not consent to go to Iraq.

In June, 1990, Mariann went to an antique show to sell some of her old games, toys, books, and dolls. She called home that evening to say goodnight to her children and tell them she would be home the following day. No one answered the phone. This scared her because she knew that Khalid never took the kids anywhere, especially in the evening. She kept calling in the vain hope that he would answer the phone and that everything was, in fact, all right. She kept trying to tell herself that the cold chills which were running down her spine did not mean her worst fear had become reality—that Khalid had stolen the children and taken them to Iraq.

When Mariann got home, she found all the children's toys and clothes intact. She could tell that he had done everything possible, including a note saying they had gone on vacation, to throw her off the trail. The cold truth of his premeditated planning to abduct Adam and Adora hit home forcefully as she began receiving bills totaling over $30,000 in purchases, bank loans, and cash advances. This was further confirmed when she found papers in the garbage with notations about his flight numbers and reservation codes from which she figured out his itinerary. They had driven to Toronto, then had taken flights to London, Vienna, and finally to Baghdad.

In retrospect, Mariann realized that from the first time he has suggested to her that they go back to Iraq, he had been laying the groundwork for such a move—he had done research on techniques of international abduction, had sent for and received work permit papers from the Iraqi Embassy, and had added the two children to his passport at the last minute. This was a prime example of how the stealth and deception which is characteristic of Middle Eastern cultures came to Khalid's aid in deceiving his wife for so long before he carried out his plan to take the children away from her.

She contacted the State Department which, of course, after many words and suggestions, told her there was nothing they could do to help her get back her children.

Mariann was in terrible shape—she could not get over her grief for months, she could not stop crying at any given instant, she could not keep her food down, and she could not recover enough to be able to obtain employment. She tried calling Iraq in an attempt to speak to her children at least once a day. Finally, with the help of friends, she was able to find out that the children were all right. She was still not able to talk to them or to Khalid.

Finally a silver lining showed through Mariann's clouds of despair. Khalid wanted to put the children in school, but he needed copies of their birth certificates authorized by the State Department. A deal was struck: if Khalid agreed to talk to Mariann, the State Department would issue the authorized copies of the desired birth certificate.

Several days later, the phone rang. It was the go between for the exchange calling. He had Khalid on the phone, ready to talk to her. The first thing Mariann wanted to know, of course, if the children were all right and healthy. Khalid reassured her that this was so. Then Mariann asked what was, for her, the crucial question: could she join them in Mosul, where Khalid and the children were living?

"Of course, said Khalid. "That was what I wanted all along."

Mariann was ecstatic; Khalid promised to help through any snags that might occur when she tried to obtain a visa through the Iraqi embassy.

Mariann sold everything she had to raise money for the trip. She moved in with her brother to save money until she left. Then she waited for authorization for the visa from her husband which alone took weeks because of the bombing in Iraq to get Saddam Hussein. She bought her ticket, but then could not use it because the United States had closed its embassy in Baghdad and all commercial sir traffic was suspended.

Khalid phoned to tell her to wait until after the war was over to come and that the children were safe. All she could do was wait out the interim, watching newscasts, and finding out as much as possible about Mosul and Iraq in general so she could feel closer to her children and their lives in Iraq.

While Mariann was waiting, she was advised to try to reach out to the Iraq community where she lived so that she could better understand them. It was very difficult for her at first, but as she became acquainted and began to know them as individuals, understanding and empathy developed; soon this empathy became mutual which turned out to very helpful to Mariann.

She became friends with the community's vice president, Shakir al-Khafaji. He was very sympathetic with Mariann's need to get to Iraq so he said he would see that she was added to a group scheduled to leave in June. He was better than his word—not only did he get space with the delegation, he was able to raise $300 to help defray her expenses during the layover in Jordan.

She was able to at last actually arrive in Baghdad after what seemed like forever. She set out the next day to try to locate her family. She went to a boarding house she knew Khalid used on business trips to ask the clerk if he could help her get word to her husband. He said he would do his best.

Later the same evening, when the group she was with went to a restaurant, a man came to the table to tell her that her husband and children would come tomorrow and pick her up. She was so overcome at how soon she would get to see her children again that she began to cry. Her group was so sympathetic that they shed a few tears along with her.

The next morning in her hotel, she was anxiously waiting in the lobby when, all of a sudden, when she turned, there they were—her two darling children. Adora was utterly beautiful with dark hair and a heart-shaped face. Adam was thin, with new teeth and a sweet smile. While she was still angry with Khalid, he was a familiar face in the strange part of the world and he was a link to home. She hoped that their marriage would have a chance now.

"'If I'd wanted to, I could have sent you divorce papers in the mail, and you would never have seen the children again,' he told her early on. 'But I didn't want to do it like that. I know that they need you, but I wanted you to come here.'"[16]

When Khalid took Mariann to where they were living, she was appalled at the shabbiness and dirt. And the bathroom! It was literally nothing more than a foul-smelling hole in the ground that did not even have a flushing system in place.

She let Khalid have it when he got home. She could not understand why he left their quite decent living situation in the United States for this ghetto-like environment. He felt terrible about the living quarters being as bad as they were, but went on to explain that everyone in Iraq was barely surviving and living on crumbs. Food supplies were severely rationed. The bombing had destroyed or disabled so many basic utilities and services that living was crippled drastically for everyone.

To help with the food problem, Khalid's relatives visited regularly—all two hundred of them, bringing food when they came so at least the children did not go hungry. These frequent visits, however beneficial as far as food went, prevented Khalid and Mariann from having any private time to learn know each other again.

Mariann was very unhappy at how disjointed Adam's and Adora's lives were. They had not celebrated any birthdays after arriving in Iraq because Muslims do not celebrate birthdays. They did not even know how old they were. There was no school for them to attend because it was closed and there was nothing for them to do. Their daily routine, such as it was, consisted of doing the laundry by hand since they had so few changes of clothes, and of looking forward to Khalid's return for lunch and dinner.

Mariann found herself a classic dilemma. When she tried to discipline the children in order to get them under control, Khalid would tell her off for yelling at them; when she was having fun with the children and showing them love and affection, Kahlid would become annoyed and complain that she did not care about him and that she had only come to Iraq to be with the children.

Paradoxically, she found herself learning to admire and appreciate the Iraqi people as a whole. They were much more welcoming and friendly to a stranger than most Americans are. Their sense of hospitality was extremely generous—if they had food, they shared it with you. If there was something you wanted while you were in their house, they would go to the store and get it for you.

Mariann was having tremendous difficulty eating since her arrival in Mosul. She could not keep anything down and she had no appetite for anything except watermelon. By the third week after her arrival, she was not even able to swallow. She could not understand it. When she went to a doctor to find out what was wrong with her, the doctor said her ailment was purely psychological. Whether or not her sickness was psychological, the effects were all too real. By the time a month had passed, she had lost forty pounds.

Mariann kept getting sicker and sicker. By the end of July—barely a month since she had arrived in Iraq—she could barely get out of bed. It was obvious to her that if she stayed, she was going to die and there was nothing she was going to be able to do about it. She had to return to the United States in order to stay alive. She had no strength to do even the simplest things such as cook a meal or play with her children.

She had to go, and quickly. The group she had come with had left and her visa was about to run out. She could not delay much longer. She had one hope—to take Adam home with her. He wanted desperately to return to the United States. He missed everything he had had to leave behind when Khalid had abducted him and his sister. He missed his friends, he missed the food, he missed his stuff—he was ready to leave in a heartbeat given the opportunity. But would Khalid let him go?

Khalid appeared to agree to letting their son return to the United States with his mother. For mother and son, every second of the rest of the week after Khalid said they would get Adam's visa in Amman, Jordan, seemed like an eternity. They planned their welcome home party down to the last detail.

As the end of the week and their departure time approached, Khalid changed his mind. Adam would have to stay. Desperate, Mariann called Shakir in Baghdad, who as it turned out, knew Khalid from student days. Shakir said he would arrange for a Red Crescent (Middle Eastern Red Cross) letter of safe passage for Mariann and Adam. Khalid agreed to go along with it. However, as the day came to leave for Amman, Khalid stalled. He said they would go tomorrow. Tomorrow came and he stalled if off until the next day, which was a Saturday. When Mariann wanted to know when they were leaving, he told her they had to talk in the other room.

"'I've made a decision. I'm not going to split up the family. If you want to stay and be a proper mom, you're welcome to stay. If you want to leave, you're welcome to leave. It's your choice. Besides, you no longer have the financial means to support Adam.'

Mariann started screaming at him. The children, who'd been playing outside with hearing range, were terrified by their mother's loss of control. They had never seen her like this. As Mariann's weeping gradually subsided, Adora entered the room and asked if her mother was leaving.

'I love you, I love you, go out and play,'

And then Adam came in, and he kissed me on the cheek, and he said,

'Don't worry, Mom, when I grow up I'll come back to you.' He said it matter-of-factly, and then he walked out."[17]

Marianne was being torn apart by grief and heartbreak at the thought of leaving Adam behind when he wanted so desperately to go with her. There is no heartbreak like that of feeling like you are deserting your child. You want to die, but you can't. At the same time, Mariann knew she did not dare delay. Her visa was about to expire and she did not know whether Khalid would allow her to leave if she stayed past the departure deadline, whether she would be trapped in Iraq until she died. She did not dare take that chance.

Sunday came and Khalid drove to Baghdad. He tried one last time to get her to stay. When she refused, he told her harshly that she had asked to come to Iraq, that he had not asked her. Then he walked away into the afternoon light of Baghdad, stiff and unyielding.

All the way to Amman in the taxicab, Mariann pondered on how her children would cope with her departure; would she be able to get out of Jordan with no complications; how would the group she had come with react to her appearing in time to return to the United States with them?

Her friends were glad to see her and helped her get through the five-day layover in Amman, which was a godsend for Mariann because she was so short of money. Her two Iraqi-American women friends and she went around all of Amman to see what it had to offer, including some wonderful restaurants with live entertainment all of which enchanted her. Khalid had told her about none of this nor had he shared it with her. Ironically, had she and Khalid been friends only when she came to Iraq, he would likely have taken her to Amman as a tourist and visited all of the most interesting spots, but as his wife, it never occurred to him that she would like to go.

Mariann may have returned to the United States, but she was not the same person who had left. She had learned firsthand that every friend she had there had had someone in their family killed or bombed. She lived in an economy that was decimated and getting worse because of the sanctions in place during the war. She saw the effects of the shortages of food and medicines. Marianne learned that the people of Iraq do not hate American people; it is the governments that cause them so much horror they want something done about.

Mariann is able to talk to Khalid and the children whenever her budget allows for the expense. If he is serious about pursuing his U.S. citizenship and about the children's passports, there is a chance he will return to this country and bring the children with him. She is saving money for a trip back to see her family. She has to battle constant guilt feelings about leaving her children in Iraq and returning home. When a mother is half a world away from her children, her heart is torn out; the wound never heals. It stays raw, possibly for the rest of her life.[18]

*   *   *

Most Arab/Muslim-American marriages result in the children of these star-crossed unions being abducted by their father and taken back to his country, there to remain for the rest of their lives whether or not they wish to stay. Usually the mother is not allowed to speak to her children nor is she allowed to follow to be with them.

Most cases of abduction to the Middle East are not made public by the left behind mothers. For every abduction that is publicized, there are at least twenty kidnappings that are not.

Perhaps the mothers hope that if they do not go public, it will help them in their efforts to find and be reunited with their children. Perhaps they have tried to find their children with the help of someone or some agency claiming to be able to find and recover the children for several hundred thousand dollars; after receiving the money these agency child finders disappear, leaving the mother without her money and her children and the mother feels like too much of a fool to speak up. Maybe someday they will find someone or some agency that will help them recover their children.

CHAPTER 17

SUCCESSFUL ESCAPES AND REUNIONS

A S HIGH AS the odds are against it, there are a few instances where the mother and children are reunited and are able to live in the United States. In other cases, a child who was abducted by the father grows into adulthood and is able to be reunited with his or her mother in the United States. Rarest of all are the mothers who have been able to escape the countries they are trapped in, with their children, and return to the United States.

Even though return to the United States has been accomplished, the lives of these mothers and children will never be the same. Most have assumed new identities in an effort to protect themselves from further attempts at abduction. They have relocated for the same reason, but always they will live in fear and keep track of each other's location at any given moment. Always they will be looking over their shoulders for suspicious, unknown individuals to appear out of nowhere.

*   *   *

Cathy Mahone married Ali Bayan. Her daughter was taken by her father to Jordan. Cathy recovered her daughter and returned to the United States where they live in hiding with new identities.

Cathy Mahone met and married Ali Bayan in Dallas, Texas. Their marriage appeared to be successful—Cathy worked in real estate and Ali worked in a restaurant. He persuaded her to visit Jordan and meet her family who accepted her with as much joy as Cathy's family had accepted Ali. They then returned to their home in Dallas.

After Cathy became pregnant, Ali visited his home in Jordan again. But this time when he returned, he was a different person. His behavior had changed to the type of behavior change which is common among Arab/Muslim males, that of reverting back to the traditions they grew up with once they become parents.

Ali was determined to move everyone back to Jordan to live. Cathy refused to go because she wanted to raise their child in the United States. As happens so often with this kind of disagreement in intercultural marriages, the infighting between the couple led to serious deterioration of their relationship. Their estrangement did not change after Cathy had her baby, a daughter, so the couple finally obtained a divorce.

One would have thought Ali would have left for Jordan to live, but he did not. He went into a new business with his brother and eventually married a second time. Ali had been granted visitation rights with Lauren, which he took full advantage of. He enjoyed fatherhood and spent as much time with Lauren as he could. This pleased Cathy very much; she thought of him as a great father.

In the late 80s, Texas economy went bottoms up. As a result, Ali and his brother had to close their business which was the end of their economic stability. This was to have repercussions for Cathy which she did not anticipate.

Ali continued to visit with Lauren; he had more time now to spend with his daughter since he was no longer running a business. However, he had not been idle. One day in November, 1987, when he had Lauren, now about 10 years old, for an overnight visit, he did not bring her back home to Cathy. He took her home—to Jordan. It had taken a great deal of careful planning on his part. He had needed either to obtain a passport for Lauren or include her on his. He had to obtain a visa to allow her entry into Jordan, and he had to gather together the finances to pay for the journey. And he had accomplished all of this without Cathy ever catching on.

Cathy was totally taken by surprise; she was devastated and knew that without her daughter, life was worth nothing to her. After she went to the State Department and obtained a list of Jordanian attorneys that the department kept on file, she began remembering how useless the State Department was when it came to realistic help in retrieving children for left behind parents. She also remembered that to go through the court system was to encounter endless delays and wasted time. She determined to take a more direct, expedient, and faster way to rescue her daughter.

Cathy withdrew her life savings of around $200,000 and hired a professional who specialized in counter abductions. He sent a team of commandos to Jordan to find Lauren. Their job was made easier by the fact that Cathy had visited Ali's family in Jarash, Jordan, so she knew where her daughter was, in all likelihood. Cathy went with them as far as Cyrpus. There she waited by a phone in a hotel room, hoping, hoping to hear that they had found her daughter. As she later told Betty Mahmoody:

"'I took your book to Cyprus, and every time I doubted I could go through with this, I read further and got the courage to carry on.'"[1]

The Phone Call came. Her daughter had been found. Cathy flew into Jordan where the commandos were waiting, disguised as tourists to the Holy Land. They found the school bus that Lauren was on, stopped it, and disposed of the keys in the sand while Lauren got on the bus and claimed her daughter. The commandos then drove them across the border into Israel, and from there Cathy flew home with her daughter, hugging her during the entire trip from Jordan, to the United States.

Cathy and Lauren went into hiding the minute they returned and assumed new identities. Even so, their lives did not settle into peace and contentment, at least not for the first few months after their return.

Cathy contacted Betty when they had found a new apartment:

"'If it weren't for your bravery in telling your story, I would not have my daughter back today,' she told me [Betty], sobbing over the phone. But Cathy's crisis was by no means over:

'Now I'm locked inside an apartment, with my daughter huddled in a corner and screaming each time someone comes to the door, 'Mommy, please don't let them take me!' I'm pacing the floor with a pistol in my hand. What do I do from here? What will the rest of our lives hold?'"[2]

Betty went on to say that she had not heard from Cathy after that phone call.

Hopefully, life went back to a semblance of normalcy for Cathy and her daughter even though they will never completely recover from the trauma which followed Lauren's abduction. If I ever have a chance to meet and talk to Betty Mahmoody, I will certainly ask her.

Carmen met and married Yeslam bin Ladin from Saudi Arabia. When living in Switzerland, they were divorced and she was awarded custody of the children. They are still in Switzerland today.

Carmen met Yeslam bin Ladin for the first time in Geneva when he came to sign a summer rental agreement for the top floor of her mother's house in which he was going to stay. Carmen and her sisters could not visit their grandmother in Iran as planned because she injured her right leg, so they had to live part time in an apartment in Lausanne and part time in their mother's house.

As Carmen became acquainted with Yeslam, she began to find him beautiful and fascinating, with an air of calm confidence about him. They found that they shared Iranian backgrounds— both their mothers were Iranian—which drew them closer to each other.

As the summer passed, the friendship between Carmen and Yeslam became a love affair. Yeslam began drawing her into his family gatherings which were large, even by Saudi standards—he had twenty-four brothers and twenty-nine sisters. When they became formally engaged in October, her mother was delighted.

Yeslam stayed on at her mother's house after summer passed which pleased Carmen's mother very much since her household had consisted of women only since her divorce years ago. Furthermore, now that Carmen was engaged to be married, she was more Yeslam's responsibility than hers and she enjoyed the respite from tracking Carmen's every movement.

While still engaged to be married, they went to the United States to go to college. Carmen loved the freedom and the easygoing approach the average person had toward life, especially in California where they went to school at UCLA. Yeslam would be studying business and Carmen would be pursuing remedial English.

Carmen met an American woman, Mary Martha Barkley, the wife of the director of international students, while she was a student. Mary Martha was to become Carmen's surrogate mother and a lifelong friend and moral support for her in later years.

Carmen and Yeslam loved living in the free new country of the United States. Carmen wanted to believe they were beginning to build a life here which would be permanent for them. After all, Yeslam had spent more time living overseas than he had in Saudi Arabia so Carmen assumed that living in the kingdom simply was not in the cards.

Carmen's mother wanted them to get married. She thought he would influence Carmen to become more collected in behavior and she wanted a man in the family. Because of this, Carmen and Yeslam decided to marry after the semester at school ended. She wanted to get married in Geneva where her friends and family were. Yeslam, who had gone to Saudi Arabia to get permission to marry from the King, said that they should get married in Saudi Arabia to prove to everyone there that he, indeed, had royal permission to marry a foreigner. Furthermore, respect for her would not be given unless she submitted to feudal rituals which had been in place in that country for centuries.

Carmen had no concept of what Saudi Arabia was like. She had never been there and she had never made any inquiries about their customs. But her mother was delighted that she was going to get married, and Carmen was in love, so she went along with Yeslam's wish. Only members of her family, including a male relative from Iran, were going to accompany her to the kingdom. The male distant cousin was essential so he could represent the bride in the men only ceremony. Without him, Carmen could not be married to Yeslam—a concept which she thought quite funny in the beginning.

Before they left Switzerland, Carmen went shopping to find her white wedding dress which she would take with her as well as black cotton which Yeslam said had to be made into an *abaya* for her to wear once they landed in Saudi Arabia.

The day came when Carmen, Yeslam, and one of Carmen's sisters boarded the plane for Jeddah. Before they left the plane, Carmen and her sister had to put on their *abayas* to avoid serious consequences when they alighted from the plane. Both women were in shock because it was virtually impossible to see out of the black gauze and their every step was badly hampered by the long folds of black cloth. When her sister Salome fell down alighting from the plane and spilled her cosmetics all over the floor, no one came over to help her up or to help her retrieve her things. because no man is allowed approach any woman in public for any reason.

Carmen found out in short order that the men had complete freedom to come and go as they pleased while the women were confined—literally—to the house. She could not even go across the courtyard without a male escort because it was not allowed for any woman's face to be seen by any man who was not a relative. And being inside the house all the time was no pleasure because, instead of being elegant and refined as one would find in homes of the wealthy in Europe or the United States, it was gaudy looking and the furniture, while perhaps expensive, was in very poor taste. Carmen was to find these characteristics to be consistent in every house she entered while in Saudi Arabia.

During the days before the wedding was to take place, Carmen was scrutinized from head to foot by every female relative in the

Bin Laden family all of whom felt themselves infinitely superior to her. "They had been born in the land of Islam's holiest site—the homeland of the Prophet Mohamed. They believed they were the chosen guardians of the world's most sacred places. They were the chosen people of God."[3]

From time out of mind, untold misery and devastation has been heaped on civilizations by self-righteous marauders of every nation who considered themselves "the chosen people of God." The politico/military history of pre-Islamic and Islamic Middle Eastern civilizations indicates clearly their penultimate skill, thoroughness, and brutality when slaughtering thousands upon thousands of poor souls, including women and children, who were unable to defend themselves or their loved ones, and so perished beneath the sword of the misguided, misbegotten, unconscionable, and evil illusion that "God is on our side so we can do what we like to anyone who gets in our way."

The wedding procedures which took place could only have occurred in Saudi Arabia. Yeslam and his brother took Carmen, in her *abaya*, to an administration building and parked in the sandy parking lot. Carmen was required to wait in the car while Yeslam and his brother went in to register the wedding. After it was registered, they brought the registry book out to the car so that Carmen could sign it in Arabic She had practiced writing her name in Arabic so she was able to do so. The book was taken back inside. That was it. They were married.

The wedding celebration which she was sharing with one of Yeslam's sisters, occurred a couple of days later in the only hotel in Jeddah. Before appearing there, however, she had gone to the sister's house to put on her wedding dress. There were only women and hairdressers present. Carmen put on her wedding dress which had been passed around and commented on disparagingly before she arrived and put her hair up in a classic chignon. Her bridesmaids readied themselves also. Of course, before she could step out the door and head for the car, she had to put on the *abaya*.

When she and her bridesmaids arrived at the hotel, they stepped out and went to the garden which had been screened off to prevent the gaze of any passing male. The women's area of the garden had been strung with strings of naked light bulbs and there were about 600 women present, dressed in jewelry and Western dresses suitable for a ceremonial ball complete with headscarves for some women. As Yeslam and Carmen walked in, the women gave the traditional ululations and looked the couple up and down.

After the couple had greeted all the guests and food had been served, the women danced, Bedouin style, to an all-woman orchestra playing traditional Arabic music clad in their Western clothing.

It was brought home forcefully to Carmen just how different the culture from which Yeslam had come was from hers as a Swiss citizen and resident. She could not wait to return to the United States and a normal, sane life style.

Back in California, Yeslam and Carmen took up classes again at UCLA and enjoyed everything that life has to offer in California. They were happier than they had been for a long time. Then Carmen discovered she was pregnant.

Of course Yeslam wanted a boy as do all Arab/Muslim males. So did Carmen because of the lack of men in her household. She had never had a brother and did not have a close relationship with her father whom her mother had divorced years ago.

Carmen noticed that Yeslam did not seem as pleased as he could have been by the coming birth. He did not do what most expectant fathers do—pay lots of attention to her growing tummy or get very involved with what he would do with the baby after it was born.

Carmen's friend and surrogate mother, Mary Martha, was wonderful to her during what seemed like interminable months of pregnancy. Carmen was not allowed to work while pregnant, so she was happy to be with Mary Martha's family for celebrations and outings which opened Carmen's eyes about people being acknowledged and valued for themselves and their individual opinions, whether or not one might disagree with another.

When Carmen gave birth to her first child, a girl, it was Mary Martha who was with her, not Yeslam. Carmen was ecstatic with her new daughter who was a beautiful baby by any standard. However, Yeslam was not pleased at all; when he heard that his new child was a girl, he walked out of the hospital.

Yeslam's dissatisfaction was not to end there. He was jealous of the close bond between mother and child—he wanted Carmen's attention to be directed at him as his mother's had been when he was growing up. However, he was preoccupied with obtaining his degree in business as quickly as possible because he wanted to return to Saudi Arabia to take advantage of the new business opportunities that were appearing because of the rise in crude oil prices. He told Carmen that it would be a great situation for them and, because she did not think through the effect of the abrupt change in lifestyle and freedom that such a move meant, and that it just might be a permanent move, she let him talk her into agreeing to go.

She was to pay the price for her lack of objective analysis.

They moved into his mother's house as was the custom. It was like walking into a cocoon. She could not play music, she could not go for a walk, she could not go shopping, and basic necessities such as the proper milk for her daughter were not to be found. If she needed something from the store, a man was sent out with a list and would come back with a suitcase full of items she had to choose from. If nothing was right, he took the things back and brought home another suitcase full of things to select from.

The restrictions and constraints for women were endless—they were not allowed to do anything, on their own, for themselves. Men avoided contact with her like the plague, simply because of her sex. Her only activity was that of taking care of Wafah, her daughter, but even that could not take up twenty-four hours a day, seven days a week, every week of the year.

"I needed activity. I needed to read. I longed for some stimulation of my mind, and my body. The two TV channels broadcast an imam chanting the Koran all day; for lighter fare, little boys as young as six or seven, who had won prizes for their Koranic knowledge, recited the whole texts from memory. Foreign newspapers were Magic Markered into fragments. Any comment on Saudi Arabia or Israel, any photo or advertisement showing even one inch of a woman's limbs or neck was blacked out by the censors. I held them up to the light, to divine the forbidden words veiled by the censor's pen.

There were no books. There were no theaters, no concerts, no cinemas. There was no reason to go out, and in any case we could not go out: I was not allowed to go for a walk, and legally could not drive. Much as I loved my role as a mother, taking care of Wafah was not enough to fill my mind and my days."[4]

When she could stand it no longer, Carmen would talk Yeslam into taking her to Geneva for a visit. Every time, it was like visiting another planet full of light and sound and color—and freedom of movement! She went on huge shopping sprees, talked to her friends;

in short, everything she used to be able to do without thought before moving to Saudi Arabia.

Had Yeslam not treated Carmen more or less as his equal, Saudi Arabia would have been unbearable. He shared what he was doing and thinking with her when he arrived at home at night. He asked her advice about things and discussed politics and any other subjects that came up endlessly. He even told her about some of the problems in the Bin Laden family organization. She knew that while there were no outright arguments, there was a lot of competition among the brothers. She felt that he considered her his strength and his equal.

Carmen was able to make friends with the wives of some of the Bin Laden men which helped a lot to relieve the tedium. Then Carmen discovered that she was pregnant again, which delighted her enormously. As members of the Bin Laden family heard, all extended congratulations saying that this time it would be a boy.

As the time drew near, Carmen went back to Geneva to make sure that she and the baby would have the best of care. She loved being back with her mother and sisters. Wafah responded with equal ease and loved being in the garden just as Carmen had when she was a toddler. She and Yeslam, who came to visit her often, hoped for a boy.

Carmen gave birth to a little girl who was the easiest baby to care for that one could wish for. Even so, for Yeslam's sake, she wished she had given birth to a boy. He insisted it did not matter, but Carmen knew differently.

Carmen was to come to be very glad she had two daughters to look after because their existence made her very sensitive to the cultural conditioning which girls in Saudi Arabia cannot escape and to motivate her sufficiently to escape from the kingdom. Her concern became suddenly active when she heard about three women of her acquaintance who had been divorced by their husbands and had lost their children to their husbands because, in Saudi Arabia, it is the husband who has uncontested custody.

Another thought occurred to Carmen. What if something happened to Yeslem and he was killed? What would become of her and her daughters? She knew she would be utterly dependant on the Bin Laden family for survival. Which of the males would take custody of her daughters and how would they be treated? When she brought up the subject to Yeslam, he did not take her fear seriously and that scared her even more. She knew it was up to her to find a solution to save her daughters from becoming mindless, subservient, fearful victims of this ferociously tribal patriarchy. When Princess Mish'al fell in love with a young man and tried to escape with him, she was shot six times in a downtown parking lot to "save the family honor", Carmen knew that she had to work out something as soon as possible.

Yeslam's business acumen was beginning to bring him into a more and more central role in the Bin Laden organization which did not always go over well with his older brothers. They continued to prosper, as did Saudi Arabia. Restrictions against women were relaxing, bit by bit, and life was more pleasant.

In January, 1979, came the rebellion against Shah Reza Pahlavi in Iran. He and his family were forced to flee Iran to save their lives. The following month, the Ayatollah Khomeini came from France to Iran and took charge of the government. Almost overnight, Iran changed from a country where women could walk the streets freely without being shrouded in a chador from head to foot to a country where acid was thrown in the faces of women who wore makeup and women were beaten if a square inch of skin showed anywhere.

The ruling family in Saudi Arabia, the al-Sauds, panicked. If the Iranian citizens could revolt and overthrow the ruler, the Saudi citizens might decide to try the same thing. They had too much to lose to take any chances, so they did not take any chances. They needed to placate the fundamentalists quickly so they clamped down on the small freedoms which had begun to make an appearance. In Iran and in Saudi Arabia, women were again required to veil from head to foot and to cover every inch of their body in black, including feet and ankles. Shopkeepers had to run to prayer when the muezzin called or they would be hauled before the religious police. Children's dolls were prohibited unless they were faceless and shapeless. Radios and stereo sets were taken from private homes and destroyed. In short, everything that made life bearable was prohibited as blasphemous and sinful. Even the young people stepped backward in time and demanded more restrictions.

Then in November of the same year, the Grand Mosque in Mecca was attacked and taken by a group of Islamic fundamentalists who declared that the al-Sauds were being corrupted by the West and that it had to stop. The ruling family immediately cut off all contact with the outside world; they wanted to control the dissemination of this catastrophe as long as possible because it was a disastrous blow to their prestige and credibility as the protector of the holy places. Newspapers that got wind of it held up their articles for several days because of the sensitivity of the issue. After the world's fastest conversion to Islam, French paratroopers were allowed near the Mosque to dislodge the extremists from the building. They did so, killing many of them in the process.

Three weeks later, Russia invaded Afghanistan. This, after the revolution in Iran, the taking of the Grand Mosque in Mecca, and growing radical fundamentalism in the kingdom, was enough to give everyone in Saudi Arabia, especially the royal family, nightmares. Saudi Arabia decided to fund the Afghans' defense against the Russians.

All the while, Yeslam was beginning to change. He had been working very hard in the Bin Laden organization and, along with the revenues from his own businesses, Yeslam's worth had risen to something like $300 million. He was one of the richest members of the Bin Laden family and this was bringing him under censure from two of his older brothers.

His personal ambition, initiative, and success in business, which would have gained Yeslam respect and stature in the West, was almost unpardonable in the eyes of his family and flouted the unwritten Saudi social and family codes of behavior.

In Saudi Arabia, it is not done to strike out on one's own as an individual. A male family member neither confronts nor separates himself from his brothers for any reason, including business ventures. Yeslam's stepping out of his allotted position in the family earned him censure from the other members of his family, especially his brothers, who were fiercely jealous of his accomplishments. He was the younger brother who was supposed to be submissive to their wishes and give them primary pride of place in all things.

As a result, "Yeslam was split between two utterly irreconcilable impulses: the modern Western ambitions encouraged by his life abroad, and the tradition-bound immobility of the Saudi way of life."[5]

Yeslam's inner conflicts were slowly destroying his stability and equilibrium. He grew afraid of flying, he could not bear being in crowds, and he was experiencing an internal nervous breakdown. Another indication of his deteriorated mental state was when Carmen became pregnant with their third child and he seriously wanted her to get an abortion because he felt he could not cope with an additional child. She did so, but at the cost of peace of mind to herself because she wanted the child terribly and hoped it was a son this time.

Carmen's daughters were growing older and became of school age. She hated sending them to any school in Saudi Arabia because of the lack of anything but rote learning without understanding of the content of what they were learning. There was no fun to be had at school, either. Relentless mental conditioning to hate Jews and religious intolerance were the worst part of the school routine.

Wafah and Najia were also drawing nearer to puberty every year. As in most Arab/Muslim countries, girls must veil in public after they have had their first menstrual period. Carmen was very frightened for them because their future as happy, fulfilled adults was at extreme risk as long as they lived in Saudi Arabia. She knew she had to get them out soon, before they were molded into the role demanded of all Saudi women—lowly, obedient, submissive, at once manipulative and terrified of the men in their families, uneducated—everything Carmen hated and wanted to free herself and her daughters of. She did not want them to live in a dependent, sleepwalking kind of life. Most of all, she did not want her daughters to become fanatical Muslims with black gloves and hatred for anyone who believed differently from them.

As Yeslam's business life flourished and grew, his personality became more Saudi orthodox and Carmen worried that he would take sole charge of their daughters away from her and impose the suffocating restrictions on every detail of their behavior as so many Saudi fathers did. It did not help that Saudi society in general was wildly contradictory. In fact, as Saudi Arabia became wealthier, it's government and citizens became more schizophrenic. Because of the contrast between making billions of dollars Western style, which was out of control, Saudis thought they wanted to go back to that with which they were familiar—7th century behavior patterns and beliefs. Like oil and water, the two directions could not mix.

Fortunately for Carmen, she and Yeslam had been taking the children to Switzerland every summer during school vacations for years, and this year was no exception. The power struggles and the family pressures had made Yeslam an unwell man and he was not ready to return to the kingdom. He delayed and delayed until Carmen knew she had to put the children in school in Geneva—which she dearly wanted to do. They were back in civilization and that was where she wanted to stay, though she said nothing to her husband.

They stayed in Geneva. Yeslam had an office in Geneva and met with Saudi princes there regularly. He seemed becoming less and less Western—he was sharp and clear thinking when he was with Saudis doing business, but in a funk when he was at home. He could not even face going out for a social evening. Then he began seeing other women. When she faced him with this, he denied it. It turned out that when she thought he was with the Saudi princes, he was not. He was with his ladyfriend.

Carman became pregnant again and this time she knew she would never get an abortion. Yeslam wanted her to have another abortion, but she categorically refused. It was at this juncture that the marriage was basically over even though the process had begun while they were still in Saudi Arabia. A great many self illusions on the part of the Saudi government and of the Saudi citizens had crumbled into dust when Mecca was attacked. The chasm between traditional Saudi Arabia and Westernized Saudi Arabia was too wide. All of this had affected Yeslam and had shredded the balance he had achieved between his Western self and his Saudi self

Their relationship grew more distant. Yeslam had lost interest in being a husband and father. After Carmen's third child, another daughter, was born, she again saw Yeslam with another woman which destroyed the marriage. After many bitter confrontations, they divorced in long and drawn out proceedings which gave Yeslam time to hide his assets to keep his financial support of his family to a minimum out of spite. Yeslam also tried to deny that he was Noor's father so Carmen has everyone tested to prove his fatherhood. Carmen has custody of the children and barely scrapes by on the alimony awarded to her by the Swiss court.

Virtually none of the Bin Laden family will have anything to do with her, even the ones she knew the best and whose children play with hers. Yeslam has nothing to do with his daughters which has hurt them very much. Carmen thinks it might be because they have grown up to be bright, beautiful, free thinking, and educated. She counts her blessings every day that she and her daughters are free and living in Switzerland.

Christy met Riaz Khan from Pakistan while both were students at college. Her three children were taken by their father back to Pakistan. She was awarded custody and brought her children are back in the United States where they are today.

When Christy took a June break from her studies to visit a friend in Oklahoma, she met Riaz Khan, who was attending law school in Tulsa. He was tall, well-built with black hair and a cleft chin.

He and Christy hit it off and they dated frequently. He was gallant and chivalrous and constantly complimented Christy in a way that made her feel very feminine. They talked a lot about the differences between living in Pakistan and the United States. When Christy asked him about his family, Riaz was evasive and claimed they were not interested in what he was doing. In spite of the fact that Pakistan is a Muslim state, Riaz also claimed that he was a Christian in the process of learning more abut his faith.

After Christy returned to Michigan in September for school, Riaz began calling her. This developed into weekend visits back and forth and in December, Riaz, met her parents. By this time he was already asking her to marry him, saying he couldn't live without her.

Riaz's student visa expired in January so he had to go back to Pakistan to reapply for a new one and come back as soon as possible. Christy, who had become very emotionally attached to him, said she would marry him when he returned to the United States. After he left, she missed him terribly. On impulse, she talked herself into going to Pakistan to be with him before graduating from school.

For her, this was going to be a wonderful adventure—the kind you read about in storybooks and classic books of travel such as Richard Halliburton's *The Royal Road to Romance.* Peshawur sounded exciting; it was in a part of the world she knew nothing about, but which she thought would be interesting and exotic to visit with a man who was as intriguing as the part of the world from which he came.

Christy arrived safely, but it was not to the exotic place she expected to see; Peshawur was primitive, dirty, dusty, crowded with refugees from Afghanistan, and polluted with diseases. The Pathans, renowned throughout history as warriors, who were in control of the area, were hard-bitten, coldly military, and totally inhospitable.

Riaz introduced Christy to his family who were delighted that she came. They were warmly welcoming to her, especially since she was soon to be Riaz's wife and a new member of the family. He was pressing her to marry him now, in Pakistan, since she was here. They could be married, he said, in a Muslim ceremony in Pakistan and in a Christian ceremony when they returned to the U.S.

This is not what Christy had in mind when she came; she came only to be with him and because she thought traveling to this part of the world would be fascinating. She preferred to continue dating him while finishing school back home. Why was he pushing her so hard to marry now?

That was when some unpleasant truths came to light. Riaz had cut so many classes that he was dropped from school and the authorities had refused to renew his visa. He would not be allowed back into the Unites States unless he married an American.

"'If you love me and you're going to marry me in America,' he pressed, 'why can't you marry me here? Then we can be together.'"[6]

The very next day, he told her that she would have to marry him now or return without him. Unbelievably, he had already arranged for an imam to come to the house to perform the ceremony—and he had already arrived! They were to get married now—and Christy was not even out of bed yet!

Christy was manipulated into the marriage by a master of deception. She was in love with him and imagined that his feelings for her were genuine. She was deluding herself, as she was soon to find out. She found out before she left Pakistan, for instance, that now she was his wife, she was no longer welcome in the same room with her husband when his friends came over. It was not customary for women to join men's conversations.

Christy left for home in August. She wanted to believe their relationship would go back to what it was before he left in the first place.

Riaz had been able to obtain his new visa and he arrived just in time for their first Christmas Eve together with their baby boy. It was a wonderful interlude for them.

Christy began to notice that Riaz tended to tell little lies about himself. For example, he told people that he was older than he really was and he told his family he owned the gas station he, in reality, worked at as an employee. The reason he gave for this was that he wanted people to respect him

Money went through Riaz's hands like water. There was never enough. Even so, he found money to buy excellent clothes, to dine at nice restaurants without Christy, to rent expensive cars, and to buy expensive jewelry. However, it was Christy who was paying the rent and everything else at home out of her paycheck. She never saw any of the money Riaz always seemed to have available and she let him know about it.

Christy became pregnant again and the pressure of expenses forced her to continue working. When she called her mother to discuss it with her, she told her mother she could not afford to cut back on her working hours.

The marriage was disintegrating and the arguments were becoming more and more frequent. One night, Riaz lost control and choked her until she lost consciousness. It was then she remembered one of Riaz's cousins asking her if she wasn't afraid of his temper. Now Christy knew what the cousin was referring to.

Attacking Christy became business as usual even though she was pregnant with their second child. During a visit to her obstetrician, the doctor suggested to her that she go to one of the safe houses because Riaz's beatings were dangerous to the health of her and her baby. Christy wanted to stick it out and try to make the marriage work and she managed to succeed for a while after Riaz saw a psychiatrist and was put on medications to smooth out the mood swings.

One day, the phone rang and Christy answered it. The caller was a woman named Nicole, asking for Riaz. The woman asked who Christy was, Christy told her. Then the woman said that she was Riaz's girlfriend; she did not know about the existence of Christy and Johnathon and was outraged at Riaz's lies. He had told her that he was living with a wealthy relative.

When Christy confronted Riaz about his affair, he came up with some weak excuses and suggested that they would have to get a divorce. Christy was six months pregnant. She needed to get this marriage patched up if it was at all possible. Riaz was willing to work on saving the marriage, but Christy insisted that he not hit her anymore and that she give up his mistress. Riaz agreed.

Prophetically, Christy told him that if there ever was a divorce, there would be very strict visitation terms because she was aware of fathers who abduct their children and take them out of the country. Riaz responded in typical extravagant terms:

"'As Allah is my God, I would never take these kids away from you. I didn't go through the agony of childbirth. You carry the children in your body, you nurture them, you take care of them.

You're the best mother in the world. I could have many women, but no woman could be a better mother.'"[7]

Riaz began talking constantly about Pakistan and his family. Christy thought this odd, considering the fact that he had been indifferent and derogatory about his origins. Then he arranged to go back to Pakistan a month before the second baby was due. Riaz's excuse what that he did not want to be around during labor. When he did return sometime in May, he took a look at his new son, Adam, and accused Christy of the baby not being his because he had blue eyes. When Christy pointed out that both Riaz's brother and grandfather had blue eyes, Riaz ignored her. And he stayed away from Adam from then on.

Then Christy got pregnant again, two months after Adam was born. It was too much for Riaz. The idea of more kids meant even more expense.

Riaz said he needed to go to Pakistan again so Christy suggested they all go after the new baby was born. She could take time off from work. Things were going well at home even though Riaz appeared to be indifferent toward his children. and never offered to help take care of them. That he might abduct them seemed ridiculous.

On December 28, when Christy was at work, Riaz called. She was having a difficult time with the pregnancy and thought she might come home early. He was very sympathetic and suggested that she stick it out at work and do nothing but rest when she got home. She decided to follow his suggestion.

Christy got home from work about 6:00 and found the apartment empty. There was a note saying that Riaz and the boys would be home in about half an hour, that they were in Hollywood to see a friend. This was unusual and alarming since Riaz had been so absentminded lately and was likely to forget anything or anyone.

9:00 came and went. Still no Riaz and the boys. John was barely two years old. Adam was only eight months old. Were they all right? By the time midnight came, there was only one conclusion she could come to—the boys had been taken. She called the FBI which referred to a federal hotline which in turn told her that passports had been issued for both boys and sent to a post office box rented by Riaz well before they left the country.

Riaz finally called her from Karachi to say they had arrived safely.

"'I-I'm sorry, I'm sorry,' Riaz stammered, over Christy's bitter weeping. 'But wait, wait, I didn't take the children away from you. I left a ticket for you, sweetheart. It's in the cedar chest in the dining room. Believe me, things will be better for all of us here.'

'How can they be better?' Christy cried.

'Here I have money, and you won't have to work,' Riaz said. Then he put John on the phone.

The toddler sounded disoriented; he wasn't used to spending so much time with his father. 'I want you, Mommy,' John said' 'When are you coming?'

'I'll be coming really fast,' Christy said, straining to keep the panic out of her voice. 'Take care of your baby brother till I get there.'

Now that she knew the truth, Christy was stunned. Riaz had covered his tracks remarkably well. Through all his frenzied rages he had never threatened to abduct the children—the act he knew would hurt her most. His cold calculation made the deed even more shocking."[8]

This was only the beginning for Christy. She was to find out about how secretive and deceptive Riaz was to everyone, not just her. She went to Pakistan and was appalled to find her children neglected and ill. She was outraged at the Riaz's lack of interest in the suffering of the children he had dragged across the world. She was horrified when she found out that he controlled the exit visas and that none of them could leave without his permission, which he was not about to give. He had lied to his family about their living conditions in America so he would gain their support. He had lied about how her parents felt about their grandchildren— that her parents hated them. He had taped Christy's phone conversations and had played them to his family to give them the impression that Christy was planning to take the children from him after divorcing him.

Christy found out that the main reason Riaz had taken the children was for entirely selfish reasons—to save face with his family, with the tribe he was a member of, and among his business associates. He would have been seen as less than a man needs to be to command respect and status.

Despite what they had been told, Riaz's relatives were getting fed up with his physical abuse, arrogance, bullying, and demanding ways. He had the nerve to try to boss them around with the family business they had run for years without his help or support. The female relatives were very sympathetic to Christy's plight, but could do nothing to interfere between man and wife. They were also afraid of being beaten up by Riaz

The boys' health was not improving. Their nutrition was so bad that they developed sores in their mouths. They were thin and high strung from neglect and erratic daily lives and their mental and physical health was steadily deteriorating, day by day.

Christy was not doing well either. She could not eat the spicy food common in Pakistan because it gave her stabbing stomach pains. Her pregnancy was not as it should have been; she was not at all sure that the fetus was developing normally.

On top of all that, she was having a hard time with prenatal strain because of the heavy water buckets she had to carry every day just to wash clothes. As a result, her labor pains started three weeks early.

The hospital she had to go to was horrendous by Western standards. The delivery room, for instance, consisted of a bare wooden table that was simply wiped off between patients. Inexcusably, the two inexperienced midwives who were assigned to her first gave her drugs to slow down the contractions. Then they decided to give her drugs so speed up the contractions. They would have never have been allowed in any hospital in the United States.

Christy's baby took eight hours to arrive. He was dangerously weak as evidenced by the muted crying when he was born and by the difficulty he had moving his arms. He was not even six pounds in weight. Riaz's cousin, Rabina, who was a medical intern, was worried about the newborn so she had her medical professor look at him. The doctor diagnosed Eric within five minutes as having a major heart defect and Downs Syndrome. He had to go to the United States for heart surgery immediately or die.

Riaz did not want to send his wife and son to the U.S. for the surgery, but when the doctor told him off he backed down in the face of greater status and authority. At first, the whole family was scheduled to go, but then Riaz decided to stay in Pakistan and keep John and Adam with him. Even so, Christy dared not delay because her new baby was so weak he had to be fed with an eyedropper.

When Riaz found out that Christy had flown first class, he was more preoccupied with that than with the confirmation of his son's condition. As she began thinking about Riaz's preoccupation with this, she began to remember how much he loved the convenience of living in the United States and, by comparison, how primitive their life style was in Pakistan. His excuse that he was in Pakistan because he wanted to hold on to his children and to preserve their marriage did not make sense—he loved his comforts too much. There was something else, but she could not figure out what.

After Eric was operated on, he was still far from well. His heart would need further operations in the future so there was no way he could ever go back to Pakistan. When Christy went back to Pakistan, her father went with her. They were appalled at what they saw when they saw the two boys left behind—they were so thin their ribs stuck out, their hair was down to their shoulders, they were completely undisciplined, and they had no language skills. In short, they had been living in ghetto conditions and it showed.

Christy knew she had to be with them—they needed her every bit as much as her newest child did, but at least he had good care and loving grandparents who would look after him properly.

Over the next ten months, she watched her two sons gradually fading. Adam withdrew to the point where he had no interest in anything and John grew ever more high strung about everything. Christy's own life was exhausting and draining—she did the cooking, cleaning, and washing, all by hand, and as a result lost twenty pounds. Christy began to lose hope of ever being able to leave and go back home to civilization.

Then a light appeared at the end of the tunnel of Christy's despair. Eric not only needed another operation, but some state of Michigan social workers were going to get him made a ward of the state unless one to two things happened—either legal guardianship be given to Christy's parents or Christy and/or Riaz could come to vouch that they were the parents and reinstate their son's state subsidized medical insurance.

This lit a fire under Riaz who, though embarrassed by Eric's ill health, could not stand to have his pride punctured by letting his son become legally claimed by someone else. This, combined with a business opportunity he said would make him a lot of money, galvanized him to go to Michigan. As his departure date drew closer, he became extremely paranoid about everything. He would not take late phone calls, he would not go outside, he would not let the boys outside alone, and he was afraid for his life. He never confided to Christy why he was so strung out.

After stops in Germany, Britain, and New York, Riaz was met by Christy's father when the plane landed in Detroit, Michigan. They reached home about 8:00 pm. Riaz immediately called Christy in Peshawur to let her know he was all right. She could tell he was feeling as though he was in control by the tone of his voice and, oddly enough, she was relieved. This was the Riaz she was familiar with. It was the last time she ever talked to him.

About two hours after he arriving at home with Christy's father, he had some friends pick him up, suitcases and all. He said good-bye and hurried out into the night, saying he had already made other plans.

About six hours later, he was found dead in a park near the Indiana state line. Christy was contacted by the police department, but could not help them because she was totally ignorant of her late husband's activities. When she called her father to find out any details he might have, she received grim verification that he was dead.

"Christy called the police back, and this time got through to a detective on the case. He told her that Riaz had been 'traumatized.'

'What does that mean?' Christy asked, as half a dozen relatives cried out, 'Did the police shoot him?' Christy tried to correct them, to pass on what she'd been told, but they would not listen. Riaz had been shot, they were sure of it. As the news sunk in, the family began to mourn their prodigal son. Most of them walked about with a blank look on their faces, staring at the walls, every now and then striking themselves to vent their grief.

'He had a very pure heart,' his mother wailed. 'He had the heart of a king—he wanted to give everything to everybody.'"[9]

The environment in Riaz's family home changed from one day to the next. The women wanted the jewelry back that Riaz had given to her because they claimed the jewelry pieces were family heirlooms. A brother-in-law tried to make advances, telling her that she and her children belonged to him now, Christy told him she was returning home. He was insulted because she rejected him and became her fervent enemy. But she was still treated as a fellow family mourner by the family at large.

When the body reached the village on the 16th of August, and the family found out from the death certificate that Riaz had, in fact, been shot and in the back of the head, the attitude toward her did an about face. First, she was accused of lying to them about the manner of his death. Then, when they saw the state of the body after the coroner had finished doing an autopsy, they went berserk. One uncle ran over to her and choked her, calling her a murdering American. Everyone else looked at Christy with hatred and blamed Riaz's death on her, saying he died because he had married her.

Then the family went after Christy's children. They tried to blame Riaz's death on Eric, the baby back in the United States who Riaz had gone to claim as his son. They were going to make Adam and John suffer by keeping them in Pakistan. On August

26th, a large group of Riaz's male relatives stormed in and did their best to take Adam and John away from Christy. They did not succeed; John screeched bloody murder and clung to his mother and Adam threw up all over everything. Christy punched one uncle in the neck, which made him and the other men retreat because they were not used to women fighting back.

Fiaz, the rejected brother-in-law, got an injunction out on Christy to prevent her leaving the country with her children. At first, she was not going to be bullied into going anywhere without them, but was cautioned by one of the female cousins that she would be safe from the male members of the family and would be able to better fight for her children if she was in the United States.

Christy left Pakistan under protest only because she did not know of any way she could safely fight for her children if she stayed in the country. As usual, the U.S. Consulate was of absolutely no help whatsoever except for one individual who helped her find a place to stay overnight and escorted her to the airport the following day.

It was to take two years before Christy was able to claim her children forever and in the safety of the United States. She wanted to avoid a full-blown court battle which would take two years to resolve (she had to get the boys back before either of them turned seven years old). She rejected the use of mercenaries to try to extract the boys because she knew strangers would be noticed in the village and would fail in their mission. She did decide to declare herself a Muslim to strengthen her position in the civil courts. She urged all of her friends to write to the Pakistani embassy, urging the release of Christy's children from Pakistan. And she waited to be notified by her Pakistani lawyer that her case was on the court docket to be heard.

When Christy did hear from her attorney, she was told that it would start any day and that her presence would probably influence the judge in her favor. She received advice from friends and advisors about the danger involved in going back again to Pakistan because of Desert Storm, but she was not to be deterred. She went.

Upon arrival, her lawyer told her that her in-laws had finally accepted that Christy's father was blameless in the death of Riaz and gave her lawyer the idea that they would like to settle out of court. Christy was definite: no way would she settle out of court. She wanted her children free and clear.

In this court case, the judge required that Christy's children be present so, when the Khan family did not bring them the first time, the judge adjourned and ordered the family to bring the boys to the hearing the following week. When they appeared in court, she could hardly hold back the tears, but she knew she had to be strong. The judge was kind enough to allow her and her sons to meet in his chambers. She was overjoyed when John came right to her and then Adam followed suit, holding out his arms to her and gluing himself onto her lap.

The Khan family kept asking for adjournments in attempts to force Christy to come to a settlement to their liking. Meantime, Adam contracted viral meningitis, a highly fatal disease in Pakistan. Christy bent all her efforts to getting Adam the kind of treatment he required to survive, leaving all the legal matters in the hands of her attorney. Adam reached his crisis point and turned the corner toward recovery with Christy by his side night and day.

Nasir, her attorney, told her that now the Khan family wanted to keep Adam and let John go with his mother. It was at this point that the judge put an end to the delays created by the repeated adjournments.

"'This is no good for the kids,' the judge had said, 'no good for the mother, no good for anyone.'

At that point, Fiaz lost all control. 'What do you mean, this is no good for the mother?' he snarled. 'The mother doesn't matter!'

The judge peered at him gravely. 'If the mother doesn't matter, what is this sheet of arguments I have in front of me?'

Fiaz had committed a colossal blunder; his family's basic contention was that Christy's sons should remain in Pakistan for their own good and that of their paternal grandmother, who needed consolation after losing *her* son. A flimsy argument to begin with, it now lay exposed in all its hypocrisy."[10]

Christy had won, at last. She had free and clear custody of her sons. She was free to take them home. Final details of the settlement were worked out. One stipulation was that if Christy married again, she would lose custody of her children.

Fiaz drove her to the airport in Peshawur, and from there she and her children flew home.

Back home, Christy still had to help the boys readjust and recover from their fragility as much as possible from their years in Pakistan. It took both boys about four months before they were no longer afraid their new life was going to prove to be a dream the next morning when they woke up. Sometimes jealousy has been shown toward Eric because he was the reason the boys' mother had to leave them on more than one occasion. Christy has had to work hard to help Adam especially get over the feeling that maybe Eric was the favorite. Eric, as a downs Syndrome child, is the most loving of all of her sons. Over time, the boys have healed to the extent that Christy can leave them with a sitter for a short time without them, dreading that she would not return.

Where the Riaz's murder was concerned, the detectives working on the case say that he owed money to everyone on the planet. They think he was involved in drug dealing—after all, Peshawur is a distribution center for opium coming out of Afghanistan. Christy believes that the Khan family knew more than they ever let on and have kept their knowledge very quiet in order to save their reputation. They will not release his telephone records and they won't give any specifics about his movements.

Christy was working toward a certification in court recording and hoped to be working by the time her three children were in school. Her life will never be the same nor will she ever forget the past few years. Now that she and her sons are safe, she can think back when she is able to and mourn for Riaz to the extent that she wishes to.

She feels that her faith saved her. She knows that by comparison to so many left behind mothers, she is one of the lucky ones.[11]

Anne-Marie and Brahim Houache from Algeria were divorced. Anne-Marie lived in France with their sons while Brahim lived in Algeria. When the sons spent the summer with their father, he then did not allow them to go home to their mother.

Anne-Marie and Brahim met and were married in a Catholic church in Anne-Marie's home town. Brahim spoke French very well which worked out nicely because they co-managed his business for years until she took an outside clerical job which eventually developed into an administrative secretary Brahim was uncomfortable with her independence away from his business and when it was bought out by a supermarket, he became resentful. Their marriage began to unravel.

Not only did he feel excluded and isolated, he was afraid that his sons would become as independent from him and out of his control as his wife now was. He became so hostile to French society and culture that eventually he and Anne-Marie separated after having two children. Their sons stayed with her in a suburb of Paris and their father lived and worked elsewhere.

When Brahim Houache invited his two sons, Amar and Farid, to come with him to Algeria for summer vacation, they thought it would be an adventure and that they would be home to start school in the fall. They had been to Algeria before and liked their father's family. They loved and trusted their father as well so they went with him gladly.

When September came, Brahim pleaded illness and said he needed to postpone their trip home to France. They were at ease with this at first, but began to wonder why their father did not show signs of illness. He enrolled the boys in an Islamic school which they did not relate to and did not care about—their school was waiting for them in France and they were looking forward to returning home very soon.

When Anne-Marie received a letter from Brahim saying that he was staying in Algeria and that the boys would be staying also, she could not believe what she was reading—it was a bolt out of the blue and she was in shock. At first she thought that there was no way he could get away with this—the boys were French citizens, living in France. When she called the Ministry of Justice, the only answer they gave her was that hers was one of an overwhelming number of such cases.

When she went to Algiers, the French Embassy was good enough to arrange a meeting between Brahim and herself and to see her sons, her sons being the priority. The boys returned to their father's apartment and were surprised at seeing their mother waiting for them.

When they saw their mother, Amar and Farid were both excited and fearful. Why was she here? Had something terrible happened?

Then they saw her pained expression—and they knew, before she'd said a word. 'Your father wants you to stay her for good,' Anne-Marie began.

'But Mom, we want to go home!' Amar protested. 'We have to go to school!'

Anne-Marie did her best to calm them: 'You can't come home just yet, but I'll do everything I can to get to get you home.'

It was a promise, as future events would prove, that this mother would not take lightly.

The boys asked Brahim what was happening. Why did he want to keep them here? What were his plans? Amar, who was generally more assertive (and louder) in confronting his father, said 'Dad, we want to go back to France.'

'Shut up!' their father replied. 'It is none of your business!'[12]

When Brahim had brought their sons to Algeria, he had thought he was doing the best thing for them and that they would appreciate being there in Algiers with him. As he began to realize that he had been badly mistaken, Brahim became more dictatorial than he had been in the past in an effort to control the situation.

In reality, they resented his deceiving them and taking them away from their mother, their life in France, their friends, and their school—in short, everything that comprised home for them. The

Islamic values and cultural living patterns meant nothing to them. They realized they and been duped and they felt guilty about having come gladly.

Furthermore, it now became obvious to Amar and Farid that everyone in their Algerian family was in on the scheme. What appeared to them at first to be socializing with everyone was, in actuality, a concerted plan to watch them, to guard them, and prevent a possible escape. It also occurred to them that their father might have been planning this since their last visit.

The boys had thought their father to be a wonderful person and worth copying in every way. As the harsh reality of what he had done to them and was trying to make them into hit home, the respect and trust evaporated. They wanted to get away from him and Algeria, which they had begun to hate, and go home to their mother who loved them without reserve and without ulterior motives.

Anne-Marie considered staying in Algeria to be near her children, but reconsidered. If she stayed, she would have to convert to Islam which she was not about to do. She was also dismayed when Brahim showed her where she would be living if she stayed— alone and separate from her sons whom she would not be able to see. All in all, she would be much wiser to go back home, even without her children for the time being. In France, she hoped to rally the French courts to her aid.

Brahim wanted to live in Algeria now that he was divorced and had no reason to stay in France where he felt displaced and unwanted. Algeria was where he had grown up and where the values were what he thought they should be. Not the least of these values was that the father was sole guardian of his children whether or not there was divorce.

When Anne-Marie went to see her sons, she was treated as inferior and unclean because she was Christian. She was not allowed to touch anything in the house, she was never allowed to see her sons alone, and Brahim was suspicious of her every move. Amar and Farid noticed all of this, resenting how limited their access was to their mother and how she was treated.

When Anne-Marie's sons informed her that Brahim was going to get married again, Anne-Marie obtained a divorce and custody of her children through the French court system. However, the French custody papers were worthless in Algeria. When she tried to obtain custody in Algeria, she was turned down because, as in every Muslim country, the father is always awarded custody. The court, however, did rule that Brahim must pay her alimony every month.

Brahim's relatives and friends working at the post intercepted all mail from both directions between Anne-Marie and her sons, had his new wife search the boys' belongings for any pictures of their mother, and destroy any that were found. Brahim tried to eliminate any contact between them.

No matter what Brahim tried, Anne-Marie visited her son every six months. She realized that she was never going to be able to accomplish her goals of getting back her children without help and support, so she became part of an organization of left behind mothers called Mothers of Algiers. Its purpose was to engineer visitation rights and influence the government into creating a system to enforce those rights for French mothers whose children had been taken to Algeria by their fathers and kept there. They had demonstrations, sit-ins, marches—anything and everything to draw attention to their plight and what they wanted done about it.

The government stalled as governments always do. Anne-Marie tried to speed up some visitations by planning to pick up some Belgian children and bring them across the border to France where they would be reunited with their mothers and from there to Belgium. There was an informer so the driver of the car was stopped by the police who took the children back to their relatives.

Confrontation and negotiation went on for months. Finally, after much international publicity, the French and Algerian government agreed to a treaty.

"As it evolved, the treaty sold itself. World opinion had become an irresistible force for enactment. The catch-as-catch-can transborder visits were too erratic. Most important, the treaty was presented in a way that allayed Algerian fears. It was not a French ploy to wrest all parental power from the fathers. Rather, it provided that both parents *share* power through custody and visitation—and that both be held responsible in assuring their children's rights.

After seven years of grindingly slow progress, the historic breakthrough came suddenly. Three days later, on June 21, the Franco-Algerian Convention was signed, sealed, and delivered. A temporary bi-national commission was appointed to advise on all abduction cases already in dispute, including those of the Mothers of Algiers. Future cases would go directly to the courts.

This was a significant event in the history of human relations. It was the best kind of victory, for there were no losers. The Mothers of Algiers were no longer severed from their children. The Algerians won new respect from the world by breaking the chains of mutual bad faith and by accommodating the values of another culture. They could no longer be cast as the villains.

Best of all, the children won—all the children who had two parents instead of one, all the children who would avoid the trauma of abduction in the future. And in this ringing affirmation of their rights against such formidable odds, the winners were all the children of the world.

No loophole can tarnish the phenomenal, unprecedented achievement of the Mothers of Algiers. They achieved what no group or government had ever done before—an effective agreement on child custody between Christian and Muslim states. With their deep commitment, their willingness to risk body and soul, and their ability to enlist the people in power, they truly moved mountains.

Since the Franco-Algerian Convention was ratified, parental abductions have been reduced to a trickle. Its shining success is a model for other agreements between Islamic and non-Islamic states, and for other nations with significant difference."[13]

Anne-Marie's sons, who are very close to each other, spend as much time as they can with their mother, almost as if they are trying to make up for those years they were forced to spend separated from her. Their relationship with their father will never be what it was—they have no interest in the country which was their prison and they will never be able to respect and look up to him as they did before he deceived them.

Alexandria Davis, formerly Yasmeen Alexandria Shalhoub, was taken by her father to Saudi Arabia. She managed to escape two years later.

Miriam Hernandez met Khalid Shalhoub from Saudi Arabia in Miami, Florida, where they met and eventually got married. The marriage broke down because Khalid expected Miriam to become a "good Saudi wife", obedient, submissive, and always on call. Miriam gave birth to a daughter and, when Alexandria was two years old, Miriam and Khalid got a divorce. Mother and daughter moved in with her mother and grandmother. As Alexandria grew older, she went to a Catholic school, went to church, and participated in sports and other extracurricular activities with her friends.

Khalid had moved to London and worked there; however, he kept in contact with his daughter. They exchanged visits for several years, especially during her school vacations.

During her eleventh summer, when her father came to pick her up for their flight to London, she thought, he straightaway took her to Saudi Arabia without warning and without asking her whether she would like to visit the kingdom. He told her that she was going so that she could meet family members and she assumed that she would be on her way home in time to start school in September.

After she had asked him several times when she was going home and he did not commit himself on when she was leaving, she began to realize that she had been abducted, that her father had no intention of sending her home. When she continued to plead with him to send her home or begged to speak to her mother, Khalid beat her. Once he started hitting her, he beat her up every time she brought up wanting to go home or wanting to speak to her mother.

Alexandria's every movement was watched and confined to the house. She was not allowed even to play outside. When the family left for an outing of any kind, she was locked in the house by herself. Khalid's family also attacked her Catholic faith, saying to her that she and all her family were going to hell and burn there which gave her nightmares every night. They also made her eat on the floor because her Christian beliefs made her too "unclean" to eat at the table with the rest of them.

It became very apparent to her that her father hated the West, he hated Christians, and he hated her mother for divorcing him. He called her terrible names such as "stupid bitch" and "fatso", and that he wished she would die and burn in hellfire.[14]

Khalid took most of the phones out of the house and did something to the one left so Alexandria could not dial out. Even so, she did manage to call her mother on occasion who taped the calls so she could send them to the American Embassy to prove she was being abused; however, true to form, the embassy ignored them. Khalid, who tapped in to the calls that Alexandria made to her mother, beat her every time she succeeded in making the calls. More than once, the poor girl was afraid to wake up in the morning because she knew she was going to be beaten.

Alexandra knew that her mother was trying everything to set it up so that she would leave Saudi Arabia forever and go home which she did not understand. How could her country do nothing to help her? As with so many other women in similar situations, she felt herself betrayed by the very institutions that were supposed to look out for their countrymen and women.

While her country did nothing to save her, Alexandria's grandmother sold her house and enlisted the help of her family to raise $200,000 to pay for her escape, probably with the help of reliable mercenaries or abduction specialists. Alexandria does not give details about this. She knew she was taking her life in her hands. If her father had caught her escaping, he would have beaten her to death right there, but it was worth the risk to her—better to die than to be forced to live in bondage as a Saudi adult woman.

When Alexandria gave this testimony, she was sixteen years old. She had changed her name to get rid of the Saudi names and so she might have a chance to start over again. Whether she can ever forget is another matter, but she loves every minute of the three years she had been back home in the United States. She knows she was one of a fortunate few to escape from Saudi Arabia.[15]

Sarah Saga, abducted at six years old by her father and taken to Saudi Arabia, was able to leave the kingdom and return to the United States, but she was required to leave her children behind.

Sarah Saga's mother, Debbie Dornier, married a man from Saudi Arabia when both were students at a California university. Within a few years of the marriage, Debbie gave birth to a daughter. However, the marriage eventually disintegrated as her husband struggled with the pressures of school and family life and because the combination of trying to pay for school and living expenses created unrelenting financial pressures. The couple got a divorce which was extremely humiliating for Debbie's husband because of the traditional values he had brought with him to the United States.

Sarah lived with her mother in California during the early years of her life. Her father had visitation rights and had taken advantage of them to remain a part of his daughter's life. In September 1985, her father arranged with her mother for their daughter Sarah to accompany him to Saudi Arabia for a month's visit to become acquainted with relatives. When Debbie went to the San Francisco Airport to pick her daughter up when she was supposed to arrive back in the United States, Sarah never alighted from any flight coming from Saudi Arabia. She simply never showed up.

Debbie was frantic. Where was Sarah? Why had she not arrived?! In a blind panic, she called Saudi Arabia until she finally was able to talk to her ex-husband. He was extremely hostile when speaking to her.

"'Don't think you'll ever get her back. I'll slit her throat her before I let her return.'"

Debbie's mother had no idea how to get her daughter back. The State Department was of no help, of course, and there was no way she could afford the huge sums of money required to by commando help to retrieve Sarah. Also, her ex-husband had threatened to kill Sarah rather than see her returned to her mother, which made Debbie too frightened for her daughter to pursue her return over a long period of time.

Sarah was forced to live in Saudi Arabia with her father and his family for eighteen years. He had more than one wife as is common in the Arab/Muslim countries, so Sarah had to live with several stepmothers, none of whom liked her. Her father and stepmothers were extremely abusive so Sarah was beaten regularly, threatened with a knife, and locked in a room for two years.

When she was eighteen, a devout Muslim, Adham Jad, wanted to marry her. In order to escape the tyranny of her father, she accepted his proposal and they were married. They moved to Mecca where they eventually had a son, Ibrahim, and then a daughter, Hanin.

When her daughter was born, Sarah started thinking about her mother and missing her terribly. Her father had long ago threatened to kill her if she searched for her mother, but she was now married and somewhat safer. Her method was rather ingenious—Sarah began her search on the internet since she could not write, did not know where she was or if she was still alive. As she began to think back over the years, she miraculously remembered her mother's last name and this was the key which eventually led to success in her search. She found the name and phone number of her mother and grandmother! She went out and bought a phone card and then called the United States. Her grandmother answered the phone.

"'Hello, this is Sarah. Is it too late to call you grandma?'

That began the long, intimate reunion between a little girl who longed for a mother's love and an American mother's hope that she and her daughter would once again be able to hug and kiss and cry and laugh and get to know each other again. Debbie and Sarah had hope again for life together that they could share in America." [16]

Sarah knew that if she tried to escape, it could cost her her life. She knew her father would kill her for the attempt alone. She also thought her husband might do the same thing since he was becoming more domineering and abusive as time went on. She knew she had no civil rights—her husband could divorce her and take the children at any time he wanted to or he could kill her— there would be no interference from anyone.

After a lot of thought, Sarah determined that the only chance she might have to escape would include somehow getting to the American Embassy in Jeddah. Her husband had refused to take her to Egypt to see her mother so she had no alternatives left. She decided to risk it.

Very early in the morning of June 15th, Sarah gathered her children from their beds and had a taxi take them to the U.S. Consulate in Jeddah. The consulate officials were not very happy to see them, but Sarah refused to leave, saying that her father would kill her if she was returned home by consulate officials.

Sarah's mother called the U. S. Ambassador's office to remind Mr. Jordan that he had promised that no American woman would be thrown out of the embassy while he was in charge. As a result,

Sarah and her children were allowed to remain in the consulate for five days in a small apartment so she and her children would be safe, temporarily at least.

During that period, she was forced to see three officials from the Saudi government who demanded a meeting with her. They had her intimidated to the point where she signed a paper saying that she would be allowed to leave the country but she had to leave her children with their father. Then she changed her mind because she could not fact the thought of her children staying there and being subjected to what she had been through. The Saudis would not let her leave with her children.

"Sarah realized too late that she had to make an impossible decision. She could seek her own freedom and fulfill and eighteen-year dream of seeing her mother. Or she could stay in Saudi Arabia with her children and face the likely vengeance of her father, who was disgraced by her decision to flee."

Saga made her choice. She returned to America, leaving her son and daughter in the care of her estranged husband. 'I wish I hadn't left them,' Saga said this week after reuniting with her mother in Fresno. 'I wish I had had a choice.'"[17]

Now, even though she is free, Sarah faces a bittersweet future without her children, just as her mother faced the last eighteen years wondering about her daughter.

Betty, a divorcee with two sons, met Dr. Bozorg Mahmoody when she was in a Michigan osteopathic facility to receive manipulation therapy for debilitating migraine headaches. They dated for three years; then they married and had one child, a daughter. When Mahtob, their daughter, was four

years old, Moody suggested they visit Iran and his family for a two-week vacation. Betty hesitantly agreed to go. When they had been in Iran for about a week, he announced that they were staying for good. After harrowing adventures and with the help of some good people, Betty Mahmoody and her daughter were able to escape Iran and return to the United States where they live under assumed names today.

Betty was getting her life re-established after an arduous divorce. She was working at ITT and had been promoted up in the company hierarchy. This was a source of great satisfaction to her and provided her and her two sons with a comfortable living. Then she started getting plagued with migraine headaches so debilitating that her doctor had her check into a hospital several miles away. The group of doctors handling her case decided to have her receive physical therapy and manipulative treatment therapy. Then she would go back to her quiet dark room where she could curl up and try to sleep off the headaches.

The physician assigned to give Betty the manipulation treatments was very gentle and effective. He was able to give her some blessed relief from the pain of her headaches, which, as it turned out, was all that she was afflicted with. The doctors thought they would disappear after a while with the therapy treatments she was receiving.

The doctors' surmise was correct. Betty did recover from her headaches. However, a new element had come into her life. During the course of her manipulation therapy, she and her therapist had become acquainted. He was caring, kind, gentle, and mature—the ideal combination of traits to be around when she was in so much pain. During her last manipulation treatment before leaving the hospital, he asked for her address and phone number so he could check on her condition, which she gave willingly.

As they became acquainted, he told her about his religion and about Iran. He was very emphatic about not wanting to return to Iran. He told her that he had changed so much during his twenty years in the United States that his family no longer understood him and he did not fit in anymore. As Betty got to know Moody better, she encouraged him to call his family and to visit his home. When he did go, he called every day to tell her he missed her.

Moody was brilliant—he had obtained degrees in mathematics and engineering and was interning to became an anesthesiologist when he had Betty as his patient. He was also capable of dark confused moodiness and disregard for anyone but himself as Betty was to learn later.

Betty was working toward her college degree—a source of great satisfaction to her—and, at first, so was her job. She was not interested in marrying again and, at first, neither was Moody. But, three years later, after a spectacularly successful birthday party she planned and carried out for him, Moody proposed to her and she accepted.

Their marriage had its ups and downs as does any marital relationship. Betty eventually became pregnant and gave birth to a daughter, Mahtob. Her two sons by her former marriage accepted their new little sister with enthusiasm and love. Then, when Mahtob was four years old, Moody's nephew suggested to Moody that he bring Betty and their daughter to Iran for a holiday so she could meet her Iranian family relations.

Betty hesitated. The thought of taking Mahtob to Iran scared her because she was afraid Moody was decide not to bring them back. But her friends did not think he would ever do that; after all, he had lived in the United States for twenty years and his medical practice was here as well. They thought he was thoroughly Americanized. As Betty said in her book:

"Moody had every reason to take us back to America after the two-week vacation. And he had every reason to force us to stay in Iran."[18]

So why did Betty decide to take her daughter and go with Moody to Iran? For what would normally have been a good reason—so Mahtob could meet her grandparents and so they could meet her. This decision changed her life and that of her daughter's forever.

Betty and Mahtob hated being in Iran from the moment they stepped off the plane. Everywhere they looked, they saw what looked like black moving tents—those tents were women in chadors, a large black cloth in the shape of a half moon which is wrapped around the shoulders, forehead and chin. Only the eyes, mouth, and nose showed. When Betty took Mahtob to the airport bathroom, they were confronted with a hole in a cement floor, surrounded by defecation and flies the smell of which was foul beyond belief.

When, after four hours, they stepped outside the building, they were mobbed by relatives everywhere, especially Moody's hysterically crying, joyous sister who wrapped herself around him with both arms and legs and hung on him, chattering in Farsi.

By the time they arrived at the Mahmoody home, Mahtob was desperate to go to the bathroom:

"Quickly I [Betty] located a bathroom for Mahtob, just down the corridor from our bedroom. When I opened the door, both Mahtob and I recoiled at the sight of the largest cockroaches we had ever seen, scurrying about the damp marble floor. Mahtob did not want to go inside, but by now it was an absolute necessity. She dragged me in with her. At least this bathroom had an American-style toilet—and even a bidet. In place of toilet paper, however, was a water hose hanging on the wall.

The room reeked of mildew, and a sick-sour stench wafted in through a window that opened onto an adjacent Persian-style bathroom, but it was in improvement over the airport facilities."[19]

There was a huge feast prepared in honor of Moody's arrival—salads of all sizes and varieties, rice, chicken—all prepared with care and effort by his female relatives which Betty noticed because she was no stranger to Persian dishes. Moody had already introduced Betty to Iranian food when they were living in Michigan. She had learned to prepare many dishes as well as learn to like the food. The whole family enjoyed Persian food thoroughly the way it was cooked in the United States. However, on this occasion:

"Sitting on the floor cross-legged or perched on one knee, the Iranians attacked the meal like a herd of untamed animals desperate for food. The only utensils provided were large ladlelike spoons. Some used these in tandem with their hands or a portion of bread folded into a scoop; others did not bother with spoons. Within seconds there was food everywhere. It was shoveled indiscriminately into chattering mouths that spilled and dribbled bits and pieces all over the *sofrays* and carpets and back into the serving bowls. The unappetizing scene was accompanied by a cacophony of Farsi. Every sentence seemed to end with the phrase '*Ensha Allah*,' 'God willing'. There seemed to be no disrespect in invoking the holy name of Allah while unwittingly spitting bits of food all about.

No one spoke English. No on paid any attention to Mahtob and me.

Moody had taught me how to cook many Iranian dishes. Mahtob and I had both come to enjoy food not only from Iran, but from numerous Islamic countries. But when I tasted this feast, I found the food incredibly greasy. Oil is a sign of wealth in Iran—

even cooking oil. Since this was special occasion, the food was swimming in copious amounts of it. Neither Mahtob nor I could eat much. We picked at the salads, but our appetites were gone.

The meal dragged on. As the adults continued to shovel food into their mouths, the children became restless. Squabbles erupted. They threw food at one another and, screaming in high-pitched voices, ran back and forth across the *sofrays*, their dirty bare feet sometimes landing in dishes of food. I noticed that some of the children suffered from birth defects or deformities of one kind or another. Others had a peculiar, vacant expression. I wondered if I was seeing the consequences of inbreeding. Moody had tried to tell me that it had no deleterious effects in Iran, but I knew that many of the couples in this room were cousins married to cousins. The results seemed obviously apparent in some of the children."[20]

Betty and Mahtob could not wait to get into bed, away from the heat, the noise of the loud and endless chatter, and the smell of the crowd of people. As they finally were able to settle into sleep, they were praying that this two-week vacation would pass quickly so they could go home where it was clean and peaceful and stench-free.

Betty got up from sleep, hoping that she, Mahtob, and Moody could shower and wash off yesterday's perspiration from the heat. In the bathroom, there were no towels so Betty tore up a sheet to provide makeshift towels for them to use.

After Betty was dressed and groomed, she went into the kitchen to find Ameh Bozorg (sister of Bozorg) bustling about the kitchen. She was in a chador which was wrapped around her body and gathered under her armpits. She had to hold her arms to her sides to keep the cloth tucked in place while she worked.

"Thus shackled, she worked in a room that, like the entire house, had once been beautiful but had now fallen into a general state of disrepair. The walls were coated with the accumulated grease of decades. Large tin cupboards, similar to those in a commercial American kitchen, were rusting away. There was double sink of stainless steel, heaped with dirty dishes. Pots and pan of every description were stacked on the counter and on a small square table. With no counter space available, Ameh Bozorg simply used the kitchen floor as a work space. The floor was tan-colored marble, partially covered by slab of red and black carpet. Scraps of food, gummy residue from spattered oil, and mysterious trails of sugar covered the floor. I was surprised to see a GE side-by-side refrigerator-freezer, complete with icemaker. A peek inside revealed a jumble of additional dishes, uncovered, the serving spoons still in place. The kitchen also featured a front-loading Italian-made washing machine and the household's single telephone.

The biggest surprise came when Moody boasted to me that Ameh Bozorg had cleaned the house completely in honor of our arrival. I wondered what the house looked like when it was dirty."[21]

This is the slovenly setting into which Betty and her daughter were plunged—it compared beautifully with Charles Dickens in terms of sheer squalor for anyone accustomed to cleanliness, good manners, food cooked with a minimum of grease, everyday hygiene, decent all around behavior from adults and children alike, basic amenities in the bathroom, and respect for every individual.

This was only the beginning. There were bugs in the food, there was a continual stench in every room of the house, the food was always so greasy that neither Mahtob nor Betty could stand to eat it, and there was continual filth everywhere

Since the appearance of Khomeini, religious fundamentalism was in full swing all over Iran. Women had to cover themselves from head to foot in black stockings gloves, chador, overcoats, etc and there were gangs of male thugs out to spy on the women everywhere to make sure they complied with the new restrictions on dress.

The exchange rate from dollars to rials was 100 rials for every dollar so everyone had to carry stacks and stacks of money on their person when they went out to shop. Moody always carried a tremendous amount of rials to buy anything.

Betty was constantly required to wear a chador when any man who was not a relative was around and she was consistently subjected to awkward statements and questions about American politics at every social occasion that she and Moody participated in. Long before it was time to leave the country, she was fed to the teeth—she and Mahtob hated Iran with every bone in their bodies.

The day for departure drew nearer and nearer. Betty and Mahtob were counting the hours. Moody, Betty, Mahtob, and Majid, a relative, went for an outing to the local park on the last day before they were due to leave. It was then that Moody began dropping bombshells on Betty.

He told her he had lost his job a short time before they left the United States. Betty knew he had had trouble in the past, partly brought on by his personality and partly from prejudice, but Betty reassured him that he would find another job and that she could go back to work.

The following day when Betty and Mahtob were packing with joy and thanksgiving that the time had finally come to leave, another bombshell was dropped. Because the passports had not been taken to the airport three days previous to the schedule departure, they could not leave as scheduled. She turned on Moody and asked him what was going on. It was then that he knew he could no longer delay.

"He sat down on the bed next to me [Betty] and attempted to put his arm around my waist, but I pulled away. He spoke calmly and firmly, a growing sense of power in his voice.

'I really do not know how to tell you this,' he said. 'We are not going home. We are staying here.'

I jumped from the bed. 'Liar! Liar! Liar!' I screamed. 'How can you do this to me? You knew the only reason I came here. You have to let me go home!'

Indeed Moody knew, but he apparently did not care.

With Mahtob watching, unable to comprehend the meaning of this dark change in her father's demeanor, Moody growled,

'I do not have to let you go home. You have to do whatever I say, and I say you are staying *here*.'

He pushed my shoulders, slamming me onto the bed. His screams took on a tone of insolence, almost laughter, as though he ware the gloating victor in an extended, undeclared war.

'You are here for the rest of your life. Do you understand? Yu are not leaving Iran. You are here until you die.'"[22]

From that moment on, Betty behaved in survival mode. She had to do so or she and Mahtob would be destroyed by Moody and the country in which they were imprisoned.

The first serious obstacle confronting her was that Moody held their passports and birth certificates. She knew there was no way he was going let her have them. The second problem was somehow figuring out how to escape in spite of the high odds against her.

When she tried to persuade Moody that both families could help with their problems, Moody's response was that since Betty's family was not Muslim, it did not count. Furthermore, the problems Betty was referring to were hers, not theirs, as far as he was concerned. He was becoming more sullen, threatening, and capricious and, as time went on, he took his moods out on Mahtob and Betty both, beating them when he chose to.

The branch of Moody's family they were living with did not like Betty and they ignored her. Ameh Bozorg did not want Betty involved in anything to do with the household, not even when Betty tried to clean up some of the filth. Every move Betty made was watched with suspicion; Moody ordered the family not let her out of their sight. He also forbade her to use the phone.

The longer they were in Iran, the worse Moody's behavior became. He beat Betty on many occasions and even abused his daughter by hitting her so hard that she bled or hurt for days afterward.

When she tried to seek sanctuary at the Swiss Consulate for her and her daughter, she was turned away. The woman in the consulate said that because she was married to an Iranian, she was officially an Iranian citizen as long as she was physically in the country. They were forced to leave; fortunately, Moody was not aware of where they had gone so Betty was able to come up with an excuse as to why they were gone. Moody was very suspicious anyway, so much so that he ordered his family not to let her out of the house again.

The Iranian school year began and Moody decided that Mahtob had to go to school. Mahtob was scared to leave her mother after all that had been going on since they had arrived, but Moody was determined. However, since there was a six-month waiting list, Mahtob could not start school immediately to her infinite relief.

Betty determined to begin the long road to regaining Moody's confidence to the point where he might let his guard down and allow her a little more freedom. The first thing to do was to get out of Ameh Bozorg's filthy house. So Betty began working on Moody about this until she talked him into taking up his nephew Reza's offer to have them stay with him and his wife Essey. Essey, while a cleaner housekeeper than Ameh Bozorg, still allowed the baby to crawl around on the carpets without diapers, urinating on them whenever he had to relieve himself with the result that the house smelled like stale urine all the time.

Moody was getting lazier and lazier, reverting to the Iranian ways he had grown up with as the spoiled son. He did not look for employment; instead, he sat around reading the newspapers and drinking coffee.

Betty was trying to adapt to everyday life as part of her plan to lull Moody into giving her the freedom she needed to formulate and eventually execute an escape plan for her and Mahtob. It was going to be difficult because, as she was finding out firsthand, The Iranians made life convoluted and inconvenient, even when it came to such a simple thing as shopping. For instance, it was impossible to go to one or two stores and pick up everything that was needed. Betty had to go to a different shop for each item that she was looking for on a given day. When on one occasion Betty went out to buy sugar, this seemingly simple errand ended up taking all day. This is because every Iranian has his or her preference for the type of sugar they use in their tea. Mammal, another relative, gave Moody several months' worth of ration coupons with which to buy sugar.

"The shop owner checked the coupons and then ladled out a few kilos of granulated sugar from a small mountain that was piled on the floor in an open invitation to vermin. Then, with a hammer, he hacked off a chunk from a large boulder of sugar.

At home I had to fashion 'cubes' (Manmal preferred sugar cubes to granulated sugar in a spoon) out of this by first bludgeoning it into small pieces and then cutting the cubes with a plierlike instrument that raised blisters all over my hands."[23]

Moody had forced Betty to call her parents to give them the idea that everything was all right and it was then that Betty found out that Moody had told her parents they were leaving for Iran as they walked out of their door to go to the airport. Betty's mother knew all was not all as it should be so both parents were doing what they could to help Betty escape and come home. When Moody received two certified letters from the Swiss Embassy telling him to bring Betty into the office so they could ascertain that she and Mahtob were all right, he did not tell her. She found out when she called Helen, a woman who worked at the embassy, who asked her if she had received the letters.

She was able to call from a local menswear shop because the owner, Hamid, could see that Betty was being held against her will and wanted to help her. He was to prove a godsend for her in terms of establishing contacts in the following months.

When Moody and Betty left the United States, they had left behind thousands and thousands of dollars in assets since nothing had been sold. While Moody had cleaned out their bank accounts, he had not tried to sell anything because Betty would have been immediately aware of what he was doing. Moody wanted their property to be sold and the money transferred to Iran, but Betty had forestalled him unawares. She had sent official paperwork to the State Department saying under no circumstances was any money to be transferred out of the United States.

Moody had dug himself deeper and deeper into a financial hole he could see no way out of. When they left the U.S., they left unpaid financial obligations behind—Moody had indeed charged a great deal on the credit cards to buy presents for his family to impress them, utility payments were not being paid, the rent on a new home was not being paid, and as time passed, even the IRS was after them. He also knew that Betty would divorce him in a heartbeat if they returned to America. To make it worse, his American medical degree was worthless in Iran. Moody had no job and no prospects. All of this was bringing out the worst in him, and that worst was dangerous for Betty and Mahtob to be around. He continued to beat Betty very badly on a regular basis and Mahtob almost as much. And the relatives did not interfere.

Betty kept in contact with Hamid, who was also trying to get his family out of Iran. He knew that sooner or later it would be found out that he had been in the Shah's army and things would go very badly for him. He found it easy to understand Betty's overwhelming need to escape Iran forever. He also proved to Betty that there were Iranians who appreciated the West.

Moody ran out of patience waiting for an opening in the private girls' school in which he was originally going to enroll Mahtob so he enrolled her in a government school for girls. He was going to drag her there in what was now his habitually threatening manner, but Betty managed to persuade him to let her accompany them.

"*Madrasay* (school) Zeinab was a low cement-block building painted a dark, drab green, appearing from the outside to be a fortress. Girls of various ages, all dressed in black and dark gray, their heads covered with the *roosarie* (scarf), scurried inside.

I [Betty] was appalled both with the school facilities and the activities that were going on there. We walked through dingy halls, past a huge picture of the scowling ayatollah, and countless posters depicting the glories of war. A favorite pose seemed to be that of a gallant soldier, standing proudly next to his rifle, glorying in the blood-soaked bandage wrapped around his forehead.

Students sat jammed next to one another on long benches and, though I understood little Farsi, the teaching technique was simple enough to comprehend. It was completely by rote, with the teacher chanting a phrase and the students chanting it back to her in unison.

I thought I had seen the filthiest conditions that Iran could offer, until I viewed the school's bathroom, a single facility for the use of all five hundred students. It was a tiny cubicle with a high open window to let in the wind, rain, snow, flies, and mosquitoes. The toilet was a mere hole in the floor that most occupants seemed to use in a hit-or-miss fashion. Instead of toilet paper, there was a hose that emitted ice water."[24]

This was the school that Moody forced his daughter to attend. His excuse was that it was better than the school he attended as a child. Mahtob hated it from the first instant and rebelled, crying at the awful conditions and behavior demanded of her. Every time she was left there, Betty and Moody got a call saying that they had to return because Mahtob was making too much noise. It got to the point where the only way the school would let Mahtob stay was if Betty stayed at the school with her.

Betty was there every day long enough to get to know some of the women working in the school and, as they became better acquainted, she found out that they held Moody in scorn for the way he treated her. But they could not let her use the phone because they had promised Moody that they would comply with his wishes. However, they did say that if she came to the school late, they would not say anything to Moody because they had not promised him they would.

One day after Betty had cajoled Moody into taking them to the park, she and Mahtob made their first contact with an American! A woman and child were there in the park. Mahtob ran over to play with the little blond girl playing on the swings while Betty hurried over to make the girl's mother's acquaintance. Moody began talking to the Iranian man with them who, as it turned out, was trying to obtain a medical visa to the States for his heart condition. As the two men became involved in their conversation, Betty took advantage of the opportunity to tell the other woman, Judy, that she and her daughter were being held against their will in Iran. The woman was willing to help so she suggested that Moody get involved in helping her companion Ali, her brother-in-law, obtain his visa. They arranged to meet at the park again.

The next time they met, Judy brought a man with her, Rasheed, who was the office manager of a medical clinic. Moody was absolutely delighted to be talking to a medical man and asked him about licensing procedures in Iran. While they were talking, Judy and Betty had their conversation. Judy told her that Rasheed knew someone who took people out of Iran through Turkey and that he would like to somehow talk privately to Betty.

Judy gave her stamps so she could write letters and mail them out of the country and lent her a typewriter so she could type Moody's letter for Ali. There was going to be a farewell party for Judy and her children in a few days to which Judy arranged that Betty and Moody be invited.

While they were at the dinner party, Judy took Betty to a bedroom so she could type the letter for Moody to send. Rasheed was in the room, waiting to talk to her. He told her that his friend took people out of Iran for thirty thousand dollars. Betty was not worried about getting the money raised—she knew her family and friends could raise it. Her prime concern was getting Mahtob and herself out of Iran as soon as possible. Rasheed gave her his phone number and told her to call in two weeks. While they were in the bedroom, Betty got Moody's letter typed as well as several of her own and gave them to Judy to mail for her.

Moody was the center of attention at the party itself because everyone felt so honored to have an American doctor present. He basked in the attention, feeling like the professional that he, in reality, was. When he and Betty were leaving, Moody told her with delight that Rasheed had offered him a job at his clinic. Finally, a professional break for him!

About a month later, Betty realized that Moody was becoming frantic about spending any money when he balked at buying Mahtob a heavy coat for winter. She found out that his job offer at the clinic had never come through. Whether or not he had gotten the job, his license was still up in the air so he might not have been able to take it anyway. He blamed Betty for his not getting a job because he had to stay home to watch her, that he did not have any freedom of movement because the CIA was after him, thanks to her parents.

It was the month of December the next time she went to the market. Betty stepped quickly into Hamid's to call Rasheed to see what he had found out. Rasheed told her that his contact said he only took men out of Iran, that women and especially children were not strong enough to withstand the difficulty. Besides, it was now winter in the mountains and travel would be impossible in the snow.

In the month of December, Betty and Mahtob were not allowed to celebrate Christmas because it was a Christian holiday. The religious police would have jailed them for certain at the very least since Muslims do not celebrate Christmas.

Betty's time at Mahtob's school was spent constructively because the women there had asked her to teach them English and in return, they taught her Farsi. She knew having some knowledge of the language would prove to be invaluable to her as time went on, especially if she could manage to arrange flight out of Iran for Mahtob and herself. Furthermore, it gave her the perfect excuse to be out of the house and out from under Moody's direct observation more often.

More than once, there were air raids in the middle of the night as Iraqi bombers flew overhead strafing various targets in Iran and more than once they came very close to hitting Betty and her little family. There was more than one occasion when she and Mahtob were in the market or on the street somewhere. One oddly positive result of Tehran being bombed was that Moody felt protective and more considerate of his family because of the danger.

Betty and Moody began to socialize with two Iranian acquaintances, Aga and Kahanum Hakim, on a regular basis. Betty liked Aga Hakim because he was a reasonable man when it came to religious views in general and Moody liked and greatly respected him. Through his connections, he was trying to help Moody find a job, either to teach medicine or to practice it once again. He asked Moody to translate his grandfather's Arabic-to-Farsi works into English. Moody immediately bought a typewriter, seconded Betty to do the typing, and set to work.

One day the Aga suggested to Moody that Betty be allowed to attend Koran classes conducted for English-speaking women every week. He knew that Betty was not allowed out of the house much and, by suggesting this to Moody, he was indirectly telling Moody that his wife should be allowed out more and to be allowed to have contact with other English-speaking people. Moody did not want to do so, but any suggestion from the Aga held a great deal of weight so Moody had to agree to let Betty go.

She was thrilled because it meant that she would have a chance to talk to other Americans and perhaps find someone who knew someone who would help her and Mahtob escape from Iran forever. Whether or not she was that lucky, she would at least be able to talk to someone who understood her position.

During a New Year's celebration at Ameh Bozorg's house, Moody began talking to one of his nephew's wife's relations, Dr.Marashi, and found out he was also a physician. When he asked Moody why he was not working, Moody told him that his papers had not yet been cleared. Dr. Marashi said the hospital where he practiced really needed an anesthesiologist and that he would talk to a friend of his at the hospital who happened to be the president of the hospital.

After New Year's Moody found out that he had landed the job. He was on cloud nine! He said that even though his paperwork had not been cleared yet, the hospital was going to ignore that and let him work anyway. In spite of himself, though, his work schedule was going to allow Betty more freedom and he was not happy about that. However, he knew his nephew's wife would report to him if Betty began acting suspiciously. So he started work.

Betty began observing that Moody was exhibiting worse and worse temper toward her and Mahtob more and more often and she could see in his eyes that he was becoming more irrational as time went by. She had been subjected to his treatment before when he was not acting with good sense and she dreaded having either Mahtob or herself near him during these occasions. Also, when he got like this, he was rabidly suspicious of everything Betty did and said, so she kept quiet whenever she could.

It was on a Saturday morning when Mahtob was getting ready for school that a very serious crisis occurred. As Moody was dropping Mahtob off at school and Betty was preparing to go into the school with her as usual, Moody told Betty to leave Mahtob at school by herself and for Betty to come home with him. Mahtob heard this and screamed in fear, clutching her mother's coat.

Betty tried to soothe her, telling her that it would be all right and that she would come for Mahtob at noon as usual. She began walking Mahtob to her classroom and, as she drew nearer to the classroom she hated and the moment when she knew her mother had to leave, she lost all composure. She wailed in terror as she had at the beginning of school. All of a sudden, Moody was standing by them with madness and rage in his eyes.

He grabbed Mahtob and kicked her. Then he pulled her around to face him and slapped her face viciously. She cried out and squirmed out of his grasp, clutching at her mother's coat once more. Betty tried to put herself between her daughter and her maddened husband. He managed to hit Mahtob a couple of times before pushing her against a nearby wall at which point the teachers on the scene formed a protective ring around the little girl.

Moody could no longer get to his daughter so he targeted his wife. He clenched his hand into a fist and hit her, hard, on the side of her head, causing her to fall backwards.

"'I am going to kill you!' he screamed in English, glaring at me [Betty]. Then, turning his gaze defiantly toward the teachers, he clutched my wrist, holding me in a viselike grip, and addressed *Khanum* Shaheen directly. 'I am going to kill her,' he repeated quietly, venomously. He tugged at my arm. I mounted a weak resistance, but I was too stunned from the force of his blow to free myself from his grasp. Somewhere in the fuzziness of my terrified mind, I was actually glad that he had turned his wrath upon me. I decided to go with him now in order to get him away from Mahtob. It's okay, I said to myself, as long as he is not with her. As long as I'm with him, she's okay.

Mahtob suddenly twisted out of the teachers' grasp and ran to my defense, pulling at my garments.

'Don't worry Mahtob,' I sobbed. 'I'll be back. Leave us. Leave us!'

Khanum Shaheen stepped forward to encircle Mahtob in her arms. The other teachers moved aside, opening a channel for Moody and me to exit. All of these women were powerless against the wrath of a single invading man. Mahtob's shrieks grew louder and more despairing as Moody dragged me from the classroom, down the hall, and out into the street. I was dizzy with pain and fear, terrified of what Moody might do to me. Would he really kill me? If I survived, what would he do to Mahtob? Would I ever see her again?"[25]

Moody threw Betty into a taxi, took her home, threw her out, and sped off toward the hospital. Betty was in a panic and knew she had some time before Moody came home. She called the Swiss embassy to talk to Helen who agreed to meet her at Mahtob's school. As she was on her way back to the school, Moody's nephew saw her and asked what was wrong. When he realized that she was determined to be with her daughter as soon as she could get to the school, he offered to take her there. After they arrived, the whole story came out in the conversation with the school teachers. As they were talking, Helen drove up in an embassy car. The school principle, who was very anti-American, was extremely displeased that the American Interest section was involved in any way and refused to let Betty have her daughter on the grounds that Mahtob belonged to her father. Hormoz said he would wait with Betty until Moody arrived and try to help them settle things down a bit.

When Moody arrived shortly after noon, he saw Betty and his nephew waiting for him. He started screaming at Betty because he thought she had dragged Hormoz into the domestic fight they were having. Hormoz assured him otherwise. After that, Betty and Moody began trading insults that steadily escalated in venom and hatred. Ellen was finally able to counsel Betty to simply not respond to Moody's yelling and Betty finally listened so, after a while, everything calmed down.

The next day, when everyone awoke, Betty knew that Moody was not going to allow her to be at school with Mahtob and, sure enough, Moody tried to take her. However, Mahtob's reaction to the level of fear and apprehension she had been feeling since they came to Iran, was to get sick and vomit. Sure enough, when Moody started to take her out the door, she broke away and headed for the bathroom. He grabbed her and headed back toward the door. At that point, Betty grabbed at Moody to stop him.

Then Moody turned on her with the vengeance, frustration, and urge to kill that had been building in him since they had come back to Iran. He threw her to the floor and banged her head against the floor several times and she in turn clawed her nails across his face. Mahtob tried to help her mother to no avail; Betty finally got Mahtob to run downstairs where she would be safe. And then Moody really started in on her. He threw Betty to the floor so hard that pain shot all up and down her back, he kicked her repeatedly, slapped her repeatedly, and pulled her hair out in bunches. And then he dashed out of the apartment, locking the door so that she could not escape. After a few minutes, she heard Mahtob's screams as Moody carried her out the door and down the street.

Betty was frantic. She talked to Reza, Essey, Hormoz, and Ellen, agonizingly afraid she would never see Mahtob again. They tried to reassure that she would indeed see her daughter again and that Moody loved them both even though all three of them knew the Moody was beyond reason at this point and becoming more deranged as time went on. When Moody walked in the door, he screamed at Betty, wanting to know what Hormoz and Ellen were doing there. When Reza and Essey said they were there to help, Moody said that he and Betty did not have problems, that it was Betty herself who had the problems, and that Hormoz and Ellen were interfering in affairs that were none of their business.

As soon as Hormoz and Ellen left, Moody dragged Betty upstairs to their apartment and locked Betty and himself in. He raved at her for several minutes, saying he would straighten everything out and that he would make all the decisions from now on. As he left for work the following morning, he took Mahtob's bunny with him to give her.

Betty did not see her daughter for a month at least. She was locked up in the apartment everyday when Moody left and he would not tell her where Mahtob was. Betty did not know if Mahtob was healthy, if she was being treated well, nothing. She tortured herself with what ifs about her defenseless little girl.

She asked every relative she talked to if they knew where her daughter was and all of them denied any knowledge of where Mahtob was. Then on an evening just after another Iraqi air raid, Moody came home carrying Mahtob in his arms.

Oddly enough, it was the air raid itself that motivated Moody to bring Mahtob home. Mahtob was ill with fever, diarrhea, and stomach pains. Betty held her all night long, sleeping as she could.

The following morning, Moody took Mahtob, sick as she was, with him to where he kept her during the day because he did not want to leave the two alone together. However, he started bringing Mahtob home in the evenings; then finally, after another two months, he began leaving Mahtob home during the day.

But Moody was changing—and not for the better. Betty could see that under the surface calmness, Moody was very concerned about money. He claimed the hospital was not paying him for the work he was doing, but Betty did not know whether to believe him.

Betty was playing a game of deception so that Moody would eventually let his guard down and allow her more freedom. She and Mahtob were going through hell together and there wasn't anything Betty would not do, or pretend to do, to eventually pave the way for her to execute their escape from Iran. She said her prayers to Mecca every day, she played the role of a submissive Iranian wife, she supported him in all issues, she flattered him, she was obedient—all of which, over time, was effective.

One day, when Moody took his family over to Ameh Bozorg's house and left them there for a short time, Betty received the surprise of her life. After Moody left, Ameh Bozorg followed her and Mahtob as they strolled out onto the balcony. Ameh Bozorg put her arms around Betty and said how very sorry she was for the way Moody was treating her. Then she told Betty to call her family to which Betty replied that she couldn't because she did not have permission to do so. Ameh Bozorg looked at her for a minute and then called in her daughters to translate for her. She told Betty to call everybody and talk as long as she wished. No one would tell Moody.

Betty called and poured her love and unhappiness over the phone to her parents and to her sons, waking everyone up in the middle of the night. She found out her father was getting worse and would need more surgery. Her sons were staying at their father's house and seemed to be all right.

After she finished, Ameh Bozorg told her that it was she who had told her younger brother to take Mahtob home to her mother and that he had to stop treating Betty like this. Maybe Ameh Bozorg could see that her brother was losing mental control and was taking steps to protect his wife and child from what he might be capable of.

Inevitably, the time came when Mammal and Reza wanted their apartments back to their families could once again live at home. They asked Baba Hajji to intercede for them and let Moody know that he needed to move his family out so they could once have their own homes. Because Baba was the head of the family and made the request, Moody had to agree to move immediately. But after Baba Hajji left, Moody ranted and raved about how ungrateful his family was, that he had helped them through school, had bought them expensive presents, had provided a place for them to live, had paid for Mammal's surgery, etc. On top of that, he really was not getting paid for his work at the hospital and would not until his paperwork was in order and that further eroded his tenuous hold on rational thought and behavior.

As Betty thought about Moody's checkered professional career, she began to realize that he could not maintain balance in his life indefinitely; he had to keep changing tracks and starting over. Every time he failed at something, he blamed outside circumstances or other people rather than examining his own actions. Because of this, in his mind, Betty was becoming his only friend when things got tough—but not to the extent that she would be able to talk him into going back to the United States.

Additionally, Moody claimed that the CIA was after him for some of his partisan activities in the United States after the Shah was deposed. But the defining reason why he could not go back, Helen told her, was that his green card had expired. He had waited too long to consider that option and now, if he did decide he wanted to return to America, he would have to get permission from his American wife. She knew he would never ask her—his ego would not let him 'demean' himself to that extent.

They finally found a place to live, one that was large enough to house an office, which was perfect. Moody wanted to set up his own practice because, even though the hospital was finally paying him, it was not nearly enough. Besides, he wanted prestige that went with his own practice. That was when he gave her the freedom he had denied her all these months. He needed her to furnish the office and living quarters in a appropriate manner as quickly as possible. He did not have time to go with her or to make the selections himself so he sent her off with money and bus tickets to find what they needed. She had a couple of close calls with lecherous old men which she never mentioned to Moody for fear that he would once again limit her mobility.

Even though their life was now more comfortable, Betty did not let herself be lulled into complacency. She knew she would never be happy in Iran. She knew she hated her husband, and she knew she feared him also. What was he capable when his violent rages took him over?

A benefactor whose name Betty cannot reveal gave her an address scribbled on a scrap of paper and told her to go there and ask for the manager because word was out that Betty desperately wanted to leave Iran with her daughter. She took Mahtob and they went the same afternoon as she had received the address because she could not wait.

The man she was to meet also wanted to get out his family out of Iran, but his circumstances were filled with complexities which had to be worked through first. Amahl was basically in the business of helping other people escape the Islamic Republic of Iran. He was pleasant, successful in business, and right to the point. He told Betty at the beginning of their conversation that he would help them get out of the country—he did not know when or how at this point, but Betty was to wait patiently for word on the arrangements. She did not dare tell Mahtob because the excitement at the prospect of escape would have been very difficult to hide; furthermore, she did not want to get Mahtob's hopes up in case leaving became an impossibility.

Moody knew that he had treated his wife very shabbily; it was obvious because of his threats to Betty that if she ever told two of her American lady friends about his past actions, she would never be allowed to see them again. She agreed, of course. She did not want to rock the boat. Her response made him think that he had won—she had given up on going back home and had become happy in Iran.

Moody was also beginning to look down on his sister's family as he began to realize that some of the members such as Baba Hajji and Ameh Bozorg were quite dirty, smelly, and had no table manners at all. He even commented on how good Mahtob's manners were by comparison when they had the family over for the obligatory dinner.

While Betty was waiting for word from Amahl, she did her best to create a harmonious home atmosphere because it made Mahotb more relaxed and happy, it lulled Moody into thinking she had accepted her fate, and because it kept her busy. She never knew when word might come. She was not sure about what difficulties she and Mahtob would have to face to escape and there was certain amount of fear of the unknown.

"'Come as soon as you can.'

There was sense of urgency in Amahl's voice that set my heart pounding.

'Tuesday is the first day I can come,' I said, 'when Moody is at the hospital.'

'Call me first, so that I can be waiting for you.' Amahl said."[26]

When Betty arrived at Amahl's office, he told her that she needed to somehow get her Iranian papers from Moody's possession because they would work better than her American passports and birth certificates.

In order to mask her joy at the prospect of returning home, she motivated one of her American friends to help her plan a Thanksgiving turkey dinner. This would justify her running to the markets to find the food and would give her the opportunity to make contact with key people. It would also please Moody because turkey was his favorite dinner. Mahtob was scared she would be left behind when her mother went home and Betty had to reassure her that such a thing would never happen.

After Thanksgiving, when Moody was working at the hospital, Betty's brother called to let Betty know that their father was not doing well; he had been so disappointed that Betty did not get home for Thanksgiving that his health was getting worse and worse every day. She hoped to be home for Christmas, but she did not want to promise again in case that fell through also.

Moody wanted Mahtob to have a nice Christmas this year even though it was dangerous to celebrate this most Christian of all holidays in Islamic Iran. This was the perfect excuse for Betty to be in and out of the house because she would be shopping for presents for Mahtob. She could easily sandwich in visits and calls to Amahl when necessary.

They were not able to get home for Christmas, but Amahl was confident that sooner or later, Betty and Mahtob would get to leave as would Amahl and his family eventually leave. It was all Betty could do not to scream in frustration.

The day after Christmas, all of Moody's relatives came over unexpectedly with goodies and presents and food. Moody loved having his house the center of the holiday festivities so Betty felt free to ask friends over for New Year's Eve. Moody was immediately a very Islamic Iranian as he demanded that there be no liquor, no kissing, and no dancing. Betty agreed so as not to anger Moody. The party was a great success, especially after Moody had to go to the hospital for an emergency operation.

In mid-January, Betty received a call from her sister to tell her that their father needed bowel surgery. Unless he had the surgery, he would not live; but, there was an equal chance that he would not live through the operation. To everyone's surprise, Moody told her to go see her father.

At first she could not believe what she heard. Then Moody said it again, threateningly, that she was going to go see her father. Then he went back to his patients waiting in the outer office of their home. When she was her bedroom crying with grief about her father, Chamsey, one of her friends, came into the room to say that it was she who had told Moody to let her go home and see her father.

When Moody finished with his patients and came back into the living quarters, Betty tried to persuade him that all three of them should go see her father. Moody said no that he had to stay to keep his job at the hospital. When she asked if Mahtob could go with her, he said that she had to go to school. Betty then told him that she would not go without Mahtob.

When Moody said he was going to book Betty a flight to Corpus Christi, Betty asked why. It didn't make sense to her since that was not where father was.

"'Why would I want to go there?'

"To sell the house. You are not going back to America without selling the house. This is not a little trip. You are not going there for a couple of days. You are going there and sell everything we own. Bring the dollars back. You are not coming back until I see the dollars first'

So there it was, the mad reasoning behind Moody's sudden decision to let me return to America. He cared nothing for my father, my mother, my sons, or the rest of my family. He cared nothing about any joy the visit might bring me. He wanted the money. And clearly, he intended to hold Mahtob as a hostage guaranteeing my return."[27]

Betty went to see Amahl the minute Moody went to the hospital. She needed advice about the wisest thing to do—or not to do. Amahl told her in no uncertain tones not to go without Mahtob, that Moody would never let her back into the country. He assured Betty that her father would not want her to come under the circumstances that Moody had dictated.

That evening at home, Mahtob confronted her mother. She told Betty that she was going to go home without her, that her father had told her so. Betty grabbed Mahtob and they went to confront Moody. She yelled at him that she was not going anywhere without her daughter. Poor Mahtob wanted to believe her mother, but she knew that Moody usually got his way. The poor little girl clung to her mother all night as she slept.

Moody was going to force Betty to pick up a passport, but Betty was not sure he had the influence to get the lengthy process speeded up. Apparently, he did, to Betty's utter dismay, because Betty was able to pick it up that day. She dashed over to see Amahl with the passport in hand to ask him what to do next. He took a look at the passport and noticed that it said she was born in Germany. He told her it would not work because it would not match her birth certificate. He advised her to take it back and just leave it because it would take time to fix.

Moody was not happy with the fact that she had to go back, but there was nothing he could do. She had to go back. Moody insisted on going with her when she retuned the following day and was able to have the passport changed in about five minutes. It looked like Betty was going to be forced to leave without her daughter in three days.

And then Amahl had news for which Betty had been waiting. His plan was in place finally; Betty and Mahtob would leave the following day. She would send him the cost of the journey when she got home. Then everything fell through.

Moody and Mammal were waiting for her as she walked to the door. Moody was so suspicious of her that he locked her in the house without the telephone, saying he was going to keep her locked up until it was time for her to leave. He was going to take the days off to stay home and watch her. Then he was going to take her to the airport and force her to board the plane.

Betty went upstairs and asked if she could use the phone. She called Amahl who said the plan had fallen through because the worst snowstorm in years had just taken place and it would be impossible to cross the mountains. He told her not to get on that plane. Chamsey later told her the same thing. She knew what Moody was planning.

When the Hakims were over for a visit that evening, Mammal showed up with the plane ticket, he taunted Betty with it. Betty screamed at him and that is when Aga Hakim intervened with questions about what was going on. It was then that Betty told him everything. Both Hakims were shocked at how Moody had treated her and not let her and Mahtob go home. When Moody joined everyone, he acted like he was going along with everything Aga Hakim said to do, but when they left, he slapped Betty so hard she ended up flat the floor and told her that if she did not get on the plane and do what he wanted, he would take Mahob away from her and lock her in a room for the rest of her life. She knew he meant it.

The day of the scheduled flight, Moody said he was taking Betty to the airport to make sure she boarded the plane. Betty said she needed to stop at Chamsey's and take care of an obligation to Chamsey and *Khanum* Hakim first; Moody knew he could not ignore a commitment to the wife of Aga Hakim so they stopped off at Chamsey's house. When Chamsey saw Betty's face, she asked what was wrong and Betty told her. Moody said Betty's father was not really sick, that it was a trick to get Betty and Mahtob back in the United States but Chamsey knew otherwise.

In the afternoon, when one of Betty's Iranian friends, Fereshteh, came over, an ambulance came charging up to the front gate to pick up Moody—there was an emergency at the hospital. This was the last thing Moody wanted, but he had no choice; he had to go. Fereshteh said she would stay with Betty until he returned.

Fereshteh knew nothing about what Betty was planning and Betty would not have dreamed of telling her in order to protect her loving, trustworthy friend. So, in order to get Mahtob and herself out of the house, she invented an excuse to buy flowers for a dinner that night. Fereshteh said she would drive them and Betty agreed because it would be faster and she could get to Amahl faster once she and Mahtob had been dropped off.

"She parked outside the flower shop several blocks away, and, as she opened the door to get out, I [Betty] said, 'Leave us here. I need some fresh air. Mahtob and I will walk home.'

To my own ears this sounded ridiculous. No one needed a walk in the ice and snow.

'Please, let me drive you,' Fereshteh insisted.

'No. I really need some fresh air. I want to walk.' I slid over toward the driver's seat and hugged her.

'Leave us,' I repeated. 'You go. And thank you for everything.'

There were tears in Fereshteh's eyes as she said, 'Okay.'

Mahtob and I got out of the car and watched Fereshteh drive off.

The cold wind bit at our faces, but I didn't care. I would feel it later. Mahtob asked no questions."[28]

Betty called Amahl. She told him that she had to leave with Mahtob this minute or she would never have her. He told an apartment address he wanted them go to and to make sure they weren't followed. After Betty hung up, she then turned to Mahtob and told her they were going home to America. When Mahtob wanted to go back and get her bunny, Betty told her that they had bought it in the United States and that they could buy a new one for her to love when they got home.

Then she asked, "Mahtob do you want to go back and get your bunny and stay with Daddy or do you want to go home to America?"

As she watched, Betty saw her daughter lift up her head and reveal the determination in her expression. She had not yet been beaten down!

Mahtob said, "I want to go home."

"Then we must hurry and get a taxi," said Betty.

When they reached the apartment, Betty called Amahl immediately. He said he would be working all night to get a deal worked out to get them on their way, but she needed to stall her husband. She needed to tell him that they had to talk further before she went anywhere.

She called Moody to say that they needed to work out their problems. When Moody told her he would call the police, she replied that she knew he was practicing medicine without a license and that she would turn him in to the authorities. He immediately backed down and asked her to come home. She told him she would think about it and hung up.

Amahl called about midnight to tell her he was getting a plan worked out and for them to go to sleep. They would need it. He showed up early the following morning with food, clothing, coloring books, and crayons for Mahtob to work on during the trip. Then he told her that they would have to be driven to Tabriz by car and by ambulance to the Iranian Turkish border—the most dangerous route of all to have to take. It would cost $12,000; Betty told him she would send it the minute she got home.

Thursday crawled by; Friday morning Amahl brought some more food, a blanket, a *montoe* (coat) for Mahtob and a *chador* for Betty He directed Betty to call her husband again and tell him that she would bring Mahtob, and her lawyer the following day to talk to him. No one else was to be present. When Betty made the call, Majid answered the phone. Betty told him what he should tell Moody and hung up.

"When I [Betty] returned to the apartment, Amahl said, 'You will be leaving tonight.' He pulled out a map and showed me the route we would travel, a long, difficult drive from Tehran to Tabriz, then farther up into the mountain country controlled as much by the Kurdish rebels as by the patrolling pasdar (religious police). The Kurds had been hostile to the shah's government and were equally hostile to the Ayatollah's. 'If anyone talks to you, do not give them any information,' Amahl warned. 'Do not tell them about me. Do not tell them you are American. Do not tell them what is going on.'

It was the responsibility of the smuggling team to get us from Tehran to the border, across into Turkey via a Red Cross ambulance, and finally to the city of Van, in the mountains of eastern Turkey. From there we would be on our own. We would still have to exercise caution, Amahl warned. We would not cross the border at a checkpoint, so our American passports would not bear the proper entry stamps. Turkish authorities would be suspicious of our documents. If they caught us, Turkish officials would not return us to Iran, but they would certainly detain us—and perhaps separate us.

From Van we could catch a plane or bus to the capitol city of Ankara and head straight for the U.S. Embassy. Only then would we be safe.

Amahl handed me a supply of coins. 'Call me at every telephone along the way,' he said. 'But be careful with the conversation.' He pondered the ceiling for a moment. 'Esfahan,' he said, naming an Iranian town. 'That will be our code word for Ankara. When you reach Ankara, tell me you are in Esfahan.'"[29]

Amahl said they would leave at seven o' clock. When the time came for departure, Betty helped Mahtob to put on the *montoe* and then put on her own *montoe* plus the *chador*, grateful for its voluminous folds which covered her completely.

At seven, two young men came. Amahl asked one more time if this is what they wanted to do. Betty said, "Yes." Then they were escorted to a very ordinary-looking car and their journey began.

At the end of half an hour, they swerved into an ally and switched cars. In the car were several people who were part of their cover as an Iranian family. Well past midnight, they drove up to a gas station and café somewhere in the wilderness for a rest stop. Betty and Mahtob stayed in the car for safety's sake. The drove into a snowstorm and kept driving. Betty and Mahtob fell asleep along with the rest of the passengers during the night journey, not responding to any questions from a woman in the car.

When they arrived in Tabriz the following frozen morning, they were stopped at a checkpoint and, fortunately, waved through without having their passports checked. They dropped off the boy in the car, but the woman stayed, much to Betty's relief. At a busy intersection in downtown Tabriz, the driver stopped the car. Everyone climbed out hurriedly and got into a car directly behind them. The car they were in drove off while the driver of the first car argued with the policeman to distract him while the second car made its escape.

They drove through Tabriz and on into the wilderness. Sometime that afternoon, they drove up to an abandoned farmhouse and stopped. Immediately, a truck pulled up behind them. Betty and Mahtob were told to get in the truck quickly and, as they did so, the car they had come in sped down the road. They were now in a truck with a new driver and another strange man. The truck drove a short distance and then turned into a trail toward a small village. The truck stopped sharply, the driver got out, and ran to look over a brick wall to see if the coast was clear. When we waved, the second young man in the truck slid into the driver's seat and drove forward slowly. The gate behind them was closed and locked instantly. Then Mahtob and Betty were herded through some mud into what was basically a barn. They huddled by a kerosene heater, but the air was so icy that the lamp was not that effective. The woman working in the barn brought Betty and Mahtob some tea and rancid cheese which they did their best to eat.

Mosehn, the young man, came back after many hours had passed and wanted to know what was in Betty's bag. She dumped everything out—she had to trust his motives. She had no choice. He told her to give the contents of her bag to him so she handed everything over to him. He kept some of the jewelry and told her he would need the rest tomorrow.

After several hours, Mosehn came back in the barn, and commanded the woman to bring as much Kurdish clothing as she could carry. She came dashing back in and bundled Betty up in about four dresses; Mosehn brought her some men's pants to wear since they were going to be riding, and socks and boots for both she and Mahtob. They were now Kurds to all intents and purposes. Mosehn then asked for Betty's money, her gold necklace, and their passports which she gave to him without hesitation.

They had to leave. There was no time for the hot meal Betty and the woman had cooked. They climbed back into the truck which was backed out of the gate and started back down road from which they had turned off. Mosehn told her in Farsi that she would pose as his sister when they were crossing over the border. When they met a truck coming from the opposite direction, both trucks stopped. Mosehn gave Betty the passports and told them to get in the other truck which made a U-turn and drove up beside them. The instant the passengers were aboard, the truck took off, up into the mountains. After a couple of minutes, the truck was stopped and Betty and Mahtob were motioned into the back of the truck, which was open. The truck then drove on in the freezing, freezing temperature. Then the truck stopped and Betty and Mahtob were motioned back into the cab. They drove over rocky, bumpy ground on an invisible trail. After they got past that, the truck made its own trail.

The sentinels which the men had spotted fired a warning shot. The truck stopped immediately. The driver and the other man were scared of who they were going to confront and it showed. As a soldier came toward them, Betty told Mahtob not to look at them and not to say a word. After what seemed like forever, the soldiers bought the story the driver gave them and motioned the truck on.

When a checkpoint in the distance ahead was spotted, the jeep stopped and everyone but the driver got out. Because they needed to avoid the checkpoint, they walked through snowy fields and down the side of another highway. After about an hour, the man stopped them and had them sit down while he walked over the crest of an icy hill.

Betty and Mahtob sat there for a long time. Betty was sure that the man who had left them was not coming back and that they were going to freeze to death. Yet, there it was, a red car coming toward them. It zoomed up to them and stopped. It was their driver—he had not deserted them, after all! They climbed into the car and drove for about fifteen minutes and then up to a house off the road. They went inside the cement house and sat in the foyer. They were brought some cold hard bread and some tea and then blankets. The driver came back in and sat down beside them, saying nothing. All three sat there for four hours. Then the ruler of the house came into the room and sat on the floor not too far from Betty, Mahtob, and the driver.

Four hours later, an older man came in, full of energy and conversation. The women brought in a complete change of clothing—four different dresses plus Betty's own clothing. She and Mahtob were so bundled up they could hardly move.

Then they were taken outside where they climbed on small mountain ponies, led by the man who had driven the red car. The old man who had come in last kept warning us not to let the horses step on ice patches that would crack and make noise. He did not want to alert the *pasdar* patrols which were on constant duty.

They moved from icy hills to even icier, colder mountains. Going uphill was safer and somewhat warmer than trying to go downhill. One slip could mean the end of them. The wind cut at their faces, the snow felt like buckshot, and the passage of time was far too slow. Betty could not believe they were still alive because she and Mahtob were so frozen. During the middle of the night, they were turned over to a sheepherder who took the reins and continued to lead them forward.

Both Betty and Mahtob had lost all feeling in their bodies— everything was frozen with cold. Betty hugged Mahtob close to her, trying to keep her warm, at least. During this part of the trek, they heard voices somewhere off in the distance and paused and waited until the coast was clear to continue.

One group of voices the shepherd recognized and headed toward. There were four men talking as if casually and they had three additional horses with them. One of them was Mosehn, keeping his promise to cross the border with them! Since they almost got caught once, they were not going to use the ambulance and risk being stopped again. They were going to continue on horses. Mahtob would need to ride with one of the men.

At this point, Mahtob broke down. She had been so brave, but to ask her to part from her mother was too much. She started to cry. Betty talked to her quietly, reminding her that the border was not too far away. They had to be brave to make it or they would have to go back to Daddy. At that, Mahtob steeled herself. She was going to get to America, to do whatever it took. She said she hated her father for making this necessary.

As they climbed, Betty kept asking repeatedly, "Turkey? Turkey?" The answer she got was "Iran, Iran." They kept climbing, up, up, up. Then they came to gaping hole separating the mountain they were on from the next one. The guide moved carefully forward and through the hole. Then he came back and talked to Mosehn. Mosehn then said to Betty that each person had to go through one at a time because the path was too narrow and dangerous for more than one person at a time.

Betty's horse was led first before she had a chance to say anything. The path was barely wide enough for a horse, leading down into the ravine and then over, up the slope to the other side of the plateau. The trip was completed in about ten minutes. Then they went back for Mahtob. When she was safe in Betty's arms, the guide pointed to the ground and said, "Turkey! Turkey!" Betty thanked God with all her heart.

Their journey was far from over. They had to keep climbing for hours to reach their goal until, finally, the last one was ahead. Betty had been falling off her horse because she was so numb with cold. The last time when she slid off, she simply did not have the ability to walk. She wanted to rest, but the men would not allow it. The guide and Mosehn each took hold of Betty and propelled her forward up the steep incline. She wanted them to leave her and take Mahtob over but they refused. They pulled her to her feet again and dragged her up the mountain. They stumbled often, but the men forced her forward. When they reached the top of the mountain, it was possible to ride so they put her on one of the horses where she perched like a frozen scarecrow and they continued down the mountain.

Then, miraculously, there was light ahead. It was the shelter they had been straining to reach in spite of the danger and difficulty confronting them at every step of the way. When Mahtob was set on the ground, she ran to help her mother who was crawling agonizingly toward the shelter. The men seemed to have forgotten them as they struggled to reach warmth and safety. It was only after they reached the threshold that Mosehn noticed Betty crawling in the door. They dragged her in the door and pulled off her boots which caused her to cry out in pain.

The men carried Mahtob and Betty to the center of the room in front of a huge hot woodstove where they lay for many minutes, allowing the warmth to slowly seep into their frozen bodies. Once they were able to walk, they were led to a separate where the women slept. There they were given wonderful feather-filled blankets to burrow down into and eventually fall asleep, thanking God again for their rescue.

The next morning they were put into a van and driven down, down further into Turkey. They stopped at a farmhouse where they were offered bread, tea, and strong, rancid cheese to eat. They drank tea with as much sugar as possible for the energy.

A woman came in with yet another change of clothes for Betty and Mahtob—Kurdish style with Turkish variation and helped her get into the numerous skirts.

Mosehn had gone into town and returned with a car and activity became a scramble. He handed Betty a packet which she stuffed into her purse. Then they all climbed into the car to pass as a Turkish family on an outing, going down the mountain at breakneck speed.

At the checkpoint, the guard looked them over and waved them on. Checkpoints occurred every twenty or so minutes and they passed through every time with ease, thanks to the disguises. Further on, the van stopped and Mosehn climbed out. The van continued then stopped. This time, Mosehn's mother climbed out. The van continued on then stopped further down the road. The driver motioned Betty and Mahtob to take off their Turkish clothes. When they were stripped down to their American clothes, they were now American tourist with passports but no visas. The van continued on and pretty soon, they approached Van. Betty, with Mahtob's help, told the driver to go to the airport. Since the next plane was not leaving for Ankara for two days, Betty asked about a bus. The driver understood. He took them to the bus depot and went in to inquire about trips to Ankara. When he came out, Betty gave him some money so he could go in and purchase the tickets for them. Then, when he came out with the tickets, they asked him about food. He took them to a nearby restaurant. Then he said, "Finished." Betty offered him her heartfelt thanks to which he responded with tears in his eyes.

Betty and Mahtob went into the restaurant and ordered something which turned out to be delightful barbecued chicken and rice which they ate and ate until they could not move. As they were talking, their driver came back in to order some food and sit with them until they were on their way to Ankara because he wanted to make sure they would be on the right bus and make the trip successfully.

When everyone had finished eating, they went over to the bus station. There the driver found the station manager and explained their situation to him. So, when he was checking everybody's papers and knew they had passports, he did not ask to see them. Then the announcement for Ankara came through a loudspeaker. Betty and Mahtob climbed onboard for a twenty-hour trip to Ankara, thanking their driver effusively for a second time.

This trip took place through ice and snow, twisted mountain roads, a blizzard, snowdrifts on the road, and, of course, blistering cold. With the weather the way it was, the delays were inevitable. Finally, they arrived intact in Ankara at 2:00 am. The bus trip had taken thirty-two hours instead of twenty-one. But they had reached their destination. The day was Wednesday, one week to the day after their dash for freedom from Moody and Iran.

They caught a taxi and had the driver take them to a hotel. The first one they were dropped off at could not let them have a room because their passports were not stamped. However, the clerk did let them use the phone to call the American embassy and to call home collect so Betty could tell her parents they were safe in Ankara. Betty also called her caseworker with the State Department to have them call the embassy in Ankara so they could get her papers in order to enable her and Mahtob to come home. The hotel clerk also gave Betty back her money and had a taxi take them to a hotel that would let them stay the night, no questions asked, as long as they were not in trouble with the police.

In the morning, she called Amahl to let him know they had successfully made the trek out of Iran. He was ecstatic to hear her voice as she told him with vaulting joy that they were in "Esfahan" and continued to thank him fervently. He was terribly happy for them and wished them Godspeed home. After Betty hung up, she and Mahtob went to have a real American breakfast with real American coffee.

When they went back to the embassy, the vice-consul was right there to help them out. He had been contacted during the night and knew exactly what to do to get their passports taken care of and the on a plane for home.

As Betty and Mahtob waited in the lobby, they caught sight of the American flag and thanked God for their deliverance.

Betty and Mahtob arrived home in Michigan on February 7, 1986. They were in time to see Betty's father who was so overjoyed to see them he rallied and was with them until August of the same year when he finally could not battle the cancer wracking his body any longer and passed away. During the two years Betty was in Iran, her sons were now young men.

Betty has never contacted her Iranian friends for fear their safety in their ignorance of her plans will be compromised, except for Hamid who was her pipeline to Amahl and the others who helped her and Mahtob escape the tyranny of both husband and his country.

Betty and Mahtob live under assumed names today and have various safeguards in place so that Moody can never get to them again.

Betty is a heroine for women all over the world. It is impossible to say how many women her book, *Not Without My Daughter,* has saved before they made irrevocable mistakes. Hers is the story of the rare success of a woman escaping *with her child* from an intolerable situation in a Middle Eastern country. While I have told some of Betty's story to let you know that escape with one's children is possible on the rare occasion, it is best that you read her book because no one can do justice to her harrowing story except Betty Mahmoody herself.

*   *   *

In every story of American and European women who have met and married individuals from the various Arab/Muslim societies from Saudi Arabia over to the depths of the African continent, the pattern of the relationships after these marriages is virtually identical in every case with the characteristics I have listed at the end of this Part.

The tragic reality of these relationships is that even though the couples may no longer be married, psychological and physical damage has been done to the women and children which can never be erased. Their lives are forever changed, and, in the case of those women and children who cannot escape from tyrannical husbands and fathers in male dominated societies the governments of which *do not care,* it is impossible to conceive of a more hellish existence, every moment of every day of every year, which does not cease until death comes at last as a blessed release. Rarely is there a happy marriage when the wife and children are forced to stay against their will and desire to go home.

The sorrow and despair of parents such as Patricia Roush who was never able to rescue her daughters from Saudi Arabia is beyond the ability of language to express. She knew they were abused, she knew they were terrorized, and she knew they were twisted and manipulated at every turn for someone else's benefit and *she could do nothing about it.*

There is now an added element of danger for any American woman who chooses to date or marry Arab Muslim males, especially Saudis. Many of these individuals now come to the United States and other Western countries and proceed to set up terrorist cells to recruit fellow Muslim students and receptive Americans for membership and terrorist activities against their host countries. Marriage to citizens of their host countries is very important to achieve in order to obtain a Green Card and have access to the freedom of movement that goes with its possession.

The following is a prime example of how such a marriage can victimize and terrorize the woman who marries such an individual:

Saraah Olsen, 35, was duped into a sham marriage to Hisham Diab from Saudi Arabia, one of Osama bin Laden's men unbeknownst to her, so that he could have an effective cover for the al-Qaeda sleeper cell he set up in her Southern California apartment.

As she said in an interview:'I married a terrorist! I married somebody who did not like America, who didn't like Americans. I really loved him.'

'I was just a stepping-stone to a Green Card,' said Saraah, who had a son from a previous marriage, and who had found out the hard say that 'was the wife, so he looked like a typical guy married to an American girl with a little blond-haired, blue-eyed boy in tow.'

She was also to learn that her husband was involved in setting up a false charity organization to be used as a front to provide money to al-Qaeda.

One of their neighbors and a partner of Diab's, Khalil Deek, was arrested in Jordan while planning to blow up the U.S. Embassy there at the end of the millennium.

Before leaving the United States to fight alongside al-Qaeda officials in Pakistan, Diab managed to convert Adam Gadahn, a Californian who was believed by al-Qaeda experts to be 'Assam the American', who appeared on a recently released terror tape and vowed in his message to the United States, 'Now it's your turn to die. Allah, willing, the streets of America shall run red with blood.'

Saraah Olsen described Adam Gadahn as an innocent teenager and 'fresh meat' for Diab and Deek. She said that 'they took this really nice individual and began teaching him about their belief of Islam [and indoctrinating him] with their warped thought processes.'

In October 1992, just four months before the first attack on the World Trade Center, Saraah stated that Diab had a special guest over for dinner—the blind Sheik Omar Abdel-Rahman, who is now in prison for his plots.

When Saraah called the FBI and tried to them what was going on, they weren't interested in her story so, finally, she gave up trying to contact the authorities.

She also says that Diab beat her and she was too terrified to go against his schemes. 'I'm in hell,' says Olsen. 'I have entered the bowels of hell and I'm going to be here forever.'"[30]

Some individuals have been lucky enough to escape—but the reality of the extreme difference between the average Arab Muslim mentality and that of the average American mentality is a chasm too wide and too deep for the effects of the experience to be forgotten or sloughed off.

Such a mentality as the one we are facing is beyond the experience of most people. But those of us who have lived around them and/or been married to one of them have learned the difference as a long, endless nightmare beyond one's most dreaded conception of hell.

Every one wants to marry and have beautiful children to love, cherish, and raise to adulthood. This is entirely possible provided you marry someone who shares your values, cultural attitudes and standards of behavior. Momentary fascination with someone who does not share these characteristics can all too easily lead you to make an irreversible mistake which will change the course of your life forever and who, if possible, will steal your children and take them where you can never rescue them.

Compared to these women, my time in Hell with an Arab husband was nothing—it at least took place in the United States where I had recourse to laws and attitudes which treat women and children as though they are thinking, intelligent, equally worthwhile beings deserving of rescue and assistance. I was able to keep my son though I admit I took precautions for years afterwards against the possibility of a kidnap attempt by his father.

There are a few American women, however, who have been fortunate enough to escape from relationships with Arab/Muslims before they got married or had children by these individuals. I have included two such examples.

CHAPTER 18

ESCAPES FROM RELATIONSHIPS WITH MUSLIM/ARABS BEFORE MARRIAGE

ARIELL CHOY WAS 16 years old when she became acquainted with an Arab/Muslim foreign student and his friends going to school in Canada. While she did not marry him, the treatment she received at his hands has scarred her for life.

Ariell was a normal teen-aged girl of 16 when she became interested in being a part of adult society. This of course included the desire to begin dating and to learn about the opposite sex. Interest in learning about people from other cultures led her to begin associating with several Arab students attending the nearby university.

She was to find out what that meant for her as a woman and as an independent, thinking individual by any standards.

The Arab students, one in particular, wasted no time letting her know what they would and would not let her do and what was expected of her on a daily basis.

In her article, "Women's Non-Existence in the Arab World", Ariell wrote that the list of what she was not allowed to do was lengthy—she was not allowed her own opinions about anything; she could not get a job; she could not watch television, read, write, go outside, speak for herself or discuss politics, religion, history, or anything else of an intellectual nature. When she was given permission to speak, the Arab students humiliated or ignored her.

What she was allowed, or rather forced, to do was submit to the Arab students' sexual demands on a continuing basis and to look after all of their other wants or desires. One Arab student in particular considered her their property and tool for whatever pleasure he wanted her to provide him and his friends.

For a bright, talented, and well brought up young Western woman such as Ariell, the shock of learning how Arab males treat their women as a matters of course was traumatic. She learned that from her Arab acquaintances that women in their part of the world are taught from birth that any worth they may have derives solely from providing their husbands with sons, preferably, and serving as a slave, first to her husband and then to the other men in the family was enormously traumatic.

She also was confronted with the Middle Eastern concept that "women, being sub-human creatures, especially in the Arab world, are seen as unfit and too immature to participate in society because . . . a woman's forgiving, caring, loving, generous nature disables her completely from functioning fully" and that "an independent woman, free to live her life for herself and be autonomous is the ultimate sin in Arab cultures". What made it worse was that these students she was involved with were enacting out these beliefs on her.

In addition, she found them to be "incredibly lazy and irresponsible" and preoccupied continually with having sex with any woman they could find; the injustice of their being able to immigrate to Canada and abuse French Canadian women was almost more that she could bear and angered her terribly.

The presence of Arab Muslims in Canada is pervasive enough that the Islamic Shar'ia, which tramples on and destroys any semblance of Canadian Muslim women's rights, has been secretly passed and will undermine the Canadian Charter of Rights and Freedoms.

Ariell Choy's life became such emotional and spiritual torture as the result of being dominated by one of the Arab males in particular that it took her years to move forward with her life. She has since become a poet and writer and has found someone who admires and respects her for her strength of character and accomplishments.

She fervently hopes that "women, although afraid, weak, and dying come forth and speak the truth about their Arab abusers even though women around the world fear being ostracized . . . . This is the first step towards healing ourselves" in Ariell's view.[1]

Andrea met Mohamed, who had come to the United States to get a degree in computer technology. She was political science student and had been studying a little about Islam. As they became better acquainted, Mohamed looked like he might be marriage material until differences of viewpoint became apparent.

Andrea had grown up as a Christian and felt that it had little to offer her. She also hated attending church regularly every Sunday.

Because she was very interested in learning about other cultures, other people, and other religions, she began exploring alternatives to her religion and soon discovered the existence of Islam.

The books about Islam that she read presented Islam as a religion of peace and the websites that she chose to read were those that had been created by individuals who knew exactly what would entice a naïve spiritual searcher closer to Islam. Someone thinking of conversion to another religion is usually interested in a belief system which does not actually dispute scientific truths, is basically peaceful, which promotes the concept of one Supreme Being, and which has followers with strong moral convictions. Therefore, when Andrea happened onto websites which pointed out violence oriented facts about Islam which she was not interested in learning about, she dismissed them as radical and inaccurate.

She also became acquainted with many Muslims on chat room websites with whom she became united in declaring that "Israel stole Palestine's land, the West was corrupt and evil, and that Jew were behind all evil acts."[2]

Then Andrea met Mohamed online. He was a student from Morocco who had come to the United States to study computer science and who lived not far from her apartment. As they became acquainted, they had numerous conversations about Islam as they listened to music on voice chat and used the webcam to look at each other while they talked. They agreed that women should not be forced to hear *hijab* (head covering), that women should be able to work if they chose, and that polygamy was outdated. Mohamed also told Andrea that he had a fiancée back in Morocco who lay around all day on the beach in her bikini. They both agreed that the fiancee was corrupted by Western values and that women should not exhibit their bodies in the presence of men.

When Mohamed told Andrea that he had broken off with his fiancée, they decided they were perfectly suited to each other for marriage. When he visited her in person, they decided that he would move with her to Connecticut after her graduation, and after he became financially secure, they would get married. Andrea thought it was wonderful that he would be willing to give up going back to Morocco after finishing his education and stay in the United States with her. She could not understand why anyone ever thought Muslims always wanted to control women.

Their relationship continued to improve. They planned that she would pursue a career in political science while Mohamed worked in the computer field. Then one evening while they were discussing wedding plans, Andrea made the following remark:

"I just can't get over these men who want more than one wife. That is really stupid and demeaning towards women."

Andrea was not speaking of any one group in particular; actually, she was thinking of Mormons and other beliefs that favored polygamy. She was startled when Mohamed's face changed from a happy expression to one of scorn as he said,

"How could you argue with Allah's words?"

"Well," Andrea replied, "In the days of Muhammad, culture was different and so he didn't see anything wrong with having more than one wife. The wars left many women as widows and they caregivers." She had unconsciously given the typical Islamic response to the question before she thought about it and did not realize it at the time.

When Muhamed asked her if she thought Islam was outdated, Andrea responded,

"Well, even you agree that cutting off people's heads is barbaric, and that women working can be a necessity in this society."

"Yes, but I do not argue that it is Allah's will. You say Allah is wrong by saying polygamy is wrong and those who don't fully believe in all of Allah's words are Kaffirs [unbelievers] and Kaffirs go to hell."

Andrea realized immediately that it was wise to say good night and went home. She was not about to tackle dealing with such irrational statements.

The next day, she received an email from Mohamed, apologizing for his words and asking her forgiveness. Andrea accepted his apologies and their relationship seemed be back on good footing. And she was worried about how she was going to pay for her extremely expensive education.

Mohamed's words about Kaffirs stuck with Andrea to the point where she became uneasy about some of what he had said and began doing some additional research about Islam. When she found out about how Muslims were not supposed to become friends with non-Muslims (Kaffirs), about their being commanded to lie to infidels, to murder non-Muslims whenever possible, and about the true nature of women's status in Islam, she was shocked and tried to discuss on the chat line what she had found out with Mohamed. This was too much for Mohamed. His boiling point had been reached. He sent her an email the next day. Andrea's words are bolded.

"What in the hell is your problem? I am willing to give up everything for you—my country, my life, my pride . . . and whenever I ask you to make one sacrifice, you get scared of it, scared of Allah's will. **(Note—The sacrifice he is mentioning is my disapproval of being a housewife)** How can you dispute what Allah has laid out so clearly? You care only about money . . . Care? No, that's not the word . . . You are obsessed with money just as badly as the Jews. Your dreams are not of how to worship your God, and submit to his will, but how you can make money, and get power.

When I dream, I dream of coming home to you after a hard day of work and I see you cooking for me, a clean house, and after that, we have our time in bed. When you dream, you dream of how you get more money, how you can get hour husband to buy what you want. That is the mind of a sick woman. **(I'm the sick one?)** Listen here, Allah says the man is more powerful than the woman, and his job is to watch over her, yet you reject all of it. Here are my demands and you will follow them not because I demand them, but because Allah demands them. And Allah demands submission to the husband.

- You will wear *hijab* at all times.
- You will not befriend Muslim girls without *hijab*, and you will absolutely not befriend Kaffirs.
- When a male friend or colleague of mine enters the house, you will go to a separate room and stay there until he leaves unless you serve him food or drink.
- You will not work, even if I am not able to financially support you. You will be around Kaffirs at work and they will look at you lustfully and tempt you to do wrong. Women are weak. You are weak and you will probably end up harassed by a Kaffir.
- If you leave, even with friends, tell me where you are at all times, and whatever you buy you must show once you return home.
- I am allowed to beat you softly, but only under extreme circumstances, such as denying sex.

- If I want to get another wife, or two or three, it is my right and Allah has recommended it, so if you are a good Muslim, you will even help me search for a wife. However, if I do find one, you cannot object to me wanting to be a better Muslim.

I know this may sound harsh, but you know it's right, even if it takes you ten years to realize. These are my demands. Meet them or you will not have the privilege to be my wife.

I love you.

Mohamed"[3]

Andrea read through the email and sent this reply:

"Dear Mo,

I feel so stupid in my ignorance, in my naivete, to not see the truth. You have laid out everything so perfectly for me. I guess seeing that I am a woman, it is somewhat difficult to come to terms with what Islam expects from me. Islam wants me to be a housewife. Islam wants me to submit to all of your requests. Islam wants me to be completely veiled, except my face and hands. How did I miss this? I really want to thank you for bringing the truth to me, for in our email, you have clearly laid out what had previously been hidden to me.

You showed me that Islam believes that women are merely sex objects and property. Islam was created by a Prophet who was indeed vile and a pedophile. Islam allows you to beat me. It allows you to be a polygamist. What does it allow me? It allows me to stay in the house because I am nothing but an object of sin. If Allah is most gracious, most merciful, he wouldn't have chosen such an ill-minded prophet. If Allah is who we worship, and whose aid we seek, count me out! I don't seek the aid of a vengeful God, who thinks beheading people is okay, who thinks beating women is okay, who thinks pedophilia is okay in this life, and homosexual pedophilia is okay in the next.

My mother always taught me to respect those whose opinions are different and understand that everyone has their own way of spiritual enlightenment. She also taught me to never use foul language. Most of all, never be angry because you will later regret what you say. Sorry Mom, I guess I failed you tonight with what I am about to say.

—you. I will not serve you and I will not serve a god who is the monster the Qur'an speaks of. Call me a Kaffir, please. I would much rather be associated with that culture than one that believes it's okay to kill 750 Jews in one day, behead non-believers, and escalate an old man who had sex with a 9-year-old girl and married her at age 6. If the *Jannah* (heaven) you speak of is full of people like you, why would I want a destination like that? The true hell would be living around millions of people such as you.

I will lock my doors now, change my name, and move . . . because for Muslims to denounce Islam and leave their religion is punishable by death.

However, once again, thank you, for showing me the light of Islam. May the truth set you free."[4]

Andrea's reaction to her narrow escape was a determination to help spread the word about the threat Islam is to American society and to help other Muslims escape. She realized that many of them are not that well informed about what their religion really teaches and that they would be shocked when they found out that Islam truly is evil. Interestingly, she made this acute and realistic observation: "Verily, jihad is the duty of all Muslim males. What we call 'good' Muslims are actually hypocrites to their religion. Those who claim peace, equality, human rights, are denouncing their religion. Those who kill non-believers, they are the true Muslims. I thank Mr. Ali Sina [an Iranian who left Islam and is the director of the website www.faithfreedom.org] for also uncovering the truth and helping me to read more about it, and making me firm in my decision."[5]

In Ali Sina's reply to Andrea's testimony, he stated:

"Welcome back to the fold of humanity. How lucky you are that Mo was stupid enough to show his had before marrying you and having a child. Other Muslims are much smarter. They wait and play the nice guy game until they know the woman is completely under their control and then they remove the mask.

Also, perhaps you should know that the story of Mo's girlfriend lying on the beach in a bikini, and that in an Islamic country, is just a pathetic lie. This controlling man could not have tolerated the thought of a girlfriend in a bikini. Also, his plan of going back to his country was another lie. Muslims kill to come out of their Islamic paradises. You were for him the Green Card. He said all those things to win your sympathy. Look how he used the 'I gave up everything for you' to induce guilt in you. I urge anyone who wants to marry a Muslim, especially a Muslim man, to study about **narcissistic personality disorders** and see how the charming man she loves, whom she thinks is different, fits that profile. The moment one becomes a Muslim, and to the degree that he follows Muhammad, he starts showing signs of NPD pathology. That is because all the Muslims have entered into Muhammad's narcissistic bubble universe. They have zero conscience when it comes to the rights of non-Muslims. The only thing admirable about this narcissist is that in a brief moment of honesty, perhaps in rage, he wrote that email and said it all. One must read that email several times. Those are not Mo's personal views. He is stating the relationship of husband and wife in Islam.

Congratulations for not having the 'privilege' of becoming the battered wife of this sick man and congratulations for starting your site [//islamstrueface.blogspot.com] to expose the evil cult of Islam. I hope you may be able to reach other girls who date Muslim men and save them before it is too late for them. Happy endings to these stories are rare, if any. May you should go back to your church and tell your story to everyone.

What I love about Muslims converting people is that most of them leave Islam as soon as the mask comes down and they see its ugly face. These people then join the army of light and with dedication try to eradicate t his cult of hate. So Muslims, go ahead. Keep converting unwary people with your lies. Soon you'll see what you thought is the 'fastest growing religion' is actually the fastest dying insanity."[6]

Ali Sina (www.faithfreedom.org.) has received hundreds of death threats for his work. He lives very quietly and unobtrusively in order to avoid getting killed for leaving Islam (the Shari'a mandates death for ex-Muslims) and for telling the truth he discovered for himself to other Muslims.

The following is found on the website, www.jihadwatch.org., and is a typical example of the death threats received by Mr. Sina. The spelling is as found in the quote:

"Helo, Did u see the video of the American that was beheaded in Iraq?? Thats what gonna happen to you when I and my friends are gonna catch u. We are currently working on finding information about you, one of my friends is a computer genius. I have gathered muslims all over the world to dispatch any of them to your location. Once u have been beheaded we will use your head to play soccer and your body will be cut into pieces and fed to the dogs. Shut down this website, then we shall not kill you. I give you 1 month to think about it. Make your decision wisely."[7]

Robert Spencer, author of the books, *Onward Muslim Soldiers* and *Islam Unveiled*, regular correspondent on www.frontpagemag.org, and director of www.jihadwatch.org. and dhimmiwatch.org., sent out the above death threat as an alert to his readership. Mr. Spencer had this comment:

"I am not posting this just to give publicity to a death threat. Rather, it is to call attention to the very real danger that converts from Islam must live with. They must live with a legally sanctioned death sentence as a price for their freedom of conscience. Remember that the next time [public figures] start talking about Islam's wonderful legacy of tolerance and respect for human rights."[8]

CHAPTER 19

REALITY CHECKS OF MOST MUSLIM/ ARAB-AMERICAN MARRIAGES AND RELATIONSHIPS

A CHILLING PATTERN of behavior is apparent in example after example of marriages of Western women to Arab/Muslims where child abductions by Arab Muslim national fathers prove to be consistent over time. Many of these characteristics I also experienced in my own marriage. I have listed the characteristics of this pattern in bullet format to make them easier to read, remember, and use to protect yourself and your children.

It is my hope that you will heed the warning about the danger that awaits you if you become seriously involved with an Arab/ Muslim male. Should you choose to ignore what I and countless other women have experienced, you do so at your peril and at the peril of your children.

- Arab Muslim foreign national males come to the United States or to any Western country to attend college, usually to a state university. Very often they become militant Islamists who work to undermine American freedoms and remake it into an Islamic country as they are doing in Europe.

- Arab Muslim foreign national males are told to marry American girls and obtain their citizenship or Green Cards more quickly through their wives' sponsorship. (They can hold dual citizenship.) They are told also to Islamize whoever they marry so any children born will automatically be Muslim.

- Arab Muslim foreign national males living in the West are expected to divorce and remarry every five years, since polygamy is illegal in the United States, and have children by each wife.

- Almost every Arab Muslim foreign national male leaves family still living in the country of his birth so he has someone to go back home to at any time.

- Some of the Arab Muslim foreign national males are charming, fun, handsome, attentive, and different enough to be interesting to date and spend time with. This normally changes radically after marriage.

- Arab Muslim foreign national males make themselves well-liked by their American girlfriends' families and claim to be very pro-Western.

- Arab Muslim foreign national males make continuous statements about preferring the freedom possible in the United States to the unrest and limitations of life back home. This changes after they have gotten their Green Cards or their citizenship.

- Arab Muslim foreign national males make good friends as long as they respect you and as long as you keep your distance, but they make very difficult husbands. It is best not to date them at all.
- No Arab Muslim foreign national male mentions to his American girlfriends how differently women in the Middle East are treated compared to how they are treated in the United States or how limited their lives are by comparison.
- No Arab Muslim foreign national student mentions to his girlfriends that women's rights as we know them in the United States do not exist in any Middle Eastern country.
- No Arab Muslim foreign national male will tell any of his women friends that men in Arab Muslim societies are not raised to like and respect women as people; nor will he reveal that men in his part of the world are taught to look down on women as inferior and to exploit them at every opportunity. The purpose of women in the Middle East is to pleasure the husband, bear his children, bear responsibility for the family honor, and be the servant of the household's upkeep and maintenance.
- No Arab Muslim foreign national male tells his girlfriend that if she marries him and goes with back with him to his country, she and their children will be considered citizens of that country the instant they step inside the border of that country and treated as such. She and the children are his property.
- If you go to any Arab Muslim country as the wife of one of its citizens, you probably will be forced to convert to Islam.
- Arab Muslim foreign national males generally do not mention to their girlfriends that they might want their children to grow up back home and to become Muslims.

- After marriage, the Arab Muslim foreign male's personality almost invariably changes from that from that of being charming, accommodating, generous, complimentary, and open-minded to that of being domineering, abusive, possessive, cruel, critical of his wife's dress and behavior, more self-centered, selfish, deceptive, and critical of the United States.
- Arab Muslim foreign national husbands will try to isolate their wives from their family and friends so that the wives will have no outside support group to help them in order to make them more vulnerable to their husbands' domination and manipulation
- Arab Muslim foreign national husbands will revert back to their upbringing sooner or later, especially when they have families, because they feel the need to atone for their decadent lifestyles when they were younger.
- After the children are born, most Arab Muslim foreign national husbands mention wishing to go back with their wives and children to live in the Middle Eastern country of their birth. Most wives wish to stay in the United States.
- Every Arab Muslim foreign national male uses every means at his disposal to persuade his girlfriend or wife to do what he wants. He uses tears, flattery, piteous appeals to her good nature, and extravagant promises that she is the most important person in his life, trying to make her feel guilty for not wanting to do as he wishes. He inundates her with presents, dinners, attention, and charm to confuse any doubts she has about him and to get his way by wearing her down.
- Every Arab Muslim foreign national husband denies that he will ever take the children from their mother if his wife expresses the fear that he might do so.

- Every Arab Muslim foreign national male makes promises which are broken when it is convenient for him to do so, saying that any promise between a Muslim to a non-Muslim is not considered binding and does not count. This includes marriage vows.
- Every Arab Muslim foreign national has been raised to believe that all Muslims are superior to all non-Muslims. Infidels are considered unclean and impure.
- Every Arab Muslim foreign national male will lie to save face or to preserve appearances, if he considers it necessary, to anyone including the police and the government. Lying is expected to save face, to keep out of trouble, to preserve appearances, to influence women, and to help spread Islam.
- Saudi Arab Muslim males are sent to the United States to infiltrate and work to Islamize this country, using their status as students as a cover.
- No Arab Muslim foreign national male will tell his American girlfriend or wife that he is allowed to have more than one wife in his country or that he might already have one waiting for him at home.
- No Arab Muslim foreign national male will admit whether he plans to marry an American woman, have children by her, convert them to Islam, and then, about 4 years later, divorce his wife so he can marry another, intending to repeat the pattern.
- Arab Muslim foreign national husbands are secretive and stealthy, not telling their wives vital information which will keep them from making mistakes affecting their welfare and that of their children

- Every Arab Muslim foreign national male becomes vengeful when he does not get his way in a matter that is important to him, especially when it looks like he has been outsmarted or rejected by a woman.
- Every Arab Muslim male is a very bad loser, especially to a woman. He will hate her forever for having proved herself to be better at something than he is, especially if other people know about it.
- All Arab Muslim foreign national husbands who abduct the children of their marriages do so abruptly and without warning after weeks of planning and preparation which *always* includes cleaning out joint bank accounts and charging thousands of dollars on credit cards to buy tickets and whatever else is wanted. They immediately take the children out of the United States back to the Middle East, there to stay with relatives.
- In no instances do the abducting fathers give priority to the stability and best interests of the children. The fathers' perceived status in their birth families always comes first.
- Many Muslim Arab foreign national fathers will have their girl children genitally mutilated and circumcised when it is traditional in their family and their society so the daughters will be considered marriageable.
- In no instance do the abducting fathers take into account how the mothers will feel at the sudden disappearance of their children.
- The mothers of the abducted children *might* be notified after their husbands have the children safely out of reach back, home half a world away.

- The abducting fathers, especially the Saudi males, repeatedly tell the abducted child or children that if they try to escape, Allah will kill every member of their mother's families or that they will burn in the fires of Hell forever.
- The abducted children are often sodomized by the males in the father's family. Regular sexual intercourse is not inflicted on the girl children because a broken hymen would render them unmarriageable, thereby preventing the father from being able to sell his daughters for an extravagant dowry.
- In some instances, the mothers are allowed limited contact with their children, and are given the choice of following their children to be with them, but this is the exception rather than the rule. Even if the women follow, it is doubtful whether they can stand the differences in culture, in living conditions, and the treatment of women, and remain in the country.
- All of the mothers of these abducted children have their hearts torn out by the separation from their children who are half a world away. Their wounds and heartache are with them for their lifetime.

CHAPTER 20

FAMILY ORIENTED ABDUCTIONS BY ARAB MUSLIM HUSBANDS

I N ORDER TO understand why
Arab/Muslim males are so
viciously possessive of their wives, but most especially of their
children, even when they do not exhibit a deep interest in assuring
the best possible environment for them after abduction, it is necessary
to travel back fourteen centuries in time.

Desert tribal patriarchies were and still are the basic cultural
pattern for the entire Middle East and were thriving long before
early Judaism and thus even longer before Muhammad was a
twinkle in his father's eye. They have been and still are based on
absolute male dominance in the family and of possession of wealth
and authority in society.

Because these patriarchies were originally nomadic, their
definition of wealth was simple: possession of as many women,
children (sons), slaves, camels, and, later, horses as possible. Their
definition of authority was equally straightforward: absolute male

control of family possessions which included women, children, slaves, camels, horses, and other booty obtained from raiding and looting other tribes. The head of the clan, the oldest male, had absolute control and authority over all other members of the tribe; his decisions were law.

Enter the tribal patriarchies' definition of "honor" which still applies today. "Honor is focused on the absolute possession of women. Women are not free in any way—not even free to have emotions such as love or longing. A disobedient woman dishonors her clan and is eliminated."[1] Neither are they free to do even the smallest thing without permission from the dominant males in their lives.

Honor and absolute possession of a woman or women are irrevocably linked in Arab/Muslim cultures, not to the woman as a whole person, but only to the state of a particular part in the lower half of her body, specifically, her hymen—is it intact? Is the woman a virgin?

Honor is never linked to the behavior of the Arab/Muslim *males*—they do not take responsibility for any of their actions. The fault is always laid at the feet of a woman and it is always she who suffers.

Honor, status, and prestige in society are not only dependant upon the virginity of the women in an Arab/Muslim's family, they are dependant upon the appearance of the males having complete control over every action of the women in the household. Appearances are everything—it doesn't matter what the truth happens to be. If the males can make it look as though they have their women completely obedient, submissive, and under unyielding control, they are well thought of in society and looked up to as "real men". Lying is justified in order to preserve appearances and to maintain status in society as is keeping secrets and being deceitful.

Honor, status, prestige, and standing in his society are further increased by the number of sons an Arab/Muslim male has. If the wife produces only daughters, she is considered worthless and will be either supplanted by an additional wife or divorced. There is nothing a male won't do to ensure the birth of male children to carry on his name and family. The more sons an Arab/Muslim male has, the wealthier he is considered to be.

While girl children are not valued as such and are treated as slaves from the day they are born, they are eventually a source of income for their fathers because he will sell them into marriage. After the marriage of a daughter has been consummated, the groom is then required to give to the father the agreed upon dowry price for his bride.

In Saudi Arabia and adjacent oil-producing countries, children are an additional source of wealth for Saudi fathers, especially if they are part of the royal family, because the government (the al-Saud family) doles out yearly stipends to *each member* of the Saudi families and relatives. The amount each individual receives is dependant upon age, rank, status, and gender. Thus it follows that the more members a male has in his immediate family, the more money that particular household receives just for existing.

As Carmen bin Ladin says in her book, *Inside the Kingdom*, "Like every other one of the thousands—perhaps ten thousand [now about thirty-thousand strong]—Saudi princes and princesses . . . supported their lifestyle almost wholly out of the stipend they received from the Treasury every year. Even small children receive this income: It is calculated by age, ranking in power, and gender. Girls receive half the share of boys. In addition, all public utilities are free for princes."[2]

To sum it up briefly: Every Muslim/Arab husband in every Middle Eastern society abducts his wife and children to save face in his society, increase his wealth and prestige, to force his family to convert to Islam, and to prove he is in control of his family. In the case of a Saudi husband, if he is a member of the al-Saud family, he will receive added stipend money to live on for each additional family member.

When just the children are abducted, it is for revenge against the wife in addition to the reasons just stated.

CHAPTER 21

WHY MUSLIM/ARAB FOREIGN NATIONALS MARRY AMERICAN WOMEN

MUSLIM/ARAB FOREIGN students, mostly Saudi males, attending schools in Europe and the United States are well known to be bad students who lack any kind of academic initiative and throw wild parties well beyond the means of average students because of the huge allowances they receive on a regular basis.

The Muslim/Arabs who do go abroad for college because they are motivated by the educational opportunity, are often also looking for a way to avoid having to go home eventually, if they so choose, and bring their families over al well.

While they want to remain Muslims, they want to do so in a Western country. They don't want to be sternly devout Muslims as they must be back home where the neighbors and religious police watch everyone closely to see that they hew the religious line. Western life is much more comfortable.

The solution to their problem is simple: find a naïve woman who is a citizen of the country he is living in and marry her. They find, preferably, girls who know nothing about Arab males, spend a lot of money on them, get them pregnant as quickly as possible, and then marry them 'to save their reputation' whether or not the family likes it. They will sweet talk the girls into sponsoring their citizenship or Green Card process so that they don't have to wait so long to get the papers and then they have it made. Marriage to a an American born girl, any girl, will do, especially if he and his friends are setting up terrorist cells in this country and need a cover of respectability.

Most of these fast marriages end up in divorce because of the chasm between cultural values and because of abuse on the male's part. If he has been smart and treated her well until he has his citizenship or Green Card, by the time of the divorce, he can stay in the country forever, especially if they have children. He can do what he likes and lead the lifestyle he wishes to.

The darkest side to this, besides the lack of decency where his wife in concerned, is that if and when any of these students decides he wants to raise his children back home, (and get even with his wife for divorcing him and making him look bad) he always abducts the children from their mother without warning and takes them back to the Middle East where the children's mother cannot rescue them. He doesn't care that both mother and children are living in degradation because of his actions. Instead, it gives him a feeling of power.

Is it possible to be more sadistically cruel and unfeeling, more self-centered, and more primitive than an Arab/Muslim male, especially a Saudi male, where women are concerned?

I leave it to you to decide whether you wish to keep your freedom of action and choice or if you wish to have every part of your life dominated and controlled by someone who tells you that you are worth nothing and that he owns you because you are his wife.

PART III

CHAPTER 22

RECOMMENDATIONS FOR PERSONAL SITUATIONS: WHAT IF . . . . ?

S OME OF THE recomendations I will be offering may sound hard and unfeeling at first reading. They are not intended to be; they are intended to help you avoid great unhappiness and pain. Hard experience teaches one that even though the price of preventive precautions may be high, the price of non-prevention is far higher and of longer duration.

*   *   *

General Recommendation: Have your friends read this book *Escape! From An Arab Marriage*, from cover to cover.

If you do this, and if all of you take advantage of the Bibliography and Recommended Reading List to do some independent research of your own, I believe that the information will answer many of your questions. This will also inform you of what you need to know about Arab/Muslims in order to draw intelligent conclusions about whether you can afford to spend time with them.

What if I have children who are very interested in the Middle East and would like to meet some people from that part of the world?

First of all, have your children read this book. This will give you and your children an idea of what kind of culture people from the Middle East come from, and, especially, how women are thought of and treated. It will help you make a decision about whether you wish to meet Middle Eastern students.

After you have some background, you and our children might visit a university campus where you can observe groups of Middle Eastern students in the student union building or you might attend holiday celebration dinners put on by students for the general public.

What if I or friends of mine do not know any Arab/Muslim males yet, but are curious about them?

Interest and appreciation of other cultures is wonderful for learning about the world and all its endless varieties of people. However, it is equally important to obtain as much knowledge about the cultures you are interested in before you meet them, if possible. This way you are not taken by surprise.

I understand very well why you might be curious about them—they are different from the people you have grown up with and some of them are often attractive in a way you are not used to.

If you and/or your friends will read *Escape! From An Arab Marriage* will give you an accurate picture of how women are thought of and treated—this is important so you will not be taken by surprise and make some unsafe choices out of ignorance of the consequences.

What if I am already dating a Middle Eastern Arab student?

You would be extremely wise to break off the relationship immediately and firmly, especially if he is from Saudi Arabia. The Saudis especially have a built-in contempt for anyone who is not a Muslim. His motive for dating you is probably to persuade you to marry him so that he can obtain either his citizenship or a Green Card so he can stay here indefinitely. Marriage will help him blend into American society. This is important for him since he could well be involved with terrorist groups planning to terror-related activities against the Untied States.

Any children you may have together will probably be taken by him back to the country of his birth where you cannot retrieve them and be forced to become Muslims.

Please take advantage of the Bibliography and Recommended Reading List at the end of this book for additional resources which will enable you to become informed about the kind of culture these young men grow up in. You will find out what they really think of women and how they treat them. Knowing what these males are really like can help you save your life and prevent a great deal of heartache for you and your family.

Another aspect of any dating relationship with Arab/Muslim males is the probability that they will learn about your personal financial affairs. If they know where you keep your checkbook, how to access your credit card numbers, and any other financial aspects of your life which they might be able to use, some will take advantage of this and either take money from your bank account or charge items to your credit cards and disappear, leaving you in debt for thousands of dollars you never spent.

What if I have been dating an Arab/Muslim male and have become pregnant by him?

First of all, if you are pregnant and have not yet told him, ***do not tell him you are pregnant*** under any circumstances, especially if he is from Saudi Arabia. And do not even think about marrying him. Break off the relationship immediately and disappear from where he normally located.

If you are pregnant, you have three choices.

1. You can get an abortion before the third trimester and be truly free of the Arab you have been dating.
2. You can take a chance and have the baby, but be aware that you will have to be looking over your shoulder for possibly the rest of your life, trying to prevent the father from finding you and abducting the child to take back home with him.
3. A very good third alternative is to have the baby's last name on the birth certificate be your parents' last name. Since the baby would not have his father's last name, it will be difficult for the father to legally claim the baby as his.
4. You just might be able to arrange for a temporary marriage with an American man so that when the baby is born, it bears his last name thereby preventing any legal claim being made by the natural father.

If the Arab Muslim boyfriend he finds out you are pregnant, he is going to do all in his power to talk you into marrying him so that he can get a Green Card, stay here indefinitely, and have a legal claim on the baby after it is born. He will probably then abduct the child after it is no longer nursing and take it back to his country. You will probably never be able to see or talk to your child again and you will certainly never be able to get him back with you. If you go back to his country with him, you will become his property to do with as he wishes.

Read *At Any Price* by Patricia Roush to become aware of how the Arab/Muslim males think and behave before you do anything else. Read stories of other women who have married into the culture and what happened to them. You will learn that the Arab/Muslim males have been raised from childhood to consider women as animals for them to use and abuse as they wish. Ask friends who have been through the experience of being married to an Arab/Muslim.

What if I am already engaged to an Arab/Muslim and am seriously thinking about getting married?

Stop right where you are and postpone the nuptials. If you return with him to his country, you will be forced to live with as the wife of a Muslim Arab male, especially if he is from Saudi Arabia.

It is doubtful that he has told you much about himself. It is very likely that he is involved with people who would like to overthrow the American government and make our country an Islamic state. If he marries you, it will provide him the perfect cover for any terror-related activities he may be involved in.

Be sure to read other stories of the women who actually married Middle Eastern males. Do not assume that it won't happen to you and that the person you are engaged to "isn't like that". After he marries you, if you go through with it, he will be exactly like that, especially if you are foolish enough to leave this country and accompany him to his place of birth. This is your future you are endangering. Find a marital prospect who is American born and raised similarly to you. Marriage is hard enough without the cultural differences.

What if I or one of my friends has already married a man from the Middle East?

To protect your personal finances, keep a separate bank account and, if you are working where direct deposit is an option for you, by all means use it. If you have a checkbook, it would be very wise of you not to keep it anywhere where your husband might be able to obtain it. Also, if you have an ATM card, you need to destroy it so he cannot steal the card to access your account with it and clean out every cent you have when he needs money. He will surely take everything you have without hesitation if and when he is planning to leave the country and take your children with him.

Whatever you or any of your friends who have married a Middle Eastern male do, do not leave the United States or any other Western country in which you are located because here you are protected by laws and attitudes which are woman friendly and where you are guaranteed the same rights as men.

This is not so in the Middle East, especially in Saudi Arabia, which is the most extreme and repressive society in the world. The moment you step inside the borders of any Arab/Muslim country, you are considered a citizen of that country and the *undisputed* property of your husband. The same is true for any children you may have brought with you. Your husband has the right to beat you, torture you, enslave you, sell you, divorce and discard you on the street without money or possession, or kill you outright. You will have no friends because you are an infidel and unclean so you will have no help if you attempt to escape.

No one will interfere with him—what goes on in his household is no one's business but his own. He is the final authority. The State Department will not help you.

While there may possibly be a faint chance of escape in countries which share borders with other countries—Betty Mahmoody escaped with her daughter from Iran by being taken over the mountains by some tribesmen in the dead of winter down into Turkey, but she is the only one I have been able to find who successfully escaped her abusive husband—there will be no chance if you go to Saudi Arabia. It is surrounded by water on all sides and *every single person* living there will be against you. You will be there to stay because the Saudi government will never let you leave.

For your safety, stay as far away from Saudi males as possible. Relationships with Saudi males are dangerous in the extreme. They will use you as a front for their terrorist activities and they will abuse you because you are a woman and worth nothing.

What if I am married to an Arab and I want to get divorced?

Don't let him know your intentions. If he knows you want a divorce, he will have no qualms about trying to get hold of any children just to get even with you.

The first thing you need to do is to reinforce your friendships, family ties, and ties to you church so that you will have a lifeline of loving support from as many directions as possible. You will encounter opposition from your husband because Arab Muslim husbands always do everything they can to isolate their wives from any ties outside of the home to make you vulnerable and without alternative resources with which to defend yourself.

Begin gathering all identification information such as numbers from his drivers' license, national ID, naturalization, license plate, bank account(s). and Social Security number if he has one. Also try to obtain family addresses in his country of origin.

It is very likely that he will have you followed and watched, hoping to catch you in a compromising situation he can use against you because he will want custody, just as you do.

He will probably do and say things that will infuriate you, but if you can keep your temper and not tell him what you are thinking or what you plan to do, it is very likely that he will make assumptions which will lead him to make mistakes and hang himself more effectively than anything you might do. If you can, expose your friends, relatives, or pastor to your husband's explosive temper and irrational behavior so they can verify statements you make about him in court or other legal situation.

If your husband is stalking you and abusing you when you are together, report it to the police and tell your parents and friends. Obtain a court order to keep him away from you and, do **not** believe him if he says he is sorry and is going to change. He will not—he will put on an act to lull you into trusting him if he can—and that is when he will disappear with the children and every asset of yours he can steal.

Have your mail sent to a post office box where you can pick it up in safety.

Be alert always to cars or people who may be following you. Drive through parking lots to see if they follow you so you will know if you are being tracked.

Keep supplies such as blankets, clothes, food, maps, and money in your locked car for a quick getaway in the middle of the night if you need to leave in a hurry.

Say things to him to distract him to diffuse anger and to get him to let his guard down, then do your best go through as many of his papers such as check register, email, rolodexes, notes, phone messages—anything to help you to know what he is planning to do, whether he is involved with terrorist groups or drugs—anything which can be used against him and get him deported from the United States. This may seem like it is sneaky and unfair—maybe it is by our standards, but remember that this is for your survival against an individual who has practiced deception to make him look good as a matter of course long before he came to the United States.

Make sure your own behavior is beyond reproach. Never be alone with male friends for any reason because your husband will use it to make you look like an unfaithful wife and/or unfit mother. This is the first thing he will seek to do—discredit the fact that you are a decent and admirable person and use these accusations to destroy you in court.

If you and the children can get away from where he is for a while, perhaps to your parents' house, it will be a very welcome refuge for you. You might also move into an active Neighborhood Watch area where you can alert the neighbors and your child's school officials about the possibility of an attempted abduction. You can pull yourself together and live in peace for a while.

Now is the time to file for divorce.

You will need to be strong but firm on the stand when you are being cross-questioned by your husband's attorney. It is his goal to break down your story and make you look unfit to have custody of the children. Keep your cool and do what your attorney advises you to do.

It would be extremely wise for you and your attorney to bring up the dangers of unsupervised visitation by the father because he will surely abduct the children and leave the country. Use the stories of illegally abducted children in *Escape! From An Arab Marriage* as examples and try to find more recent examples on the internet to use as evidence also.

After the divorce, do not let your ex-husband talk you into any unsupervised time with the children. It will be on one of these occasions when he will disappear with them, having planned everything ahead of time, and be out of the country before you realize something is wrong.

If you have not signed any citizenship or Green Card papers for him, you may be able to get him deported on grounds of abuse and harassment. If you know he is involved in illegal activities, you can use these as grounds also to get him deported back to his own country.

What if I would like to get married again and have my new husband adopt my children?

It would be an excellent idea provided you are careful who you marry. It would best be an American who loves you enough to stand by you and keep you safe, and who genuinely loves your children and wants to protect them. It would be definite plus if he was familiar with the Arab male mentality from past experience.

If adoption can be accomplished, that will be a great protection for your children. It would have to be done carefully, making sure that every possible technicality which might be used against you by your ex-husband is eliminated.

By that I mean you might time the necessary announcements in newspapers to announce the intentions to adopt when your ex-husband was out of the country so that there would be no response to the announcement.

Or, you and your new husband might consider moving to another part of the country and living there for awhile before beginning adoption proceedings. I believe announcements must be in the local newspapers for a specific length of time. You would need to check with an attorney about the legalities and follow his advice.

An alternative to actual adoption would be to simply change the children's last name to that of your new husband, with his consent, of course. This would effectively remove the legal claim from their father and it would make it harder for him to find them. If they are very young, I believe the legal requirements are minimal. Again, you would want to contact a lawyer and follow his advice.

What if my children have been abducted and taken to the Middle East?

There is virtually no instance where the mother has been successful in retrieving her children.

Appendix 1 has a list of child recovery specialists and their websites. I cannot say which is the best or most dependable. You will need to contact them directly. You need to know that the possibility of success depends a lot on which country the children have been taken to.

Saudi Arabia is impossible because everyone knows everyone, there are no street names or addresses, and everyone is paranoid about strangers. One attempt was made and was on the brink of succeeding when a truck full of gunmen appeared out of nowhere and shot down the would-be child retrieval team.

Some countries now have agreements about shared visitation and custody—I believe Algeria is one of them.

The State Department will be useless—it has helped no one escape or retrieve their children. You will most likely have more success with private sources; however, they are expensive (five or six figures) and it will be necessary to do a lot of work to find out which of these retrieval concerns is legitimate. You might contact veterans' organizations to see whether any former Special Forces experts are able to help you. They have the training and the kind of experience which will be necessary for there to be any chance of success.

EPILOGUE

THE INFORMATION WITHIN will not be outdated unless the Arab Muslim societies change radically, which is not likely in the foreseeable future. Indeed, they wish to change Western societies to be just like them. God help us all.

This book started out as a personal story to help women understand the risks of marrying into a culture so radically different from that of the United States *before they made the mistake of doing so.* Then I realized that other women's stories should be included to add credibility to my experience. It also became clear to me that it was necessary to warn readers not to enter Middle Eastern countries as the wife of an Arab Muslim because wives are considered the property of their husbands and can do nothing, let alone leave the country and return home, without the husband's written permission. It needed to be clear also that this was equally true of children.

The dominance of males in the Middle East is just the tip of the iceberg—there are many more aspects of these societies which need to be made known to Western women which will be addressed in subsequent books.

Pass this book on to your friends and families so that all of you will be better informed and more clearly aware of the price of carelessness in choosing who you date and who you marry.

Blessings upon you, each and every one of you bright and beautiful Western and American women.

The next book in this series is titled *Thirty-Two Secrets Arab Men Never Tell American Women*. It will be published in late 2006 or early 2007.

Appendix 1

Reality Checkpoints of Most Arab-American Marriages

- Most Arab Muslim males come to the United States or to any Western country to attend college, usually to a state university. Very often they become militant Islamists who plot to conquer America and remake it into an Islamic country as they are doing in Europe.
- Arab Muslim foreign national males are told to marry American girls and obtain their citizenship or Green Card more quickly through their wives' sponsorship. (They can hold dual citizenship.) They are told also to Islamize whoever they marry so any children born will automatically be Muslim.
- Arab/Muslim foreign national males living in the West are expected to divorce and remarry every five years, since polygamy is illegal in the United States, and have children by each wife.
- Almost all of Arab/Muslim foreign national males leave family still living in the country of their birth so they have someone to go back home to at any time.

- Some of the Arab/Muslim foreign national males are charming, fun, handsome, attentive, and different enough to be interesting to date and spend time with. This normally changes radically after marriage.
- Arab/Muslim foreign national males make themselves well-liked by their American girlfriends' families and claim to be very pro-Western.
- Arab/Muslim foreign national males make continuous statements about preferring the freedom possible in the United States to the unrest and limitations of life back home. This changes after they have gotten their Green Cards or their citizenship.
- Most Arab/Muslim foreign national males make good friends as long as they respect you and as long as you keep your distance, but they make difficult husbands at best. It is best not to date them at all.
- No Arab Muslim foreign national male mentions or explains to his American girlfriends how differently women in the Middle East are treated compared to how they are treated in the United States or how limited their lives are by comparison.
- No Arab Muslim foreign student mentions to his girlfriends that womens' rights as we know them in the United States do not exist in any Middle Eastern country.
- No Arab Muslim foreign national male tells any of his women friends that men in Arab Muslim societies are not raised to like and respect women as people; nor will he reveal that men in his part of the world are taught to look down on women as inferior and to exploit them at every opportunity. The purpose of women in the Middle East is to pleasure the husband, bear his children, bear responsibility for the family honor, and be the servant of the household's upkeep and maintenance.

- No Arab Muslim foreign national male tells his girlfriend that if she marries him and goes with back with him to his country, she and their children will be considered citizens of that country the instant they step inside the border of that country and treated as such. She and the children are his property.
- If you go to any Arab Muslim country as the wife of one of its citizens, you will be forced to convert to Islam.
- Arab Muslim foreign national males generally do not mention to their girlfriends that they might want their children to grow up back home and to become Muslims.
- After marriage, every Muslim Arab foreign national male's personality changes from that of being charming, accommodating, generous, complimentary, and open-minded to that of being domineering, abusive, possessive, cruel, critical of his wife's dress and behavior, more self-centered, selfish, deceptive, and critical of the United States.
- Arab Muslim foreign national husbands will try to isolate their wives from their family and friends so that the wives will have no outside support group to help them in order to make them more vulnerable to their husbands' domination and manipulation.
- Arab Muslim foreign national husbands will revert back to their upbringing sooner or later, especially when they have families and as they grow older because they are desperate to atone for their decadent lifestyles as young men.
- After the children are born, most Arab Muslim foreign national husbands mention wishing to go back with their wives and children to live in the Middle Eastern country of their birth. Most wives wish to stay in the United States.
- Every Arab Muslim foreign national male uses every means at his disposal to persuade his girlfriend or wife to do what he

wants. He uses tears, flattery, piteous appeals to her good nature, and extravagant promises that she is the most important person in his life, trying to make her feel guilty for not wanting to do as he wishes. He inundates her with presents, dinners, attention, and charm to confuse any doubts she has about him and to get his way by wearing her down.

- Every Arab Muslim foreign national husband denies that he will ever take the children from their mother if his wife expresses the fear that he might do so.
- Every Arab Muslim foreign national male makes promises which are broken when it is convenient for him to do so, saying that any promise between a Muslim and a non-Muslim is not considered binding and does not count. This includes marriage vows.
- Every Arab Muslim has been raised to believe that all Muslims are superior to all non-Muslims. Infidels are considered unclean and impure.
- Every Arab Muslim foreign national male will lie to save face or to preserve appearances, if he considers it necessary, to anyone including the police and the government. Lying is expected to save face, to keep out of trouble, to preserve appearances, to influence women, and to help spread Islam.
- Saudi Arab Muslim males are sent to the United States to infiltrate and work to Islamize this country, using their status as students as a cover.
- No Arab Muslim foreign national male will tell his American girlfriend or wife that he is allowed to have more than one wife in his country or that he might already have one waiting for him at home.
- No Arab Muslim foreign national male will admit whether he plans to marry an American woman, have children by her,

convert them to Islam, and then, about four years later, divorce his wife so he can marry another, intending to repeat the pattern.

- Many Arab Muslim foreign national males are secretive and stealthy, not telling their wives vital information which will keep them from making mistakes affecting their welfare and that of their children
- An Arab Muslim foreign national male becomes vengeful when he does not get his way in a matter that is important to him, especially when it looks like he has been outsmarted or rejected by a woman.
- Every Arab Muslim male is a very bad loser, especially to a woman. He will hate her forever for having proved herself to be better at something than he is, especially if other people know about it.
- All Arab Muslim foreign national husbands abduct the children of their marriages abruptly and without warning after weeks of planning and preparation which *always* includes cleaning out joint bank accounts and charging thousands of dollars on credit cards to buy tickets and whatever else is wanted. They immediately take the children out of the United States back to the Middle East, there to stay with relatives.
- In no instances do the abducting fathers give priority to the stability and best interests of the children. The fathers' perceived status in their birth families always comes first.
- Muslim Arab foreign national fathers will have their girl children genitally mutilated and circumcised when it is traditional in their family and their society so they will be considered marriageable.
- In no instance do the abducting fathers take into account how the mothers will feel at the sudden disappearance of their children.

- The mothers of the abducted children *may* be notified after their husbands have the children safely out of reach back, home half a world away.
- The abducting fathers, especially the Saudi males, repeatedly tell the abducted child or children that if they try to escape, Allah will kill every member of their mother's families or that they will burn in the fires of Hell forever.
- The abducted children are often sodomized by the males in the father's family. Regular sexual intercourse is not inflicted on the girl children because a broken hymen would render them unmarriageable, thereby preventing the father from being able to sell his daughters for an extravagant dowry.
- In some instances, the mothers are allowed limited contact with their children, and are given the choice of following their children to be with them, but this is the exception rather than the rule. Even if the women follow, it is doubtful whether they can stand the differences in culture, in living conditions, and the treatment of women, and remain in the country.
- All of the mothers of these abducted children have their hearts torn out by the separation from their children who are half a world away. Their wounds and heartache are with them for their lifetime.

APPENDIX 2

CHILD RECOVERY SPECIALISTS

Cobra Missing
    Children Network   www.fortunecity.com

Counter Terrorism
    International   www.cti5.com

Dabbagh & Associates   www.maureendabbagh.com

HUKO International   www.hug-ur-kids.org.au

International Child &
    Adult Recovery   www.icps.20m.com

International CTC
    Group Limited   www.ctcintl.com

Llobera & Associates   www.kidhunters.nl

Missing Children
   Investigation Center   mcic.hypermart.net

National Center for Missing
   and Exploited Children   www.charitywire.com

Parental Abduction
   Search Specialists   www.parentalabduction.com

Trojan Securities   www.trojansecurities.com

Zamora & Associates   www.zamora.nl

*   These listings are to give you an idea of what to look for should
   you need such services.

   I cannot comment on the effectiveness and integrity of any of
these groups because I was fortunate enough not to have my son
abducted. If you contact Maureen Dabbagh, Patricia Roush, or
Betty Mahmoody, they may be able to advise you.

Appendix 3

Basic Information on The Green Card

THE FOLLOWING INFOR-MATION is taken from "The American Dream" website www,greencard.info.

What are the advantages of the Green Card?

The Green Card entitles you to permanently emigrate into the United States under relatively simple and less bureaucratic conditions.

Should you desire to settle permanently in the U.S., you are entitled to do so in any of the 50 states freely and unconditionally. You are under no obligation to give up your current citizenship.

Life in the United States does provide enormous opportunities. The U.S. economy is the largest and most dominant in the world; and unemployment is below 4%. In most parts of the United States, quality real estate prices are well below the cost of comparable property in Europe. The overall environment is better and has more potential than what prevails in Europe. And last, but not least, the U.S. dollar has remained one of the most stable convertible currencies over the past several decades.

Working and Studying

There are additional perks: your tuition costs for vocational, professional, or university studies will be reduced by up to 80%. You are entitled to public assistance and, under some conditions, you might even be able to apply for special visas for relatives who wish to follow you to the United States.

You will not face any restrictions in the job market. The entire U.S. playing field of career and professional advancement is yours to explore. Furthermore, you will receive certain trade licenses quickly and easily.

Above all, with the exception of voting, you will be entitled to all the rights of a U.S. citizen without losing your current citizenship. If you want more, you can always apply for U.S. citizenship after only five years as a card holder.

If you dream of:

- living in the United States for a longer period of time,
- starting a completely new life here,
- studying at one of the renowned U.S. universities or professional institutions,
- exploring new professional and career options,

- becoming your own boss (self-employed), and
- enjoying your retirement here,

this is your chance. The future could be only an application away.

Who can participate in the Green Card Lottery?

Basically everyone can join the Green Card Lottery. There are almost no special requirements and no documents which need to be sent along with the application form.

The only exceptions are persons born in a country with a very high rate of emigration into the United States.

Any country which in average has 'sent' more than 50,000 immigrants to the United States during the past five years is excluded from participation in the lottery. This procedure ensures that otherwise discriminated against countries get a fair and equal chance as well. The list of excluded countries may very from year to year.

One's country of citizenship is not important in this process. The only important thing is the country of your birth, in accordance with current world political maps.

Individuals who were born in excluded countries may apply for a Green Card if their spouses (husband or wife) were born in one of the eligible countries, or if the individuals were born in an excluded country while parents of said individuals were only temporary residents of the excluded, non-eligible countries.

In this case, the country of birth of the spouse or parents must be listed as 'native country' in addition to your country of birth.

Other Conditions

The only other requirement is a certification of completion of secondary school education (comparable to the U.S. high school diploma), which usually means that you must have completed 12 years of education in school **or** a minimum of two years' work experience within the past five years in a profession which requires at least two years of training. Proof of these prerequisites are only necessary when you are simply submitting the application.

Is there any other way to obtain a Green Card?

Usually not unless you invest $1 million in the United States or have close relatives or an employer advocating in your favor. But even if a U.S. enterprise does credibly assure you that they are willing to employ you, it has to be proven that you are not taking this workplace away from an American citizen capable of the same job. The process of presenting such evidence at the U.S. Department of Labor is costly and can often take years.

This means that for persons without anybody in the United States advocating for them, obtaining a Green Card outside the DV-2004 program is close to impossible. However, if you consider yourself particularly qualified or able to invest in the United States, look at the category 'USA Visa Services' on our homepage. It is our aim to assist you in any immigration matters as well as possible.

How are the winners selected?

Each participant will be assigned an electronically generated random number. Then, the U.S. State Department selects all winners via a computer-generated random procedure. A total of 55,000 applicants will receive a Green Card.

If you belong to the successful participants, the American authorities will notify you directly in the spring. The subsequent correspondence will then be handles by the responsible American consulate in your country.

What could possibly go wrong with my application?

More than you would imagine. 40% of the applications in the year 2002 were rejected for non-compliance with either the very strict formal requirements or the tight deadline.

The personal information requested on the first application seems to be minimal at first sight. Thus, many applicants assume that the entry is very easy and that winning is just a question of good fortune. However, it is precisely because of the apparent ease that a lot of mistakes are made. May people apply each year armed only with their confidence in Lady Luck; but faulty applicants put them out of the running right away. In raw terms, over 3 million people applicants were disqualified last year alone.

The application requirements are very strictly enforced. The most careless error automatically disqualifies you. Given the large number of applications that are received in the United States, a first screening is done by a computer before any of the applications are handled by any staff members. Equally important is the deadline which is generally specified in August of each year. The period of four weeks that is normally given is adhered to strictly. Applications that arrive even a minute earlier or later will simply be rejected and will stand no chance at all. During the eight years of its existence, the lottery has taken place four times in February oar March, twice in November, and twice in October.

What are my chances of winning a Green Card?

The chances to win a Green Card vary from year to year depending on the number of participants and legal regulations. There are certain contingents for the regions of the world. The average winning chance lies between 1 in 20 and 1 in 25, so that about every 20th applicant does indeed receive a Green Card.

What are the educational requirements?

You can participate if you have finished at least a 'high school' or its equivalent in your country. a 'high school education or equivalent' is defined as successful completion of a twelve-year course of elementary and secondary education in the United States or, in another country, successful completion of a formal course of elementary and secondary education comparable to a high school education in the United States. Alternatively, you can prove two years of work experience in any occupation requiring at least two years of training, and you must have worked in this profession at least two years over the course of the past five years. Sometimes two years of working in a profession which usually requires a two year training is sufficient, even if you do have not actually accomplished such a training. There is no minimum or maximum age for entering the Green Card lottery.

Unfortunately, all persons who do not fulfill the above-mentioned requirements are not entitled to participate in the DV-lottery.

I do not meet the requirements. What can I do?

If you meet the conditions, you may participate. Should this not be the case, minors (under the age of 21, according to U.S. law) may simply be mentioned in their parents' Green Card application. Thus, if the parents win, they will have to fulfill the prerequisites, and you yourself can receive the visa without proof, just on the basis of family bounds.

Can a winner be accepted into the U.S. Army?

You can work in almost all professions, including most areas of the U.S. army. The few areas of army and politics which are not accessible are usually open to you after having acquired U.S. citizenship. You can usually acquire U.S. citizenship after five years of being in possession of the Green Card.

What if I do not want to relocate in the United States immediately?

Generally, the Green Card is valid for a life-time. However, if you win one you will have to enter the United States at least once before September at the latest, to confirm receipt of the Green Card. However, you are under no obligation to stay in the U.S. for a longer period. U.S. immigration laws have specifically binding provisions.

What does the Green Card mean to my family?

If you win, not only you but also your spouse and your unmarried children under 21 years of age will each receive their own personal Green Card.

That means if you and your partner submit and individual application, chances for the whole family double. Please note that each individual may only participate in the Green Card lottery once a year.

What happens if I get married or become a parent after I have won?

You have a 6-month grace period, from the moment you are notified of the award, to adjust your status. Should you get married or become a parent during that period, the new family members will automatically be entitled to get the visa as well.

If your marriage occurs after your interview at the U.S. Consulate and after the immigrant visa has been granted to you, you spouse may be expected to wait for 3 to 4 years before a U.S. residence permit can be issued.

ENDNOTES

Chapter 3—DEVELOPMENTS

1. El-Sa'adawi, Nawal. *A Daughter of Isis.* Translated by Sherif Hetata. London and New York: Zed Books Ltd, 1999. p. 20
2. Sasson, Jean. *Princess: The True Story of Life Behind the Veil in Saudi Arabia.* New York: William Morrow and Company, Inc., 1992. p. 25
3. Sasson, Jean. *Princess: The True Story of Life Behind the Veil in Saudi Arabia.* New York: William Morrow and Company, Inc., 1992. p. 25-26

Chapter 5—REVELATIONS

1. Mernissi, Fatima. *Beyond the Veil: Male-Female Dynamics in Modern Muslim Society.* Bloomington and Indianapolis: Indiana University Press, 1987. pp. 113-115
2. Goodwin, Jan. *Price of Honor: Muslim Women Life the Veil of Silence on the Islamic World.* New York: Little, Brown and Company, 1994. pp. 43-45

Chapter 10—REFUGE

1. Brooks, Geraldine. *Nine Parts of Desire: The Hidden World of Islamic Women.* New York: Anchor Books, Doubleday, 1995. p. 44.

Chapter 11—DIVORCE AT LAST

1. Brooks, Geraldine. *Nine Parts of Desire: The Hidden World of Islamic Women.* New York: Anchor Books, Doubleday, 1995. p. 60.
2. Mernissi, Fatima. *Beyond the Veil: Male-Female Dynamics in Modern Muslim Society.* Bloomington and Indianapolis: Indiana University Press, 1987.

Chapter 16—MARRIAGES MADE IN HELL

1. Sasson, Jean. *Desert Royal.* London: Penguin Books, 2000. p. 171-173
2. Roush, Patricia. *At Any Price: How America Betrayed my Kidnapped Daughters for Saudi Oil.* Nashville: WND Books, 2003. p. 12.
3. Roush, Patricia. *At Any Price: How America Betrayed my Kidnapped Daughters for Saudi Oil.* Nashville: WND Books, 2003. p. 14.
4. Roush, Patricia. "Pat Roush Commentary", Statement of Patricia Roush Before The Committee On Government Reform, June 12, 2002. www.patroush.com
5. Detrich, Allan. "Starving For her Daughter's Return." Virginia Beach, VA. www.allandetrich.com/maureenstory.htm p. 2
6. Detrich, Allan. "Starving For her Daughter's Return." Virginia Beach, VA. www.allandetrich.com/maureenstory.htm p. 1
7. Roush, Patricia. "Pat Roush Commentary", Statement of Monica Stowers Before The Committee on Government Reform, June 12, 2002. p. 1 www.patroush.com

8. Roush, Patricia. "Pat Roush Commentary", Statement of Monica Stowers Before The Committee on Government Reform, June 12, 2002. p. 2 www.patroush.com

9. Roush, Patricia. "Pat Roush Commentary", Statement of Monica Stowers Before The Committee on Government Reform, June 12, 2002. p. 8 www.patroush.com

10. Mahmoody, Betty and Dunchock, Arnold. *For The Love Of A Child.* New York: St Martin's Press, 1992. p. 51.

11. Mahmoody, Betty and Dunchock, Arnold. *For The Love Of A Child.* New York: St Martin's Press, 1992. pp. 51- 53.

12. Mahmoody, Betty and Dunchock, Arnold. *For The Love Of A Child.* New York: St Martin's Press, 1992. p. 50.

13. Mahmoody, Betty and Dunchock, Arnold. *For The Love Of A Child.* New York: St Martin's Press, 1992. pp. 55-57.

14. Mahmoody, Betty and Dunchock, Arnold. *For The Love Of A Child.* New York: St Martin's Press, 1992. pp. 61-62.

15. Mahmoody, Betty and Dunchock, Arnold. *For The Love Of A Child.* New York: St Martin's Press, 1992. p. 166.

16. Mahmoody, Betty and Dunchock, Arnold. *For The Love Of A Child.* New York: St Martin's Press, 1992. p. 180.

17. Mahmoody, Betty and Dunchock, Arnold. *For The Love Of A Child.* New York: St Martin's Press, 1992. p. 189.

18. Mahmoody, Betty and Dunchock, Arnold. *For The Love Of A Child.* New York: St Martin's Press, 1992. pp. 163-193.

Chapter 17—SUCCESSFUL ESCAPES AND REUNIONS

1. Mahmoody, Betty and Dunchock, Arnold. *For The Love Of A Child.* New York: St Martin's Press, 1992. p. 132

2. Mahmoody, Betty and Dunchock, Arnold. *For The Love Of A Child*. New York: St Martin's Press, 1992. p. 131-132

3. Bin Ladin, Carmen. *Inside the Kingdom: My Life in Saudi Arabia*. New York: Warner Books, 2004. p. 44

4. Bin Ladin, Carmen. *Inside the Kingdom: My Life in Saudi Arabia*. New York: Warner Books, 2004. pp. 58-59.

5. Bin Ladin, Carmen. *Inside the Kingdom: My Life in Saudi Arabia*. New York: Warner Books, 2004. pp. 132-133.

6. Mahmoody, Betty and Dunchock, Arnold. *For The Love Of A Child*. New York: St Martin's Press, 1992. p. 70.

7. Mahmoody, Betty and Dunchock, Arnold. *For The Love Of A Child*. New York: St Martin's Press, 1992. p. 76.

8. Mahmoody, Betty and Dunchock, Arnold. *For The Love Of A Child*. New York: St Martin's Press, 1992. p. 79.

9. Mahmoody, Betty and Dunchock, Arnold. *For The Love Of A Child*. New York: St Martin's Press, 1992. p. 90

10. Mahmoody, Betty and Dunchock, Arnold. *For The Love Of A Child*. New York: St Martin's Press, 1992. p. 104.

11. Mahmoody, Betty and Dunchock, Arnold. *For The Love Of A Child*. New York: St Martin's Press, 1992. pp. 66-109

12. Mahmoody, Betty and Dunchock, Arnold. *For The Love Of A Child*. New York: St Martin's Press, 1992. p. 200.

13. Mahmoody, Betty and Dunchock, Arnold. *For The Love Of A Child*. New York: St Martin's Press, 1992. p. 224-226.

14. Roush, Patricia. "Pat Roush Commentary", Statement of Alexandria Davis Before the Committee on Government Reform, June 12, 2002 pp.1-2 www.patroush.com

15. Roush, Patricia. "Pat Roush Commentary", Statement of Alexandria Davis Before the Committee on Government Reform, June 12, 2002 pp.1-2 www.patroush.com

16. Roush, Patricia. "Pat Roush Commentary". Article titled "Sarah and the Saudis", June 17, 2003. www.patroush.com

17. Rubin, Joel. "She Fights for Children She Left Behind in Saudi Arabia; Nation's Law Keeps The Youngsters There. Congress Begins Looking At the Issue Today" p. 1 www.house.gov

18. Mahmoody, Betty and Hoffer, William. *Not Without My Daughter.* New York: St Martin's Press, 1987. p. 4

19. Mahmoody, Betty and Hoffer, William. *Not Without My Daughter.* New York: St Martin's Press, 1987. p. 12.

20. Mahmoody, Betty and Hoffer, William. *Not Without My Daughter.* New York: St Martin's Press, 1987. p. 14-15.

21. Mahmoody, Betty and Hoffer, William. *Not Without My Daughter.* New York: St Martin's Press, 1987. p. 19-20.

22. Mahmoody, Betty and Hoffer, William. *Not Without My Daughter.* New York: St Martin's Press, 1987. p. 40.

23. Mahmoody, Betty and Hoffer, William. *Not Without My Daughter.* New York: St Martin's Press, 1987. p. 92.

24. Mahmoody, Betty and Hoffer, William. *Not Without My Daughter.* New York: St Martin's Press, 1987. p. 106-108.

25. Mahmoody, Betty and Hoffer, William. *Not Without My Daughter.* New York: St Martin's Press, 1987. p. 185-186.

26. Mahmoody, Betty and Hoffer, William. *Not Without My Daughter.* New York: St Martin's Press, 1987. p. 296.

27. Mahmoody, Betty and Hoffer, William. *Not Without My Daughter.* New York: St Martin's Press, 1987. p. 323.

28. Mahmoody, Betty and Hoffer, William. *Not Without My Daughter.* New York: St Martin's Press, 1987. p. 358.

29. Mahmoody, Betty and Hoffer, William. *Not Without My Daughter.* New York: St Martin's Press, 1987. pp. 367-368.

30. "I Married a Terrorist". (author unknown) *National Examiner*, June 27, 2005

Chapter 18—ESCAPES FROM RELATIONSHIPS WITH MUSLIM/ARABS BEFORE MARRIAGE

1. Choy, Ariell. "Women's Non-Existence in the Arab World".
www.think-israel.org/choy.arabwomen.html
www.sullivan-county.com/immigration/e6.htm
2. Andrea. "My Awakening . . ." FaithFreedom.org. p. 2.
www.faithfreedom.org/Testimonials/Andrea50716.htm
3. Andrea. "My Awakening . . ." FaithFreedom.org. p. 4-6.
www.faithfreedom.org/Testimonials/Andrea50716.htm
4. Andrea. "My Awakening . . ." FaithFreedom.org. p. 7-8.
www.faithfreedom.org/Testimonials/Andrea50716.htm
5. Andrea. "My Awakening . . ." FaithFreedom.org. p. 8-9
www.faithfreedom.org/Testimonials/Andrea50716.htm
6. Andrea. "My Awakening . . ." FaithFreedom.org. p. 9-10
www.faithfreedom.org/Testimonials/Andrea50716.htm
7. Spencer, Robert. "Islamic Tolerance Alert: Ali Sina Threatened with Death", May 12, 2004. p. 1.
www.jihadwatch.org/dhimmiwatch/archives/001924.php
8. Spencer, Robert. "Islamic Tolerance Alert: Ali Sina Threatened with Death", May 12, 2004. p. 1.
www.jihadwatch.org/dhimmiwatch/archives/001924.php

Chapter 20—FAMILY ORIENTED ABDUCTIONS BY ARAB MUSLIM HUSBANDS

1. Bin Ladin, Carmen. *Inside the Kingdom: My Life in Saudi Arabia.* New York: Warner Books, 2004. p. 103.
2. Bin Ladin, Carmen. *Inside the Kingdom: My Life in Saudi Arabia.* New York: Warner Books, 2004. p. 170-171

BIBLIOGRAPHY AND
RECOMMENDED READING LIST

Abdo, Geneive. "Re: Attitudes on Women's Rights in Iran". *Iranian Woman Brief #18*. December 1999.
www.sdnp.undp.org/ww/women-rights/msg00143.html

Abedin, Mehan. "Al-Qaeda: In Decline of Preparing for the Next Attack? An Interview With Saad al-Faqih" *Spotlight on Terror*, June 2, 2005—vol III, Issue 5. The Jamestown Foundation
www.jamestown.org

Abraham, Larry. "Clash of Civilizations and the Great Caliphate". January 29, 2004.
www.youmeworks.com/theclash.html

"A Brief Review of the Current State of Violations of Women's Rights in Lebanon".
www.1inf.org.lb/windex/brief1.html

Aburish, Said. "Why is There So Much Anti-Israel Bias in The Press and The American Educational System?"
www.afsi.org/MEDIA/reasonforbias.htm

"Academic Bill of Rights".
www.studentsforacademicfreedom.org/abor.html

Agha, Marisa. "Cal State Seeks to Offer Islamic Center". *Inland Southern California*, April 7, 2004.
www.campus-watch.org/article/id/1114

Ahmed, Ayesha. "Duplicity of Muslims".
www.islamreview.com/articles/duplicityof muslims.shtml

Ahmed, Ayesha, "Islamic Haram and Halal", July 29, 2002. *Islam Watch*
www.islam-watch.org/AyeshaAhmed/islamic_haram_ and_halal.htm

Ahmed, Ayesha. "Sharia in America".
www.islamreview.com/articles/sharia/shtml

"A Hoax of Hate: The Protocols of the Learned Elders of Zion". Anti-Defamation League.
www.adl.org/special_reports/protocols/protocols_intro.asp

Akeel, Maha. "Saudi Women Seek End to Home Abuse". *Arab News*, November 25, 2004.
www.arabnews.com/?page=1&section=0&article= 55034&d=25&m=11&y=2004

Al Araby, Abdullah. "Being A Muslim's Wife".
www.islamreview.com/articles/beingamuslimswife.shtml

Al Araby, Abdullah. "The Christian Difference"
www.islamreview.com/articles/thechriestian difference.shtml

Al Araby, Abdullah. "If Islam Ruled America".
www.islamreview.com/articles/ifislam.shtml

Al Araby, Abdullah. "Incredible Teachings of Muhammed".
www.islamreview.com/articles/incredibleteachings.shtml

Al Araby, Abdullah. "Islam: The Façade and the Facts".
www.islamreview.com/articles/façade.shtml

Al Araby, Abdullah. *The Islamizaton of America*. Los Angeles: The Pen vs. The Sword, 2003.

Al Araby, Abdullah. *The Islamization of American Schools*. Los Angeles: The Pen vs. The Sword, 2004.

Al Araby, Abdullah. "The Islamization of Europe. America, Take Note Before It's Too Late."
www.islamreview.com/articles/islamizationofeurope.shtml

Al Araby, Abdullah. *Islam Unveiled*. Los Angeles: The Pen vs. The Sword, 2004

Al Araby, Abdullah. "Lying in Islam".
www.islamreview.com/articles/lying.shtml

Al Araby, Abdullah. "Masters of Deception".
www.islamreview.com/masters.shtml

Al Araby, Abdullah. "Nothing in Common".
www.islamreview.com/articles/nothingincommon.shtml

Al Araby, Abdullah. "On the Road to The New World".
www.islamreview.com/articles/theroad.shtml

Al Araby, Abdullah. "Save America".
www.islamreview.com/articles/saveamerica.shtml

Al Araby, Abdullah, translator. *Snatched from the Lions' Jaws*. Los Angeles: The Pen vs.The Sword, 2003.

Al Araby, Abdullah. "The Terror of Islam".
www.islamreview.com/articles/terrorofislam.shtml

Al Araby, Abdullah. "The True Face of Islam".
www.islamreview.com/articles/trueface.shtml

Al-Fahad, Abdulaziz. "Understanding Saudi Islam-Wahhabism". Free Muslims Coalition.
www.freemuslims.org/document.php?id=38

"Algeria—Womens Issues"
www.paralumun.com/issuesalgeria.htm

Ali. "Comment From and Old Apostate". *FaithFreedom.org*.
www.faithfreedom.org/Testimonials/ali1940.htm

Ali-Ahmed. "Human Rights in Saudi Arabia: The Role of Women". Congressional Human Rights Caucus, June 4, 2002. www.house.gov

Almaeena, Khaled. "False Messages Drive Wedge Between Islam and the West". *Arab News,* March 8, 2005. www.muslim-refusnik.com/news/abarbnews-05-03-08/html

Alpert, Carl. "Honor Killings Plague Israeli Muslims". *Jewish News of Greater Phoenix,* Vol. 55, No. 52, August 22, 2003 www.jewishaz.com/jewishnews/030822/honor.shtml

Alphonso, Caroline. "Militant Islamists Deny Free Speech in Canada AGAIN". www.danielpipes.org/comments/5921

Al-Qaradawi, Yusuf. *The Lawful and the Prohibited in Islam.* Translated by Kamal el-Helbawy, M. Moinuddin Siddique, and Syed Shukry. Indiana: American Trust Publications, 2002.

Amanullah, Shahed. "Sudan Not Letting Genocide Interfere With Treaty Celebration". *alt.Muslim,* May 27, 2004. www.altmuslim.com/perm.php?id=1234_0_26_0_C

American Jewish Committee, "Steven Pomerantz, Former Head of FBI's Counterterrorism Unit, Takes on New American Jewish Committee Post As Senior Adviser on Conterterrorism", October 22, 1998. www.charitywire.com/charity11/00430.html

Amnesty International. "Section One What is Female Genital Mutilation?", March 5, 2004. www.amnesty.org/ailib/intcam/femgen/fgm1.htm

Amrani, Nora. "Archives: Honor Killings'"
www.vibrani.com/honorkillings2.htm

Anbar, Michael. "Misojudaism and Anti-Zionism". *Think-Israel*
www.think-israel.org/anbar.misojudaism.html

Andrea. "My Awakening . . ." *FaithFreedom.org.*
www.faithfreedom.org/Testimonials/Andra50716.htm

"An Interview with the Mother of a Suicide Bomber". *Al-Sharaq al-Awsat*
(London), June 5, 2002
www.islamreview.com/articles/interview.shtml

"Apostasy: 'Leaving Islam'. The Peace Encyclopedia.
www.yahoodi.com/peace/apostasy.html

Apostate Success. "Free At Last', February 26, 2005. *FaithFreedom.org.*
www.faithfreedom.org/Testimonslas/ApostateSuccess 50226.htm

"Arabian Nights Meets Red Dawn in Charles Welty's 'Ameristan'.
http://ameristan.net

Araji, Sharon. "Crimes of Honor and Shame: Violence Against Women in
Non-Western and Western Societies". *The Red Feather Journal of Postmodern
Criminology*, Anchorage, 2000
//critcrim.org/redfeather/journal-pomocrim/vol=8-shaming/araji.html

Atkinson, Gerald. "Threats to America's Survival". September 11, 2001.
www.newtotalitarians.com/ThreatsToAmericas Survival.html

Author Unknown. "To Kill An American".
www.islamreview.com/articles/tokillamerican.shtml

Bardach, Ann Louise. "Islamic Fundamentalism's War Against Women". *Flashpoint! Electronic Magazine*, August 1993. www.webcom.com/hrin/magazine/july96/muslim.html

Basch, David. "Wrong-Headed Vision". Abstract. www.think-israel.org/basch.wrong-headed.html

Bauer, Yehuda. "Nazis, Communists and Radical Islamist". *Jerusalem Post*, November 28, 2002 www.rickross.com/reference/islamic/islamics57.html

BBC News. "Kuwaiti Women Given Vote". May 16, 1999. //news.bbc.co.uk

BBC News. "Millions 'Forced Into Slavery'". May 27, 2002 //news.bbc.uk/1/hi/world/2010401.stm

BBC News. "US Decries 'Modern-Day Slavery". July 12, 2001 //news.bbc.uk/1/hi/world/Americas/1436329.stm

BBC News. "World: Middle East Election Defeat for Qatar Women". 2004. //news.bbc.co.uk/1/hi/world/middle_east/293171.stm

Bechor, Guy. Translated by Moshe Kohn. "The Sanctity of the Unsacred". *Yediot Aharanot*, December 4, 2003. www.think-israel.org/bechor.unsacred.html

Beckwith, Leila. "UCSC Back Islamists, Not Israel". *Santa Cruz Sentinel*, March 10, 2004.
www.frontpagemag.com/Articles/ReadArticle.asp? ID=12517

Beichman, Arnold. "Eustatic Racism in Eurabia?". Commentary. *The Washington Times*, September 30, 2004.
//washingtontimes.com/commentary/20040930-082914-7106r.htm.

Benard, Cheryl. "Civil Democratic Islam Partners, Resources, and Strategies", National Security Division, Rand Corporation, 2003

Ben-David, Jeremy. "Collegetown, U.S.A. The Next Terrorist Target?" *National Review Online*, May 22, 2003.
//nationalreview.com/comment/comment-ben-david 052203.asp

Bennetta, William. "Islam: A Simulation of Islamic History and Culture, 610-1100 Page for Page This is The Most Malignant Product That I've Seen During All My Years as a Reviewer". *The Textbook Letter*, September-October, 2000
www.textbookleague.org/114islam.htm

Berkowitz, Bill. "The Campus Crusades". *Conservative Watch*, November 2002.
//zmagsite.zmag.org/Nov2002/Berkowitz1102,htm

Bernie, Andrew. "What Does 'Palestinian Moderate' Mean? Apparently Nothing." *Campus Watch*, April 10, 2003.
www.campus-watch.org/article/id/1504

Beyer, Lisa. "The Women of Islam", November 25, 2001.
www.time.com

The Bill of Rights, Amendments 1-10 of the Constitution
//usinfo.state.gov/infousa/facts/funddocs.billing.htm

bin Hookah, Al Skudsi. "Maintaining Family Honor". January 20, 2003
www.sullivan-county.com/x/honor/_killings.htm

bin Laden, Osama, "Encyclopedia of Afghan Jihad". A synopsis.
www.multimedia.belointeractive.com/attack/binladin/1 . . .

Bin Ladin, Carmen. *Inside the Kingdom: My Life in Saudi Arabia.* New York:
Warner Books, 2004.

Bloom, Howard. "Dodging the Nuclear 9/11". *Pakistan-Facts.com*, September
29, 2004.
www.pakistan-facts.com/article.php?story= 2004092900409381

Bloom, Howard. *Global Brain.* New York: John Wiley & Sons, 2002.

Bloom, Howard. "How Allah Nipped Your Right to Know". *Islamic Censorship
in the West*, August 22, 2003.
www.referendum.1hwy.com/custom4.html

Bloom, Howard. "Islam's War Against The West". Excerpted from *The Lucifer
Principle: A Scientific Expedition Into The Forces of History.*
www.howardbloom.net/islam.htm

Bloom, Howard. *The Lucifer Principle: A Scientific Expedition in the Forces
of History.* New York: The Atlantic Monthly Press, 1995.

Bloom, Howard. "Osama bin Laden, Terrorism, and the Great Crusade Against America".
www.howardbloom.net/osama.htm

Bodansky, Yossef. "Islamic Anti-Semitism as a Political Instrument". January 1998. p. 2
www.freeman.org/m_online/jan98/bodansk.htm

Boettcher, Mike. "Jordanian Anti-Terrorism and The Al Qaeda Manuals". November 20, 2001.
//archives.cnn.com/2001/COMMUNITY/11/20/rec . . .

Boston, Andrew. "Islamic Apostates' Tales" A Review of "Leaving Islam: Apostates Speak Out", edited by Ibn Warraq, *FrontPageMagazine.com*, July 21, 2003.
www.frontpagemag.com/Articles/ReadArticle.asp?ID=9000

Bowers, Steve. "Diversity of Opinion Needed on College Campuses". *Political Gateway*, May 18, 2005.
www.politicalgateway.com/main/columns/read.html?col=358

Brooks, Geraldine. *Nine Parts of Desire: The Hidden World of Islamic Women.* New York: Anchor Books, Doubleday, 1995.

Bryson, Donna. Southern Yemeni Women Say Rights Lost Since Merger with North". *Associated Press*, January 21, 2004.
www.canoe.ca/LifewiseHeartSoulwise01/0124_south_ap.html

Burmeister, B.S., Col. "The Rise of Islamic Fundamentalism—Over or Under-rated As a Threat to (South African) National Security".
www.mil.za/CSANDF/CJSupp/TrainingFormation/DefenceCollege/Researchpapers2 . . .

Bushell, Andrew. "Pakistan's Slave Trade". February 14-21, 2002.
www.bostonphoenix.com/boston/news_features/top/features/documents/
02161800.htm

Campbell, Matthew. "Jihad Wrecks Dutch Race Harmony".
www.islamreview.com/articles/jihadwrecks.shtml

"Campus Suppression of Political Speech".
www.studentsforacademicfreedom.org/reports/CampusSuppPoliticalSpeech.html

Campus Watch. "Esposito: Apologist for Militant Islam".
FrontPageMagazine.com, September 3, 2002.
www.frontpagemag.com/articles/Printable.asp?ID=2651

"The Captive Mind". *The Nation*, March 16, 2005.
www.thenation.com/doc.mhtml?I=20050404&s=editors

Caswell, Ruth. "The Case of the Western Bride: Mixed Marriages".
www.jordanjubilee.com

Caswell, Ruth. ""Marriage Customs in Arab Society".
www.jordanjubilee.com

Caswell, Ruth. "Rules and Etiquette When Meeting the Local People."
www.jordanjubilee.com

Caswell, Ruth. "Solo Women Travelers in the Middle East."
www.jordanjubilee.com

Center for Religious Freedom House, *Saudi Publications on Hate Ideology Invade American Mosques*. Washington, DC: Center for Religious Freedom, 2005.

"Chabad's Children of Chernobyl"
https://www.ccoc.net/new/Default.asp

Chahine, Jessy. "Lebanese Women Break Down Barriers, But There is Still a Long Way to Go". *Daily Star*, January 3, 2005.
//dailystar.com.lb/article.asp?edition_id=1&categ_id=1& article_id=11458

Chesler, Phyllis. "Feminism's Deafening Silence". *FrontPageMagazine.com*. July 28, 2004.
www.frontpagemagazine.com/Articles/Printable.asp? ID=14365

Chesler, Phyllis. "The Psychoanalytic Roots of Islamic Terrorism". *Front Page Magazine.com*, May 3, 2004.
www.think-israel.org/chesler.terrorroots.html

Child Labor Coalition for Teen Workers and Students. "Iqbal Masih Remembered".
www.stopchildlabor.org/teensandstudents/iqbal.htm

Choudhury, Salah Uddin Shoaib. "Punished for Supporting Peace". May-June 2005
www.think-israel.org/choudhury.punished.html

Choy, Ariell. "Women's Non-Existence in the Arab World".
www.sullivan-county.com/immigration/e6.htm
www.think-israel.org/choy.arabwomen.html

"Christians in Egypt The Humiliation Continues". interview with Youssef Sidhom, Il Regno.
www.islamreview.com/articles/christiansinegypt.shtml

Coalition for the Defense of Human Rights. "Declaration at the World Conference Against Racism in Durban, South Africa". n.d.
www.dhimmi.com/durban.htm

"Columbia U. Releases Edward Said Chair Donors: Names Arab Government" *Campus Watch.org*, March 19, 2004.
www.campus-watch.org/article/id/1076

Committee to Defend Women's Rights in the Middle East (Azam Kamguian, editor). "Bulletin 1", May 2002.
www.secularislam.org

Cotton, Samuel. "Slavery is Alive and Well in 2002: Arab Masters—Black Slaves". *The City Sun*, February 1-February 7, 1995
www.icomm.ca/survival/slaves.htm

Christian. "A Reader Speaks Out: Sodomy and Islam". June 15, 2000. To Steve Van Nattan, editor. *Balaamsass.com*
www.balaamsass.com

Crittendon, Stephen. "Islam and Apostasy. An Interview with Ibn Warraq".
www.islamreview.com/articles/islamapostasy.shtml

Croft, Jim. "Are Christianity and Islam Equally Hostile?"
www.islamreview/articles/equallyhostile.shtml

Croft, Jim. "By Their Fruits You Shall Know Them".
www.islamreview.com/articles/their fruits.shtml

Croft, Jim. "Islamic Terrorism. What You Need to Know And What You Need To Do."
www.islamreview.com/articles/islamicterrorism.shtml

Croft, Jim. "2004 Preparations for Possible Homeland Islamic Terrorist Attacks".
www.islamreview.com/articles/preparation/shtml

Cultural Orientation Project. "Everyday Life." February 18, 2004.
www.culturalorientation.net/iraqi

Dao, Chris. "Burned Alive: A Victim of the Law of Men". *National Geographic News*, February 12, 2002.
www.twbookmark.com/books/89/044653346/press_ release.html

Darwish, Nonie. "An Islamic Reformation—(An Arab for Israel Speaks!)".
jerusalempostonline.com, December 22, 2004.
//209.157.64.200/focus/f-chat/1307624/posts

Darwish, Nonie. "'Arab' Means Never Having To Say You're Sorry". Root and Branch Association of Jerusalem
www.think-israel.org/darwish.arab.html

Darwish, Nonie. "Arabs for Israel".
www.noniedarwish.com/pages/745449/page745449.
html?refresh=1110343831443

Darwish, Nonie. "Loudspeaker Call to Islamize America".
islamreview.com/articles/loudspeaker.shtml

Darwish, Nonie. "Madrassas in America". April 5, 2004.
www.noniedarwish.com/pages/745452/page745452.
html?refresh=1110343830146

David, Alan. "Infibulation en republique de Djibouti". Thesis No. 131, Universite de Bordeaux, 1978 "Dawa in Public Schools". *DawaNet.*
www.dawanet.com/methods/publicschools.dawapublic.asp

Debra@OLN.comlink. "Egyptians Stand By Female Circumcision Tradition Flouts Foreign Pressures to Eliminate the Risky Practice". *Observor News*, December 10, 1996.
www.hartford-hwp.com/archives/32/018.html

The Declaration of Independence
www.ushistory.org/declaration/document/

Detrich, Allan. "Starving For her Daughter's Return.". Virginia Beach, VA.
www.allandetrich.com/maureenstory.htm

Deyo, Holly. "Islamic Terrorist Network in America". Map, 2002-3
www.millennium-ark.net/news_Files/NBC/Terrorist_cells.html

Deyo, Holly. "Top 120 Cities Vulnerable to Terrorism". Map, 2004.
www.standeyo.com/News/NBC/Top_120_Cities.html

Dobras, Allan. "Islam in California Public Schools". *Newa Analysis*, January 30, 2002.
www.cultureandfamily.org/articledisplay.asp?id=410& department=CFI&c . . .

Dogan, Sara. "Defending a Patriotic Arab Student's Rights". *FrontPage Magazine*, March 31, 2005.
www.studentsforacademicfreedom.org/archive/2005/March2005/
AhmadFoothillDefendingPatAra

Dowd-Gailey, Jonathan. "Islamism's Campus Club: The Muslim Students' Association (MSA) *Middle East Quarterly*, Spring 2004.
www.think-israel.org/dowd-gailey.muslimstudents.html

Dowd-Gailey, Jonathan. "Yvonne Haddad: America's 'Sensitivity' Trainer". *FrontPageMagazine*, December 14, 2004.
www.campus-watch.org/article/id/1446

Dreher, Rod. "Damned if You Do". *National Review Online*, October 29, 2002.
www.campus-watch.org/article/id/288

Dreher, Rod. "Oriana's Screed". *National Review Online*, October 8, 2002.
www.nationalreview.com/dreher/dreher101002.asp

Duin, Julia. "Islam's Idealistic Version of Itself Not Quite The Reality". Interview with Bat Ye'or, October 30, 3002
//members.tripod.com/joe_matalski/Pages/idealistic.htm

Duran, Khalid. "How CAIR Put My Life in Peril". *The Middle East Quarterly*, Winter, 2002.
www.meforum.org/article.108

Eberhart, Dave. "Congressmen Challenge 'Friendship' of Child-Stealing Saudis".
NewsMax.com, June 13, 2002.
www.sullivan-county.com/id2/child_stealing.htm

Education Committee of Worcester Peace Works. "The Background of the Current Crisis in World Affairs".
www.radicalphilosophy.org/Afghan.htm

The Egyptian Wife's Tale". to Ibrahim Sa'adeh, editor.
www.islamreview.com/articles/egyptianwife.shtml

Ehrenfeld, Rachel. *Funding Evil: How Terrorism is Financed—and How to Stop It* Chicago: Bonus Books, 2003.

Ehrenfeld, Rachel. "Jihad on the American Mind". *FrontPage Magazine*, March 11, 2005.
www.campus-watch.org/article/id/1730 //canadiancoalition.com/forum/ messages/5866.shtml

Eibner, John. "My Career Redeeming Slaves" *The Middle East Quarterly*, December 1999, Vol VI: No. 4.
www.meforum.org/article/449

"18 Tips for Imams and Community Leaders". *SoundVision.com.*
www.soundvision.com/Info/parenting/teens/18tips.asp

Eidelberg, Paul. "The Arab Demographic Problem: A New Approach". *Think-Israel*, November 2004.
www.think-israel.org/eidelberg.demographics.html

Eidelberg, Paul. "'Muslim Moderates'". Women for Israel, December 7, 2004.
www.think-israel.org/eidelberg.pipes.html

Eidelberg, Paul. (Reviewer) "The Sword of the Prophet" (Trifkovic). August 2003.
www.freeman.org/m_online/aug03/eidelberg.htm

Eliezar, "Arab Views of Female Sexuality".Comment on "Western Muslims; Racist Rape Spree", Sharon Lapkin. *FrontPage.com*, 12/28/2005
www.frontpagemag.com/GoPostal/commentdetail.asp? ID=20646&com . . .

El-Sa'adawi, Nawal. *A Daughter of Isis*. Translated by Sherif Hetata. London and New York: Zed Books Ltd, 1999.

El-Sa'adawi, Nawal. *The El Sa'adawi Reader*. London: Zed Books, 1997.

El-Sa'adawi, Nawal. *Two Women in One*. Translated by Osman Nuairi and Jana Gough. London: Al Saqi Books, 1985.

El-Sa'adawi, Nawal. *Walking Through Fire*. Translated by Sherif Hetata. London: Zed Books, 2002.

Emerick, Yahiya. "How to Make America An Islamic Nation". www.jannah.org/articles/america.html

Emerson, Steven. *American Jihad: The Terrorists Living Among Us*. New York: The Free Press, 2002.

Emerson, Steven. "Jihad in California". *FrontPageMagazine.com*. January 16, 2004. www.frontpagemag.com/Articles/ReadArticle.asp?ID=11786

Len Estrin. "Hope or Illusion?" *arutsheva.com*, November 11, 2004 www.think-israel.org/estrin.hope.htm

Evita, Emmanual. "Analysis: Syria Avoids Women's Rights Reforms". *United Press International*. News World Communications, Inc., 2004. //washingtontimes.com/upi-breaking/20041028-012033-4416r.htm

Ezzat, Dina. "Fortifying Women's Rights". *Al-Ahram*, Issue no. 695. 17-23 June 2004. //weekly.ahram.org.eg/2004/695/eg5.htm

Fadlallah, Sayyed Mohammed Hussein. "Women's Rights in Lebanese Constitution". American University of Beirut, May 1998

Falkson, Jock. "Why is Bush So Nice to Palestinian Terrorists?" *Think-Israel* www.think-isarel.org/falkson.bushandpa.html

Fallaci, Oriana, translated by David A. Harris. "Oriana Fallaci on Anti-Semitism". *The American Jewish Committee.* www.ajc.org/InTheMedia/Publications.asp?did=506

Fallaci, Oriana. translated by Letizia Grasso. *The Rage and the Pride.* New York: Rizzoli International Publications (USA), 2002

Fallaci, Oriana. translated by Letizia Grasso. "Rage & Pride" (Rabbia e Oroglio) www.borg.com/~paperina/fallacy_1.html

Farah, Joseph. Post on Al-Qaida Training Videotape. *WorldNetDaily.com*, September 4, 2002
//kissata.homestead.com/newsarticles.html

Farah, Joseph. "When 'Academic Freedom' Fails". April 15, 2005 www.worldnetdaily.com/news/article.asp?ARTICLE_ ID=43819

Farah, Joseph. "When 'Academic Freedom' Fails". posted excerpt. *WorldNetDaily*, April 15, 2005. www.freerepublic.com/focus/f-news/1384341/posts

Farmer, Leslie. "The Arab Woman—A Traditional View". www.saudiaramcoworld.com

Farooqi, M.I.H. "Status of Muslim Societies Around the World". Islamic Research Foundation, Inc.
www.irfi.org/articles/articles_251_300/status_ . . .

Feder, Don. "Islam and Violent Trends". Symposium in Washington, DC, February 15, 2003
www.think-israel.org/feder.html

Finley, Noland. "Word Games Don't Change the Facts; This Is a War on Radical Islam". July 4, 2004.
www.think-israel.org/finley.radicalislam/htm

Fitzgerald, Hugh. "Columbia Teaches 'Hate'". *FrontPageMagazine.com*, June 6, 2005.
www.frontpagemag.com/Articles/ReadArticle.asp?ID=18302

Fitzgerald, Hugh. "Lisa Anderson: Apologist for Academic Radicalism". *FrontPageMagazine.com*, May 3, 2005.
www.frontpagemag.com/Articles/ReadArticle.asp?ID=17922

Fitzgerald, Hugh. "Time to Get Cracking At the Vatican". *Think Israel*
www.think-israel.org/fitzgerald.vatican.html

Freedom House. "Saudi Publications on Hate Ideology Invade American Mosques". Center for Religious Freedom. Washington DC, January 28, 2005.

Free Muslims Coalition.
www.freemuslims.org

Free Muslims Coalition. "Islamist Websites and Their Hosts."
www.freemuslims.org/news/article.php?articles=222

Fregosi, Paul. *Jihad in the West: Muslim Conquests From the 7th to the 21st Centuries.* New York: Prometheus Books, 1998.

Fregosi, Paul. "Jihad in the West".
www.hutch.demon.co.uk/prom/jihadin/htm

French, David. "Academic Freedom for Some". *FrontPageMagazine.com*, March 4, 2005.
www.studentsforacademicfreedom.org/archive/2005/March2005/
DavidFrenchAcadfreedoomforsome . . .

FrontPageMagazine.com. "Eurabia". Interview with Bat Ye'or, *A Time To Speak*, December 2004, vol IV:12 (No. 48)
//Israel.net/timetospeak/48.htm

Gabriel, Mark. *Islam and Terrorism.* Lake Mary: Charisma House, 2002

Gaffney, Frank. "Know Thine Enemy". *Washington Times*, May 17, 2005.
www.sperryfiles.com/media.shtml

Gardner, Frank. "World: Middle East Kuwaiti Women Given Vote", May 16, 1999.
http://www.bbc.uk

Germano, Michael. "Islamic Europe? The Rise of Eurabia". *Perspectives*, July-September 2003, vol 6, no 3.
www.bibarch.com/Perspectives/6.4D.htm

Gergen, David. "Many World Orders". transcript of interview at Harvard University, January 9, 1997.
ww.pbs.org/newshour/gergen/january97/order_1-10.html

Gertz, Bill. *Treachery*. New York: Crown Forum, 2004.

Ghazali, Abdus. "Arab and Muslim Professors at US Universities Remain Target" *American Muslim Perspective*, April 1, 2005.
www.amperspective.com/html/arab_and_american_ prof.html

Gillespie, Jacqueline. "Once I Was A Princess".
www.islamreview.com/articles/onceprincess.shtml

Giniewski, Paul. "The Historic Roots of Islamism". *NRO National Review*, September 30, 2002
www.nationalreview.com/comment/comment-giniewski093002.asp

Glazov, Jamie. "Symposium: A Crack in the Saudi Berlin Wall?" *FrontPageMagazine.com*,
May 30, 2005.
www.frontpagemag.com/Articles/ReadArticle.asp?ID=18211

Glazov, Jamie. "Symposium: Murdering Women for 'Honor'".
FrontPageMagazine.com, June 10, 2005.
www.frontpagemag.com/Articles/ReadArticle.asp?ID=18370

Gazov, Jamie. "Symposium: Muslims in France: A Ticking Time Bomb?"
FrontPageMagazine.com, July 4, 2005
www.frontpagemag.com/Articles/ReadArticle.asp?ID=18631

Gazov, Jamie. "Symposium: The Death of France". *FrontPageMagazine.com*,
December 9, 2005
www.frontpagemag.com/Articles/ReadARticle.asp?ID=20504

Glazov, Jamie. "Symposium: The Future of Terror". *FrontPageMagazine.com*, April 22, 2005.
www.frontpagemag.com/Articles/ReadArticles.asp?ID=17812

Glasov, Jamie. "Symposium: The Future of U.S.-Saudi Relations". *FrontPageMagazine.com*, July 11, 2005.
www.frontpagemag.com/Articles/ReadArticles.asp?ID=8866

Glazov, Jamie. "Symposium: The Terror War: How We Can Win". *FrontPageMagazine.com*, November 15, 2004
www.think-israel.org/glazov.terror.html

Glazov, Jamie. "Infiltration". *FrontPageMagazine.com*, April 12, 2005
www.frontpagemag.com/Articles/ReadArticle.asp?ID=17681

Glazov, Jamie. "We Are All Souad". *FrontPageMagazine. com*, June 9, 2004.
www.frontpagemag.com/Articles/Read/Article asp?ID=13698

Glick, Caroline. "Europe's Arab Gambit". *The Jerusalem Post*, January 1, 2004.
www.jpost.com/servlet/Satellite?pagename=JPost/JPArticle/
ShowFull?cid=1072930907853&p= . . .
www.jihadwatch.org/dhimmiwatch/archives/000592.php

Goldberg., Jonah. "Religion of Peace? Prove It!"
www.sullivan-county.com/id3/rel_peace.htm

Goldberg, Jonah. "Return of the Nazis: Clippings on Islamic Fascism and Its Fellow Travelers".
www.sullivan-county.com/id3/islamic_fascism.htm

Goodenough, Patrick. "Feature: Blood and Honor". *Middle East Digest*, February 1995.
//christianactionforisrael.org/isreport/bloodhon/html

Goodtree, Beth. "AI PAC of Lies". May-June 2005.
www.think-israel.org/goodtree.aipac.html

Goodtree, Beth. "Taking Away Their Greatest Weapon".
www.think-israel.org/goodtree.weapon.html

Goodwin, Jan, *Price of Honor: Muslim Women Life the Veil of Silence on the Islamic World*. New York: Little, Brown and Company, 1994.

Gordon, Murray. *Slavery in the Arab World*. New York: New Amsterdam Books, 1989.

Grigg, Jenny. "In Discussing Jerusalem, History Matters" May-June 2005
www.think-israel.org/grigg.jerusalem.html

Hagmann, Douglas. "U.S. Showing Lack of Understanding—Or Honesty". May-June 2005.
www.think-israel.org/hagmann.islam.html

Halevi, Jonathan. "Al-Qaeda's Intellectual Legacy: New Radical Islamic Thinking Justifying the Genocide of Infidels". *Jeruslaem Viewpoints*, December 2003
www.think-israel.org/halevi/alqaedaintellestuals.html

Hamid. "I Found My Freedom", September 15, 2005. *FaithFreedom.org*.
www.faithfreedom.org/Testimonials/Hamid50915.htm

Hamilton, Donald. "Lies Terrorists Tell". *Think-Israel*
www.think-israel.org/hamilton.terroristslie.html

Hanson, Victor. "The Mirror of Fallujah No More Passes and Excuses for the Middle East". *Private Papers*, April 4, 2004
www.victorhanson.com/articles/hanson040404.html

Hanson, Victor. "On Being Disliked". *National Review*, April 25, 2005.
www.nationalreview.com/hanson/hanson/200504290803.asp

Hanson, Victor. "1/9/2004: The Same Old Thing".
www.littlegreenfootballs.com/weblog/?entry=9555

Hanson, Victor. "The Whole World is Watching". *National Review Online*, September 10, 2004.
www.victorhanson.com/articles/hanson091004.html

Harris, Dan. "Conservatives Censored on College Campuses? Free Speech Movement Finds New Group of Supporters". *ABC World News Tonight*, February 1, 2005.
www.thefire.org . . . /index.php/article/5208.html

Hawkins, John. "An Interview with Victor Davis Hanson". *Right Wing News*, September 11, 2001.
//rightwingnews.com/interviews/hanson.php

Higgins, Sean. "Militant Islam is Put in Class with Communism, Fascism". *Investor's Business Daily*, August 26, 2002
www.danielpipes.org/article/449

Hodges, Lee. "Moral Credibility". *The Iranian*, March 26, 2002.
www.iranian.com/Opinion/2002/March/Response/

Hodges, Lee. "Victimology". *The Iranian*, March 11, 2002
www.iranian.com/Opinion/2002/March/Victim/

"Homeland Security, State by State". Updated February 16, 2003.
www.standeyo.com/News_Files/NBC/State.defense. prep.html

Horowitz, David. "A Campaign of Lies". *FrontPageMagazine.com*, February 10, 2005.
www.studentsforacademicfreedom.org/archive/2005/February2005/
DHCAIRResponseFpage.Cam . . .

Horowitz, David. "The Campus Blacklist". *FrontPageMagazine.com*, April 18, 2003.
www.studentsforacademicfreedom.org/essays/blacklist.html

Horowitz, David. "The Professors' Orwellian Case". *FrontPageMagazine,com*, December 5, 2003.
www.studentsforacademicfreedom.org/arachive/december/
HorowitzAAUPResponse120503.htm

Horowitz, David and Perazzo, John. "Unholy Alliance: The 'Peace Left' and the Islamic Jihad Against America". *FrontPageMagazine.com*, April 13m 2005
www.frontpagemag.com/Articles/ReadArticle.asp?ID=17702

Horowitz, David. "Ward Churchill is Just The Beginning". *Rocky Mountain News*, February 8, 2005.
www.frontpagemag.com/Articles/ReadArticle.asp?ID=16946

Hosken, Fran. "The Hosken Report: Genital and Sexual Mutilation of Females". Women's International Network News, 4th Ed. Lexington, MA, 1994.

Hosken, Fran. "The Hosken Report: Genital and Sexual Mutilation of Females. 4th Ed. Womens International Network News: Lexington, MA, 1993, pp.114-115, 192-202, 216-218 (notes omitted).

Hughes, Donna. "Iran's Sex Slaves Suffer Hideously Under Mullahs". June 8, 2004.
www.activistchat.com/phpBB2/viewtopic.php?t=2678

Hughes, Donna. "Islamic Fundamentalism and the Sex Slave Trade in Iran".
www.uri.edu/artsci/wms/hughes/iran_sex_slave_trade

Hughes, Donna. "Women and Reform in Iran." February 2000.
www.uri.edu/artsci/wms/hughes/reform/htm

Human Rights in Tunisia: Options and Accomplishments. "Womens' Rights".
www.tunisiainfo.com/documents/options/chapter3.html

Human Rights Watch. "Egypt: Ensure Women's Rights To Divorce". New York: *Human Rights Watch,* 2004
www.hrw.org/english/docs/2004/11/29/egypt9729.htm

"Human Trafficking & Modern-Day Slavery—Pakistan".
//gvnet.com/humantrafficking/Pakistan.htm

Hunting, J.H. "The Protocols of Zion". reprinted from the *Vineyard*, March 1978.
www.cdn-friends-icej.ca/antiholo/protocol.html

Huntington, Samuel. "The Clash of Civilizations". *Foreign Affairs*, Summer 1993, v72, n3, p22(28)
www.alamut.com/sumbj/economics/misc/clash.html

Hurd, Dale. "Putting Tolerance to the Test: The Rise of Islam in Europe".
www.islamreview.com/articles/puttingtolerance.shtml

iafrica.com. "Five Die in Pakistan 'Honour Killing'". January 5, 2005.
www.iafrica.com/news/worldnews/402014.htm

iabolish. "A Problem We Must All Address (cont.)" .2005.
www.iabolish.com/act/abol/profile/marg2.htm

iabiolish. "Becoming A Slave". 2005.
www.iabolish.com/today/experience/becoming.htm

iabolish. ""From Home Care Nurse to Rescuer". 2005.
www.iabolish.com.act.abol/profile/marg1.htm

iabolish. "Going Free". 2005.
www.iabolish.com/today/experience/going.htm

iabolish. "Modern Day Slavery Fact Sheet". 2005.
www.iabolish.com/today/factsheet.htm

iabolish. "Slavery: Worldwide Evil". 2005.
www.iabolish.com/today/background/worldwide-eveil.htm

iabolish. "The Mental Experience". 2005.
www.iabolish.com/today/experience/mental.htm

Ibn Warraq. "Female Genital Mutilation: A Glimmer of Hope in Egypt", n.d.
www.secularislam.org

Ibn Warraq. "Islam's Shame Lifting the Veil of Tears", excerpt from *Why I Am Not Muslim*, Promethius Books, 1995.
www.secularislam.org

Ibn Warraq. "Publishers and the Fear of Muslim Fundamentalists". *ISIS*
www.secularislam.org/news/publishers.htm

Ibn Warraq. "Statement by Ibn Warraq on the World Trade Center Atrocity".
www.sullivan-county.com/news/mine/not_muslim.htm

Ibn Warraq, *Why I Am Not a Muslim*. New York: Prometheus Books, 1995.

"I Married a Terrorist". (author unknown) *National Examiner*, June 27, 2005

International Women's Health Coalition. "Victory for Women in Turkey: New Penal Code Recognizes Women's Bodily Integrity, Sexual Rights".
www.iwhc.org/programs/asia/turkey/index.cfm

ISIS. "A Declaration of the Rights of Women in Islamic Societies"
www.secularislam.org

ISIS. "About Azam Kamguian"
www.secularislam.org

ISIS. "Testimonies: Why I Left Islam"
www.secularislam.org/testimonies/

"Israel—Facts on Prostitution of Women and Children".
www.paralumun.com/issuesisrael/htm

"Islamic Terrorism".
www.youmeworks.com/islamic_terrorism.html

Isreal4Ever. "Arab Child Abuse", November 3, 2003.
www.middleeastinfo.org

"Islam-Terrorism, Inc—Parts I and II".
www.flex.com/~jai/satyamevajate/terrorist.html

"I Was Once a Muslim's Wife (A True Story)"
www.islamreview.com/articles/oncemuslimswife.shtml

Jackson, S. "Nation of Islamic Hatred-Nation of Islam Accuses the United States of Waging A War 'Against Islam'". *Frontpagemag/DiscoverThe Network.org,* February 28, 2005.
www.freerepublic.com/focus/f-news/1352602/posts

Jacobs, Charles. "Becoming Columbia". *Columbia Spectator*, April 11, 2005.
www.columbiaspectator.com/vnews/display.vART/2005/04/11/4259dce9c9205

Jacobs, Charles. "Slavery: Worldwide Evil". *World & I*, April 1996.
www.iabolish.com/today///background/worldwide-evil.htm

Jain, Sandhya. "Saudi Halo Over US Academies". *Pioneer*, May 4, 2004.
www.campus-watch.org/article/id/1260

Jehl, Douglas. "For Shame: A Special Report. "Arab Honor's Price: a Woman's Blood", June 20, 1999.
www.polyzine.com

Jehl, Douglas. "Vote on Women's Rights Shows Deep Rift in Kuwait Society". *New York Times*. December 20, 1999.
www.library.cornell.edu/colldev/mideast/kuwmn2.htm

Jensen, Derrick. "The New Slavery: An Interview with Kevin Bales". *The Sun*, 2001.
www.thesunmagazine.org/slavery.html

Jewish Virtual Library. "Women's Rights in the Arab World". *The American-Israeli Cooperative Enterprise*, 2004.
www.jewishvirtuallibrary.org/jsource/arabwomen.html

Joffe, Alexander. "Academics Against Israel". *FrontPageMagazine*, June 1, 2005.
www.campus-watch.org/article/id/2057

Johnson, Karen. "The Day the Music Died: Women and Girls in Afghanistan", n.d.
www.now.org

"Jordan—Womens Issues".
www.paralumun.com/issuesjordan.htm

Jutta. "Islam Was My Nightmare", april 26, 2005. *FaithFreedom.org.*
www.faithfreedom.org/Testimonials/Jutta50426.htm

Kamguian, Azam. "Against Hijab"March 8, 2001
http://www.secularislam.org

Kamguian, Azam. "Crimes of Honour Women's Tragedy under Islam & Tribal Customs", n.d.
www.secularislam.org

Kamguian, Azam. "Islam and Women's Rights", n.d.
.secularislam.org

Kamguian, Azam. "The Lethal Combination of Tribalism, Islam & Cultural Relativism", January 17-19, 2003.
www.secularislam.org

Kamguian, Azam. "Women in Afghanistan: What Next?", n.d.
www.secularislam.org

Kaplan, David. ":Hearts, Minds, and Dollars". Investigative Report. *U.S News, & World Report*, April 25, 2005.

Kaplan, Lee. "The Saudi Fifth Column on Our Nation's Campuses".
FrontPageMagazine, April 5, 2004.
www.why-war.com/news/2004/04/05/thesaudi.html
www.frontpagemag.com/Articles/ReadArticle.asp?ID=12833

Kaplan, Lee. "SFSU Hosts a Terrorist". *FrontPageMag.com*, May 2, 2005
www.studentsforacademicfreedom.org/archive/2005/May2005/
SFSUhoststerrorist050305.htm

Katulis, Brian. "Women's rights in Focus: Egypt". Findings from May-June 2004 Focus Groups with Egyptian Citizens on Women's Freedom. October 19, 2004.
www.comminit.com/materials/ma2004/materials-1988.html

Katz, Nikki. "Turkish Women's Equal Rights Come Into Effect". 2002.
//womensissues.about.com/library/weekly/aa010202a.htm

Karacan, Serpil. "Will Women's Rights Correct Turkish Wrongs?—Marriage Laws". Contemporary Review. July, 2002.

Khaled, Saudi Araba. "My Testmony", January 13, 2006. *FaithFreedom.org.* www.faithfreedom.org/Testimonials/Khaled.htm

Khan, Lal. "The Menace of Islamic Fundamentalism and the Hypocrisy of Imperialism". October 2000. www.marxist.com/Asia/islamic_fund_ism1100.html

Khaula, Nakata. "Veil: The View from the Inside". Albalagh. n.d.

Khouri, Ghada. "Caught in the Middle" Women in Lebanon". www.geocities,com/Wellesley/3321/win13b.htm

Knappert, Jan. "Review of 'Why I Am Not A Muslim' Far More Dangerous Than Nazism". www.secularislam.org/reviews/knappert.htm

Knight Ridder/Tribune Information Services. "Culture of Death? Palestinian Girl's Murder Highlights Growing Number of 'Honor Killings'". 2003. www.sullivan-county.com/w/cul_death.htm

Koller, Julia. "Female Genital Mutilation", 2001. www.hausarbeiten.de/faecher/hausarbeit/ena/16316.html

The Koran. Translated by N. J. Dawood. London: Penguin, 1956.

"Koran—The Ultimate Truth". www.flex.com/~jai/satyamevajayate/koran/html

Kresta, Al. "Islam and the West: The Treat, The defense". interview with Srdja Trifkovic. May-June 2005
www.think-israel.org/trifkovic.islam.html

Kurtz, Howard. "College Faculties A Most Liberal Lot, Study Finds". *Washington Post*, March 29, 2005.
www.washingtonpost.com/wp-dyn/articles/A8427-2005Mar28.html

Lafflin, John. *The Arabs as Slave Masters*. Englewood: SBS Publishing, Inc., 1982.

Lantos, Tom. "Discrininations Against Women and The Roots of Global Terrorism". *Human Rights Magazine*, Summer, 2002.
www/abanet.org/irr/hr/summer02/lentos/html

Lapkin, Sharon. "Western Muslims' Racist Rape Spree", *FrontPageMagazine.com*, December 27, 2005.
www.frontpagemag.com/Articles/ReadArticle.asp?ID=20646

Lappen, Alyssa. "Ford Has a Better Idea: One Nation Under Allah".
www.think-israel.org/lappen.fordfoundation.html

Lappen, Alyssa. "Triple-Pronged Jihad—Military, Economic and Cultural. Bat Ye'or [Eurabia: The Euro-Arab Axis]". Interview with Bat Ye'or. *Free Republic*, April 5, 2005
ww.freerepublic.com/focus/f-news/1377783/posts

Laqueur, Walter. "The Terrorism To Come".
www.worldthreats.com/al-qaeda_terrorism/The%

Latifa. *My Forbidden Face*. Translated by Linda Coverdale. New York: Hyperion, 2001.

"Lebanon's People Bring About Renaissance of Freedom". *The Daily Star*, March 15, 2005.
www.dailystar.com.lb/article.asp?edition_id=10&
article_id=1343&categ_id=17

Leibovitz, Liel. "Hysteria at Columbia Uiniversity". March 11, 2005
//peaceandjustice.org/article.php?story= 20050314215550955&mode=print()

Lewis, Jone. "Attitudes Toward Women". December 1990.
//womenshistory.about.com/library/ency/blwh_Egypt.htm

Lipkin, Lewis. "The Saudis: The Middle East Mafia".
www.think-israel.org/lew.mafia.html

Lobe, Jim. "'Anti-Islamist' Crusader Plants New Seeds". *antiwar.com*, February 25, 2005.
www.antiwar.com/lobe/?articleid=4963

Lobe, Jim. "Anti-Muslim Activist Plants New Seeds of Hatred". February 27, 2005.
www.dawn.com/2005/02/27/int12.htm

Loflin, Lewis. "Muslim Immigration Must Be Halted".
www.sullivan-county.com/id2/index0.htm

"Loving A Muslim: A Support Group . . ." Loving A Muslim Index.
www.domini.org/lam/

M.A. "My Journey To Freedom", November 13, 2005.
www.faithfreedom.org/Testimonials/MA51114.htm

MacDonald, G. Jeffrey. "Whither Academic Freedom?" *USA Today*, May 17, 2005.
www.usatoday.com/news/education/2005-05-17-collegians_x.htm

Maddex, Bobby. "Three Questions for Thomas Klocek, the Former DePaul University Professor." *The Crux Magazine*, May 25, 2005.
www.freerepublic.com/focus/f-news/1410586/posts
www.cruxmag.com/asset/klocek.html

Mahmood, Hadia. "Is the Islamic Hijab a Women's Right?", n.d.
www.secularislam.org

Mahmoody, Betty and Dunchock, Arnold. *For The Love Of A Child.* New York: St Martin's Press, 1992.

Mahmoody, Betty and Hoffer, William. *Not Without My Daughter.* New York: St Martin's Press, 1987.

Mahmoud, Houzan. "The Killing of Women by Islamic Groups in Iraq Continues Unabated", n.d.
www.secularislam.org

Mallard, Herb. "Arabian Peninsula and the International Sex Slave Trade". Issue #12.
www.sauduction.com/12issue.html

Mallard, Herb. "Can Saudi Princes Be Considered Pedophiles?". Issue #13.
www.sauduction.com/13issue.html

Mallard, Herb. "Dear Reader." Issue #13. p.8.
www.sauduction.com/13issue.html

Mallard, Herb. "Dear Reader." Issue #27. p. 6.
www.sauduction.com/13issue.html

Mallard, Herb. "Devout Muslim Speaks". Issue #32. p. 8.
www.sauduction.com/32issue.htm

Mallard, Herb. "Prince Nayef, Yet Again, Misrepresents the Truth". Issue #22.
www.sauduction.com/22issue.htm

Mallard, Herb. "State Department Child Sex Slave Recruitment". Issue #32.
www.sauduction.com/32issue.htm

Mallard, Herb. "US Children As a Target of the International Sex Slave Trade".
Issue #13.
www.sauduction.com/13issue.html

Mallard, Herb. "US Private Investigator Hunts Saud Family US Child
Kidnappers". Issue #32.
www.sauduction.com/32issue.htm

Mallard, Herb. *statedepartment.com.*
www.statedepartment.com

Manji, Irshad. *The Trouble With Islam*. New York: St Martin's Press, 2003.

Masci, David. "The CQ Researcher: Islamic Fundamentalism". Abstract. *The
CQ Researcher,* Vol 10, No 11, March 24, 2000
www.cqpress.com/context/articles/cqr20000324.html

Mason, Jackie, and Feder, Raoul. "Religion of Hate". *American Spectator*, July 8, 2004.
www.think-israel.org/mason.islam.html

Mason, M. "Egyptian Women Back Circumcision". *Daily Telegraph*, March 17, 1997.
www.hartford-hwp/com/archives/30/150.html

McCormick, Evan. "Lies, Misinformation and CAIR".
FrontPageMagazine.com, August 1, 2003.
//frontpagemag.com/Articles/ReadArticles.asp?ID=9188

McFarquhar, Neil. "Muslim Scholars Increasingly Debate Unholy War". *New York Times*, December 9, 2004.
www.rickross.com/reference/islamic/islamic65.html

Meehan, P. "The Islamic War". October 2001
www.literatus.net/essay/IslamicWar.html

Meir-Levi, David. "Arab Refugees: The Big Arab Lie". May-June 2005.
www.think-israel.org/meir-levi.arabrefugees.html

MEMRI, "Bahraini Women's Rights Activist Ghada Jamshir Attacks Islamic Clerics for Issuing Fatwas Authorizing Sexual Abuse of Infants".
Discovertheneworks.org, December 30, 2005.
www.discoverthenetwork.org/Articles/bahraini.html

Mernissi, Fatima. *Beyond the Veil: Male-Female Dynamics in Modern Muslim Society.* Bloomington and Indianapolis: Indiana University Press, 1987.

Mernissi, Fatema. *Dreams of Trespass: Tales of a Harem Girlhood.* Massachusetts: Addison-Wesley Publishing Company, 1994.

Mernissi, Fatema. *Islam and Democracy: Fear of the Modern World.* Translated by Mary Jo Lakeland. Massachusetts: Addison-Wesley Publishing Company, 1992.

Mernissi, Fatema. *Scherezade Goes West: Different Cultures, Different Harems.* New York: Washington Square Press, 2001.

Mernissi, Fatema. *The Veil and the Male Elite: A Feminist Interpretation of Women's Rights in Islam.* Translated by Mary Jo Lakeland. Massachusetts: Addison-Wesley Publishing Company, 1991.

Miles, Austin. "Public Schools Embrace Islam—A Shocker". January 9, 2002. www.islamreview.com/articles/publicschools.shtml

Millett, Kate and Keir, Sophie. *Going to Iran.* New York: Coward, McCann & Geoghegan, 1982.

Milon, Mizanur. "Americans Should Be Wary of CAIR, ISNA, ICNA, NABIC, Etc." www.prophetofdoom.net/americans_should_be_wary.html

M.L. "Awakening At Last", December 23, 2004. www.faithfreedom.org/Testimonials/ml.htm

"Mohammed—'A True Saint'". www.flex.com/~jai/satyamevajayate.libido.html

"Mohammed's High Regard for Women". www.flex.com/~jai/satamevajayate/playboy.html.

Muravchik, Joshua. "Freedom and the Arab World: Terrorism Thrives Where People Aren't Free". *Middle East Facts*.
www.middleeastfacts.com/arab-freedom-and-terrorism.php

Muslim Refusenik.
www.muslim-refusenik.com/inthenews.html

"Muslim Scholars Increasingly Debate Unholy War". National Commission on Terrorist Attacks Upon the United States. "What to Do? A Global Strategy".
www.9-11commission.gov/report/911Report_Chap12.html

Nazer, Mende and Lewis, Damien, *Slave*. New York: Public Affairs, 2003.

Nelan, Bruce. "The Dark Side of Islam". November 2, 2001.
www.rickross.com/reference/islamic/islamic37.html

Neuwirth, Rachel. "It's France Again!" *Truth News*, September 27, 2004.
www.truthnews.net/world/2004090206/htm

NGO Events/News. "Trafficking and Forced Labor of Children in the United Arab Emirates Continues".
www.mentos.net/events/04newsevernts/omanqataruamain/
children-trafficked.htm

Norland, Joseph. "Professor Merkeley On the Divestment Decision of the World Council of Churches (WWCC)" *Think Israel*
www.think-israel.org/norland.merkeley.html

"Not In Our Town" KQED PBS. Movement in response to hate crimes.
www.pps.org/niot/

Novial, Fabian. "Women's Rights in Arab World Still Lagging Behind". *Middle East Online*, April 28, 2004.
www.middle-east-online.com/english/jordan/?id=5318

Nunnally, Steven. "Nadia Dabbagh"
www.baddteddy.com/missing/nadia.htm

Oh! editions. "Burned Alive". 2003
www.twbookmark.com/books/89/0446533467/chapter_excerpt18578.html

"One Million". *FrontPage Magazine.com*, November 26, 2004.
www.frontpagemag.com/Articles/ReadArticle.asp?ID=16090

Owens, Mackubin. "Against the West: Islamic Radicals Hate Us for Who We Are, Not What We Do" Editorial, July 2004
www.ashbrook.org/publicat/oped/owens/04/occidentalism.html.

Papas, Voula. "Islam and Women's Rights" Atheist Foundation of Australia, Inc.
www.theatheistfoundation.org.au/islamrights.htm

Papas, Voula. "Islam: Scraping Off the Whitewash!"
www.theatheistfoundation.org.au/islamwhitewash.htm

Papps, Nick. "Mother Seeks Paramilitary Help to Get Kids". 5 October, 2002
www.hug-ur-kids.org.au/motherparamilitary.htm

Parker, Ned. "The Veil is Not a Barrier in an Arab Vote". *Christian Science Monitor*. March 12, 1999.
//csmonitor.com/cgi-bin/durableRedirect.pl?/durable/1999/03/12/fp7s1-csm.shtml

Parker, Randall. "Energy Policy, Islamic Terrorism, and Grand Strategy". May 4, 2003. www.parapundit.com/archives/001210.html

Parker, Randall. "Patrick Sookhdeo Describes Muslim TV and Persecution of Christians". *ParaPundit,* June 4, 2003.
www. parapundit.com/archives/001340.html

Peck, Arlene. "Arab Women and Farm Animals".
www.sullivan-county.com/id4/peck2b.htm

Peck. Arlene. "Commentary on Issues in the News by Top Opinion Writers*".
Arlene Peck Archives.*
www.arlenepeck.com/column_archives.htm#revere

Peck Arlene. "I Strive to Be Politically Incorrect!".
www.think-israel.org/peck.incorrect.html

Peck, Arlene. "Stuck Between Iraq and a Hard Place". November 2003. *Wow! It's Arlene Peck Thought Police Archives No 2.* p. 2
www.arlenepeck.com/column_archives_2htm#dysfunctional

Peck, Arlene. "What is All This Insurgent/Militant Stuff? They Are Terrorist!" May-June 2005.
www.think-israel.org/peck.islaminamerica.html

Peck, Arlene. *Wow! It's Arlene Peck Thought Police Archives #1.*
www.arlenepeck.com/column_archives_1.htm

Peck, Arlene. *Wow! It's Arlene Peck Thought Police Archives #3.*
www.arlenepeck.com/column_archives_3.htm

Perazzo, John. "Academic Appeasers". *FrontPage Magazine*, October 2, 2002. www.campus-watch.org/article/id230

Phillips, James. "James A. Phillips on Terrorism". WebMemo #5, October 2, 2001 www.heritage.org/Research/NationalSecurity/WM45.cfm

Pickthall, Marmaduke. *The Meaning of the Glorious Koran.* New York: Dorset Press, n.d.

Pipes, Daniel. "The Abu Ali Case and Balancing Liberties, Security". *New York Sun,* March 1, 2005. www.danielpipes.org/article/2434

Pipes, Daniel. "Advice to non-Muslim Women on Marrying Muslim Men", May 16, 2004. www.danielpipes.org/blog/256

Pipes, Daniel. "Amazon.com's Koran Desecration Problem". *FrontPageMagazine.com,* May 20, 2005. www.danielpipes.org.article/2634

Pipes, Daniel. "'The American Muslim' and Islamist Intentions for the United States", January 26, 2004. www.danielpipes,org/blog/168

Pipes, Daniel. "[American Muslim Group for Policy Planning] Another 'Moderate' Muslim Group". *FrontPage Magazine.com*, December 29, 2004. www.danielpipes.org/article/2315

Pipes, Daniel. "Anti-Israel Terror Backfire". *New York Sun*, April, 2004. www.danielpipes.org/article/1741

Pipes, Daniel. "A Prof[Hamid Dabashi] Tangles the Truth", *FrontPageMagazine.com*. March 31, 2005. //webmail.pas.earthlink.net/wam/msg.jsp?msgid=1410& folder=INBOX&x=1068633084

Pipes, Daniel. "A Room Full of American Muslim Citizens", December 30, 2004. www.danielpipes.org/blog/392

Pipes, Daniel. "'Become a Muslim Warrior'", *Jerusalem Post*, July 3, 2002 www.danielpipes.org/article/430

Pipes, Daniel. "[Beltway Snippers]: Converts to Violecne?" *New York Post*, October 2, 2002 www.danielpipes.org/article/492

Pipes, Daniel. "[Beslan Atrocity:] They're Terrorists—Not Activists". *New York Sun*, September 7, 2004. www.danielpipes.org/article/2066

Pipes, Daniel. "The California Congress of Republicans & Its Strange Friends", December 29, 2003. www.danielpipes.org/blog/149

Pipes, Daniel. "Can Hezbollah and Hamas Be Democratic?". *New York Times*, March 22, 2005. //webmail.pas.earthlink.net/wam/msg.jsp?msgid=1080& folder=INBOX&x=-281606473

Pipes, Daniel. "Capturing Osama". *New York Sun*, March 9, 2004. www.danielpipes.org/article/1624

Pipes, Daniel. "Christians Disappearing from Iraq". *New York Sun*, August 24, 2004.
www.danielpipes.org/article/2033

Pipes, Daniel, and Harris, Jonathan. "Columbia vs. America". *New York Post*, April 1, 2003
www.sullivan-county.com/z/columbia_u.htm

Pipes, Daniel, "Conservative Professors . . ." *Jerusalem Post*, April 12, 2005.
www.campus-watch.org/article/id/1911

Pipes, Daniel. "Conservative Professors, "An Endangered Species". *New York Sun*, April 12, 2005.
www.danielpipes,org/article/2526

Pipes, Daniel. "Constructing a Counterfeit History of Jerusalem". May 11, 2004.
www.danielpipes.org/blog/246

Pipes, Daniel. "Counting Mosques". *New York Post*, February 4, 2003.
www.danielpipes.org/article/10018

Pipes, Daniel. "The Danger Within: Militant Islam in America".
www.pushhamburger.com/militant.htm

Pipes, Daniel. :Deport Saudi Diplomats on Religious Freedom Grounds?", February 28, 2005.
www.danielpipes.org/b.og/414

Pipes, Daniel. "Europeans Fleeing 'Eurabia'", October 10, 2004.
www.danielpipes.org/blog/355

Pipes, Daniel. "Female Desire and Islamic Trauma", May 25, 2004.
//danielpipes.org/articles/1823

Pipes, Daniel. "[Fixing] Islam's Image Problem". *New York Post*, July 29, 2003.
www.danielpipes.org/article/1179

Pipes, Daniel. "Free Muslims March Against Terror", March 31, 2005
www.danielpipes.org/blog/435

Pipes, Daniel. "Girl Scouts Celebrate 'Committing to Hijab'", May 21, 2004
www.danielpipes.org/blog253

Pipes, Daniel. "Harvard Loves Jihad". *New York Post*, June 11, 2002
www.danielpippes.org/article/419

Pipes, Daniel. "Has America Learned from 9/11?" *New York Sun*, November 2, 2004.
www.danielpipes.org/article/2185

Pipes, Daniel. "The Hell of Israel is Better than the Paradise of Arafat". *Middle East Quarterly*, Spring 2005.
www.danielpipes.org/article/2534

Pipes, Daniel. "'History Alive!', Scottsdale Schools, and a Reader's Comment at www.danielpipes.org" Weblog, April 6, 2005.
www.damielpipes.org/blog/

Pipes, Daniel. "Identifying Moderate Muslims". *New York Sun*, November 23, 2004
www.danielpipes.org/articale/2226

Pipes, Daniel. "Islam Driving the Social and Legal Agenda", November 10, 2003
www.danielpipes.org/blog/160

Pipes, Daniel. "Is Turkey Going Islamist?" *New York Sun*, June 7, 2005.
www.danielpipes.org/article/21670

Pipes, Daniel. "The Islamic States of America?" *FrontPageMagazine.com,*
September 23, 2004.
www.danielpipes.org/article/2100

Pipes, Daniel. "It's Okay to 'Become a Muslim Warrior' in California Schools",
December 11, 2003.
www.danielpipes.org/blog/135

Pipes, Daniel. "Jihad and the Professors". *Commentary*, November 2002
www.danielpipes.org/article/498

Pipes, Daniel. "Khaled Abou El Fadl Reveals His Islamist Outlook", February
4, 2005.
www.danielpipes.org/blog/402

Pipes, Daniel. "[Maher Hawash:] The Terrorist Next Door". *New York Post*,
August 12, 2003
www.danielpipes.org/article/1195

Pipes, Daniel. *Militant Islam Reaches America*. New York: W.W. Norton &
Company, 2002.

Pipes, Daniel. "Muslim Europe". *New York Sun*, May 11, 2004
www.danielpipes.org/article/1796

Pipes, Daniel. "My Talk at UC-Berkeley", February 12, 2004
www.danielpipes.org/blog/181

Pipes, Daniel. "Naming the Enemy". *New York Sun*, August 17, 2004.
www.danielpipes.org/article/2021

Pipes, Daniel. "The Need to Name and Know Thy Terrorists". *New York Post*,
November 19, 2002.
www.danielpipes.org/article/943

Pipes, Daniel. "[Nepal and France:] Two Opposite Responses to Terrorism".
New York Sun, September 14, 2004.
www.danielpipes.org/article/2076

Pipes, Daniel. "Protecting Muslims While Rooting Out Islamists". *The Daily
Telegraph (London)*, September 14, 2001.
www.rickross.com/reference/islamic/islamic14.html

Pipes, Daniel. "Radical Islam's Hypocrisy [:The Ehrgott * Okashah Cases]".
New York Sun, January 18, 2005.
www.danielpipes.org/arivle/2348

Pipes, Daniel, "[The RAND Corporation and] Fixing Islam". *New York Sun*,
April 6, 2004.
www.danielpipes.org/article/1704

Pipes, Daniel. "[Samuel Huntington and] American Purposes in Iraq". *New
York Sun*, April 27, 2004.
www.danielpipes.org/article/1763

Pipes, Daniel, "Saudi Arabia Enforces Ramadan on Non-Muslims", October 11, 2004.
www.danielpipes.org/blog/351

Pipes, Danel. "The Saudi Connection: How Billions in Oil Money Spawned a Global Terror Network", December 15, 2003.
www.danielpipes.org/blog/128

Pipes, Daniel. "Saudi Religious Leader Calls for Slavery's Legalization". Weblog. November 7, 2003.
www.danielpipes.org/blog/123

Pipes, Daniel. "The Saudis' Covert PR Campaign". *New York Sun*, August 10, 2004.
www.danielpipes.org/article/2006

Pipes, Daniel. "Saudis Import Slaves to America". *New York Sun*, June 16, 2005
www.danielpipes.org/article/2687

Pipes, Daniel. "Saudi-Supported Mosques and Islamic Research Institutes in the West", January 24, 2005.
www.danielpipes.org/blog/399

Pipes, Daniel. "Saudi Venom in U.S. Mosques". *New York Sun*, February 1, 2005.
www.danielpipes.org/article/2384

Pipes, Daniel. "The Scandal of U.S.-Saudi Relations". *National Interest*, Winter 2002/03.
www.danielpipes.org/article/995

Pipes, Daniel. "Spreading Islam in American Public Schools". *FrontPageMagazine.com*, November 24, 2004. www.danielpipes.org/article/2236

Pipes, Daniel. "Spread Islam or Maintain a High Standard of Living?". May 15, 2004 www.danielpipes.org/blog/258

Pipes, Daniel. "Support the Lesser Evil [in Saudi Arabia}". *The Australian*, May 31, 2004. www.danielpipes.org/article/1842

Pipes, Daniel. "Terrorist Professors in the United States". *Capitalism Magazine*, March 11, 2003. //capmag.com/article.asp?ID=2506

Pipes, Daniel. "[Theo Van Gogh] 'Education by Murder' in Holland". *New York Sun,* November 16, 2004. www.danielpipes.org/article/2218

Pipes, Daniel. "Think Like A Muslim[, Urges 'Across the Centuries']". *New York Post*, February 11, 2002. www.danielpipes.org/article/118

Pipes, Daniel. "To Profile or Not to Profile?". *New York Sun*, September 21, 2004. www.danielpipes,org/article/2091

Pipes, Daniel. "U.S. Islamist Groups Gain from the War on Terror", November 6, 2004. www.danielpipes.org/blog/363

Pipes, Daniel. "U.S. Judge: 'You Are An Insult to the Muslim Faith'",
November 25, 2003.
www.danielpipes.org/blog/145

Pipes, Daniel. "What Are Islamic Schools Teaching?". *New York Sun*, March
29, 2005.
www.danielpiples.org/article/2489

Pipes, Daniel. "What You Can Do to Help Win the War on Terror", February
9, 2005
www. danielpipes.org/blog/404

Pipes, Daniel. "Which Privileges for Islam?" *New York Sun*, March 15,
2005.
www.danielpipes.org/article/2468

Plaut, Steven. "A Few Unfashionable Facts Worth Knowing About the Middle
East". *Think-Israel*
www/think-israel.org/plaut.facts.html

Plaut, Steven. "DeNial at DePaul—the Thomas Klocek Affair".
FrontPageMagazine.com, April 18, 2005.
www.frontpagemagazine.com/Articles/ReadArticle.asp? ID=17728

Pomerantz, Steven. "The Findings of the National Commission on Terrorism".
The American Jewish Committee, August 24, 2000
www.ajc.org/Terrorism/BriefingsDetail.asp?did= 221&pid=739

Poston, D.L. "Female Genital Mutilation", Lecture 11, Fall, 2002.
www.sociweb.tamu.edu/Faculty/POSTON/Postonweb/soci207/foll02/
Lecture11.htm

"Protocols of the Learned Elders of Zion". *Timeline*
www.rotten.com/library/hoaxes/zion-protocols/

Prusher, Ilene. "Small Stepts, But the Pace Quickens". Part 1. *Christian Science Monitor*, August 7, 2000.
www.csmonitor.com/atcsmonitor/specials/women/rights/rights080700.html

Prusher, Ilene. "Symbol of Both Oppression and Freedom". Part 4. *Christian Science Monitor*, August 11, 2000.
www.csmonitor.com/atcsmonitor/specials/women/rights/rights081100.html

Prusher, Ilene. Kuwaiti Women Seek Right to Vote". Part 2. *Christian Science Monitor,* August 8, 2000.
www.csmonitor.com/atcsmonitor/specials/women/rights/rights080800.html

Prusher, Ilene. Two Homes, Two Families, Two Wives". Part 3. *Christian Science Monitor*, December 30, 1999
www.csmonitor.com/atcsmonitor/specials/women/rights/rights123099.html

Pryce-Jones, David. *The Closed Circle An Interpretation of the Arabs*. New York: Harper & Row, 1989

Qurqas, Richard. "Fundamentalists Demand Mafia-Style Protection Money From Copts ". *Middle East Times (Egypt)*.
www.sullivan-county.com/id3/mafia_egypt.htm

Rainbo. "Reference Chart of Types of Female Circumcision/Female Genital Mutilation".
www.rainbo.org

Rashid, Ahmed. *"A Peaceful Jihad, But There Will Be War"*. *The Daily Telegraph*, January 24, 2002.
//ilicas.org/English/enlibrary/libr_07_01_02is.html

"The Religious Mindset of the Terrorists". translation of terrorist letter.
www.islamreview.com/articles/religiousmindset.shtml

Reporter. "Mende Nazer—From Slavery to Freedom". October, 2003.
www.antislavery.org/homepage/news/mendenazarfeature.htm

Reuters. Amnesty Faults Algeria on Women's Rights". January 10, 2005.
www.alertnet.org/thenews/newsdesk/N09141301.htm

Robinson, B.A. "Female Genital Mutilation in Africa, The Mddle East and Far East". Ontario Consultants on Religious Tolerance, March 13, 1998.
www.religioustolerance.org

Robinson, Linda, "Tinker, Tailor, Soldier, Spy", *U.S. News & World Report*, April 25, 2005.

Ross, Brian and Scott, David. "An American Married to Al Qaeda." *ABC News*, December 24, 2004.
//www.alipac.us/article134.html

Rossman-Benjamin, Tammi. "What Ever Happened to Free Speech on College Campuses?" *StandwithUs.com*, June 23, 2005.
www.standwithus.com/news_post.asp?NPI=349

Rotella, Sebastian. "Extremist Threats Put Netherlands in Turmoil". *Los Angeles Times*, November 22, 2004.
www.islamreview.com/articles/extremiststhreats.shtml

5555555455555

55555555555

Roush, Patricia. *At Any Price: How America Betrayed my Kidnapped Daughters for Saudi Oil.* Nashville: WND Books, 2003.

Roush, Patricia. "Pat Roush Commentary"
www.patroush.com

Roush, Patricia. "Pat Roush Commentary". Articles on Sarah Saga's escape from Saudi Arabia. "Sarah and the Saudis", June 17, 2003; "Sarah Walks the Green Mile", June 19, 2003; "Sarah Defies Saudi Thugs, Won't Leave Without Kids!", June 20, 2003; "Sarah's Choices", June 21, 2003; "State's Saudi Problem", July 2, 2003; "Out of Arabia, Sarah Saga To Tell her Story", July 7, 2003; "Saudi Embassy Suites", July 16, 2003.
www.patroush.com

Roush, Patricia. "Pat Roush Commentary", Statement of Alexandria Davis Before the Committee on Government Reform, June 12, 2002
www.patroush.com

Roush, Patricia. "Pat Roush Commentary", Statement of Monica Stowers Before The Committee on Government Reform, June 12, 2002.
www.patroush.com

Roush, Patricia. "Pat Roush Commentary", Statement of Patricia Roush Before The Committee On Government Reform, June 12, 2002.
www.patroush.com

Rubenstein, Sondra. "Book Review—On Honor Killings". The Prism Group, 2003.
www.theprismgroup.org/bookreviewhonor.htm

Rubin, Barry. "Mideast Fantasies". May 2005.
www.think-israel.org/rubin.mideastfantasies.html

Safire, William. "Sharon's Hard Choice". *New York Times*, September 22, 2002.
www.tampabay.primer.org/index.cfm?action= articles&drill=vi . . .

Sagamori, Yashiko. "The Seven Pairs of Asses". *Think-Israel*
www.think-israel.org/sagamori.asses.html

Sagamori, Yashiko. "Twinkle, Twinkle, Little Star". *Think-Israel*
www.think-israel.org/sagamori.twinklestar.html

Salem, Ali. "An Apology From An Arab". *Time Magazine*, September 1, 2002.
www.islamreview.com/articles/apology.shtml

Salmon, Magida. "The Arab Woman", excerpt from Salmon, Magida, et. al.
Women in the Middle East. London: Zed Books, n.d.
www.dhushara.com

Sasson, Jean. *Desert Royal*. London: Penguin Books, 2000.

Sasson, Jean. *Princess: The True Story of Life Behind the Veil in Saudi Arabia*.
New York: William Morrow and Company, Inc., 1992.

Sasson, Jean. *Princess Sultana's Daughters*. New York: Doubleday, 1994.

"Saudi Arabia: Number 1 Terrorist State".
www.sullivan-county.com/id2/list.htm

Schlafly, Phyllis. "Confronting the Campus Leftists". *The Phyllis Schlafly
Report*, April 2004.
www.studentsforacaademicfreedom.org/archive/April2004\
schlaflyreportconfrontingcampusleft04 . . .

Scheindlin, Dahlia. "Democrats or Devils?: A Women's Model Parliament"
www.geocities.com/Wellesley/3321/win11a.htm

Schwind, R.L. "Christian Flights from the MiddleEast".
www.byzantines.net/bycathculture/christflight.html

sciforums.com. ""Muslim Paedophiles & Female Genital Mutilation", August 13, 2004.
www.sciforums.com/showthread.php?t=39586

"Selling of Women in Pakistan".
www. paralumun.com/issuespak.htm

Senior Coordinator for International Women's Issues. "Egypt: Report on Female Genital Mutilation FGM) or Female Genital Cutting (FGC)". State Department, June 1, 2001.

Senior Coordinator for International Women's Issues. "Women and Girls in Afghanistan". State Department, March, 1998.
www.state.gov/www/global/women/

Senior Coordinator for International Women's Issues. "Yemen: Report on Female Genital Mutilation (FGM) or Female Genital Cutting (FGC)". State Department, June 1, 2001.

Sha'arawi, Huda. *Harem Years: The Memoirs of an Egyptian Feminist.* Translated by Margot Badran. New York: The Feminist Press, 1986.

Shaikh, Younus. "Islam and the Woman".
www.mukto-mona.com/Articles/Younus_Shikh/IslamWoman.htm

Shalakamy, Ahmed. "Confessions of a Former Islamist". *FaithFreedom.org/*
www.faithfreedom.org/Testimonials/AhmedShalakamy 50521.hrtm

Shalakamy, Ahmed. "Confessions of a Former Islamist", Part 2, N.M.A.
FaithFreedom.org.
www.faithfreedom.org/Testimonials/AhmedShalakamy 50521.htm

Sharon, Moshe. "The Agenda of Islam—A War Between Civilizations".
www.think-israel.org/sharon.civilizations.html

Sherman, Martin. "There Is a Solution to the Conflict". *Think-Israel*
www.think-israel.org/sherman.solution.html

Shorrosh, Anis. "Twenty-Year Plan for USA: Islam Targets America". *Koenig's
International News.*
www.think-israel.org/shorrosh.islam.html
www.worldnetdaily.com/news/article.asp?ARTICLE_ ID=33898
www.worldthreats.com/general_information/Islam
www.shea-king.com/RadioShows/IslamPlan.html
www.sullivan-county.com/immigration/rob_nothink.htm
www.freerepublic.com/focus/f-news/1364352/posts
www.unknownnews.net/030929hate.html
India.indymedia.org/en/2020/12/2585.shtml
www.hvk.org/articles/1202/200.html
www.ummah.org.uk/forum/showthread.php
www.jihadwatch.org/archives/003797.php
www.jihadwatch.org/archives/001750.php
www.rudehost.com/board/toast.asp?sub=show &action=posts&fid=1&tid=0
www.levitt.com/levletter_2002.html

Short, Tom. "Confused College Students". *ShortNotes*
www.shortreport.com/july_19.htm

Siasoco, Ricco. "Modern Slavery". *Infoplease*, April 18, 2001.
www.infoplease.com/spot/slavery1.html

Siddiqi, Shamim. *Methodology of Dawah Ilallah in American Perspective.*
Brooklyn: The Forum for Islamic Work, 1989
www.dawahinamericas.com/bookspdf/Methodology ofDawah.pdf

Simon, Ahmed. "Islam's Weakness is Islam".
www.islamreview.com/articles/islamsweakness.shtml

Simon, Ahmed. "Biography of Muhammad".
www.islamreview.com/articles/bioofmuhammad.shtml

Simon, Ahmed. "The Character of Tyrants. Similarities Between Hitler,
Muhammad, and Stalin."
www.islamreview.com/articles/tyrants.shtml

Simon, Ahmed. "Why Islam Must Defeat Islam".
www.islamreview.com/articles/mustdefeat.shtml

Sina, Ali. "Islam in Fast Demise".
www.islamreview.copm/articles/fastdemise.shtml

Smith, Grant. "At Your Service: Future U.S. Service Exports to Saudi Arabia".
www.saudi-american-forum.org/Newsletters/SAF_Essay_30.htm

Sina, Ali. "From Belief to Enlightenment: The Treacherous and Arduous Path." *FaithFreedom.org.*
www.faithfreedom.org/Articles/sina/frombelief.htm

Sina, Ali. "Lying For A Good Cause".
www.faithfreedom.org/oped/sina40428.htm

Sina, Ali. "The Traps of Islam: A Commentary on the Testimony of Never A Dhimmi". *FaithFreedom.org*
www.faithfreedom.org/oped/sina41022/htm

Sookhdeo, Patrick. "The Myth of Moderate Islam". *The Spectator*, August 2, 2005.
www.frontpagemag.com/Articles/Printable.asp?ID=18966

Sorokin, Ellen. "'Biased' Professors Posted on Web Site". *Washington Times*, October 6, 2002.
www.campus-watch.org/article/id/224

Souad. *Burned Alive.* Translated by Judith Armbruster. New York: TimeWarner Books, 2004.

Spencer, Robert. "Europe Will Be Islamic By the End of the Century". *Human Events Online*, September 16, 2004.
www.think-isarael.org/spencer.islamiceurope.html

Spencer, Robert. "Islamic Tolerance Alert: Ali Sina Threatened with Death", May 12, 2004.
www.jihadwatch.org/dhimmiwatch/archives/001924.php

Spencer, Robert. *Islam Unveiled*. San Francisco: Encounter Books, 2002.

Spencer, Robert. *Onward Muslim Soldiers*. Washington, DC: Regnery Publishing, Inc., 2003. Spencer, Robert. "Spencer on Rape and Jihad", *Jihad Watch*., September 24, 2004.
www.jihadwatch.org/archives/003309.php

Spencer, Robert. "Why They Hate Us". *Front Page Magazine*, May 6, 2004.
www.think-israel.org/spencer.muslimhate.html

Sperry, Paul. *Infiltration: How Muslim Spies and Subversives have Penetrated Washington*. Nashville: Nelson Current, 2005.

Stakelbeck, Erick. "Islamic Radicals on Campus". *FrontPageMagazine.com*, Aprail 23, 2003.
www.frontpagemag.com/Articles/ReadArticle.asp? ID=7395

"Stand With Us". A pro Israel advocacy organization for a secure future for Israel.
www.standwithus.com

"Stand With Us Campus" Dedicated to presenting facts about Israel on college campuses.
www.standwithuscompus.com

Stock, Barbara. "American Saudi Schools: Home Grown Sleeper-Cells". *ChronWatch*, March 1, 2005.
www.chronwatch.com/content/contentDispaly.asp?aid=13335

"Students For Academic Freedom Mission and Strategy".
www.studentsforacademicfreedom/org/essays/pamphlet.html

"Students for Academic Freedom Second Year Achievement Report".
June 6, 2005.
www.studentsforacademicfreedom.org/letters/LettersJan-May2005/letter-
secondyearachievementre . . .

Sudan Human Rights Organization—Cairo Branch. "On the Removal of
Women's Travel Ban". November 22, 2003.
www.shro-cairo.org/pressreleases/november03/women travelban.ht

"Sudan—Womens Issues".
www.paralumun.com/issuessudan.htm

Sun-Tzu. *The Art of Warfare*. Translated by Roger T. Ames. New York:
Random House (Ballantine Books), 1993

Taheri, Amir. "Culture of Hate".
www.islamreview.com/articles/cultureofhate.shtml

Tavernise, Sabrina. "Shielding Women from a Renewal of Domestic Violence",
October 14, 2004.
www.secularislam.org

"Terrorism Book".
www.youmeworks.com/terrorism_book.html

"Terrorism in America".
www.youmeworks.com/terrorists_among_us.html

"Terrorist Chronology". Federation for American Immigration Reform.
www.sullivan-county.co/id3/fair.htm

"The Arab 'Palestinian' Refugee: So Much Time . . . So Little Learned!"
www.masada2000.org~refugees.html

The Barnabus Fund. "Two Australian Pastors Have Been Taken to Court To Silence Their Criticism of Islam".
www.islamreview.com/articles/pastorcourt.shtml

"The Koran and Paradise".
www.balaamsass.com/alhaj/page6.htm

The Pen vs. the Sword. "The Islamization of American Schools."
www.islamreview.com/articles/islamschool.shtml

"The X-Rated Paradise of Islam".
www.flex.com/~jai/satyamevajayate/heaven/html

"This Makes Me Proud To Be An American!" Ruling by Judge William Young U.S. District Court.
www.islamreview.com/articles/proudtobeamerican.shtml

"Thomas Klocek Roundup". Minion of the Great Satan, March 9, 2005.
www.motgs.com/archives/001476.html

"3/5/2005: The United States of Islam". Map of projected Islamic takeover.
//littlegreenfootballs.com/weblog/?entry=14952_
The_United_States_of_Islam

Tortajada, Ana. *The Silenced Cry*. Translated by Ezra E. Fitz. New York: St Martin's Press, 2004.

Trangsrud, Kristin. "Female Genital Mutilation: Recommendations for Education and Policy". n.d.
www.ucis.unc.edu/resources/pubs/carolina/FGM/FGM.html

Trifkovic, Serge. "Islam and the West: The Threat, The Defense". Interview with Al Kresta, Ave Maria Radio. October 14, 2004.
www.chroniclesmagazine.org/News/Trifkovic04/NewsST101904.html

Tifkovic, Serge, "The Folly of Appeasement", *FrontPageMagazine.com,* December 10, 2002.
www.sullivan-county.com/x/appeasement/htm

Trifkovic, Serge. *The Sword of the Prophet Islam History, Theology, Impact on the World.* Boston: Regina Orthodox Press, 2002.

Trifkovic, Sdrge, "The West Will Pay Dearly For The Devastation of Christianity. Islam Has a Wild Appetite". Translated by Sergey Stefanov. *Pravda,* January 1, 2002.
//English.Pravda.ry/main/2002/01/30/26099.htm

Truthseeker. "A Truth Seeker Who Found The Truth". *FaithFreedom.org.*
www.faithfreedom.org/Testimonals/Truthseeker50510.htm

Tunisia Online (Tunis). "Increasing Role of Women in Decision-Making Process". June 2, 2003.
//allafrica.com/stories/200306020237.html

"UC Irvine Course Description: American Unilateralism Responsible for Islamic Barbarism". *Mere Rhetoric,* June 1, 2005.
www.mererhetoric.com/archives/112721417.html

"UC Irvine Muslims React to Anti-Terroirsm Memorial".
Mere Rhetoric, February 3, 2005.
www.mererhetoric.com/archives/11271271.html

UK/BM-32 Translation. "Al-Qaeda's Instructions To its Adepts". pdf document a
accessed from: Pipes, Daniel. "Is Turkey Going Islamist?" *New York Sun*,
June 7, 2005.
www.danielpipes.org/article/21670

Unger, Craig. *House of Bush, House of Saud: The Secret RelationshipBetween
the World's Two Most Powerful Dynasties*. New York: Scribner, 2004

United Nations Commission of Human Rights. "Trafficking and Forced
Labour of Children in the United Arab Emirates (UAE)". Geneva 16, June 20,
2003. www.antislavery.org/archive/submission/submission2003-UAE.htm

UPI. "Iran Reins In Women's Rights Gains". *Washington Times*. September
23, 2004.
//washingtontimes. com/upi-breaking/20040923-102112-54r.htm

UPI. "Turkey's New Year Marks Women's Rights". *Washington Times*. January
1, 2002.
www.polygamyinfo.com/intnalmedia%20 plyg%20124washtimes.htm

U.S. State Dept. "Pakistan (Tier 2-Watch List)". Trafficking in Persons Report,
June 14, 2004.
//gvnet.com/humantrafficking/Pakistan-2.htm

"University of Jihad". *The Straits Times*, December 15, 2002.
www.rickross.com/reference/islamic58.html

Van Nattan, Steve, editor. "Muslims Leaving Islam—Tip of the Iceberg" Appendix Nineteen.
www.blessedquietness.com/alhaj/append-19.htm

Walker, Alice. *Warrior Marks*. Florida: Harcourt Brace & Company, 1993.

Weltch, Liz. "A Horror Story Every Woman Must Read". *Rozaneh Magazine*, July/August 2002.
www.freerepublic.com/focus/news/742564/posts

Welty, William. "Al-Takeyyah: Lying for Allah". *The Islam Commentaries*.
//islamcommentaries.com/lying/

Welty, William. "Official Muslim Prayers of Hate Toward Israel and the United States".
//islamcommentaries.com/prayers.htm

Welty, William. "The Lie is Different At Every Level". *Israel National News*, June 14, 2004.
www.israelnationalnews.com/print.php3?what=article&id=3798

"What are 'The Protocols of the Elders of Zion?"
www.holocaust-history.org/short-essays/protcols.shtml

"Why Islamists and the Left Hate Daniel Pipes".
www.sullivan-county.com/id2/index2.htm

Williams, Carol. "The Seattle Times: 'Honor Killing' Shakes Up Sweden After Man Slays Daughter Who Wouldn't Wed". *The Seattle Times*, 2003.
www.sullivan-county.com/id4/honor_kill.htm

Windfall. "Feeling the Birth Throe", January 1, 2005. *FaithFreedom.org*
www.faithfreedom.org/Testimonials/windfall.htm

WIN News. "Tunisia: Legal and Social Status of Women—Brief Article".
Winter, 2001.
www.findarticles.com/p/articles/mi_m2872/is_1_27/ai_71563377

Winston, Emmanuel. "Identifying Islamists on Campus:".
www.think-israel.org/winston.campus.html

Winston, Emanuel, "Rice's 'Viable Palestinian State' Would Shrink Israel
Out of Jordan Valley and Most of West Bank". *Think-Israel*
www.think-israel.org/winston.ricepasstate.html

Wistrich, Robert. "The New Islamic Fascism". *The Jerusalem Post*, November
16, 2001.
www.sullivan-county.com/id3/islamic_fascism2.htm

Womankind Worldwide. "Womankind and Women's Rights in Sudan", 2003.
www.womankind.org.uk/global%20reach/East%20Africa/sudanpf.html

Women for Women's Rights. "Women, Sexuality and Social Change in the
Middle East and Mediterranean". September 2001.
www.wwhr.org/id_658

Women for Women's Human Rights. "Women's Human Rights in the New
Turkish Penal code: The Success of the Campaign for the Reform of the Turkish
Penal Code from a Gender Perspective". n.d.
www.wwhr.org/id_911

"Women's Human Rights in Egypt".
www.paralumun.com/issuesegypt.htm

Women's Issues Network. "Profile of An Abuser".
www.paralumun.com/issuesabuser.thm

"Wondrous Treatment of Women in Islam".
www.flex.com/~jai/satyamevajayate/women.html

World Health Organization. "Clitoridectomy". n.d.
www.iifhr.com/womens%20website/clitoridectomy.html

World Health Organization. "FGM Defined by the World Health Organization".
n.d.
www.circumstitions.com/FGM-defined.html

WorldNetDaily, "Muslim in 'Personal Attack' on Home Depot", December 31,
2005
www.worldnetdaily.com/news/article.asp?ARTICLE_ ID=48139

WorldNetDaily, "'Palestinians agree': Wipe Israel Off Map", January 1, 2006.
www.worldnetdaily.com/news/article.asp?ARTICLE_ ID=48146

WorldNetDaily, "PA TV: Expel Israelis from Israel", December 30, 2005.
www.worldnetdaily.com/news/article.asp?ARTICLE_ ID=48129

Ye'or, Bat. "Arafat's Legacy for Europe". *FrontPage Magazine.com*, November
16, 2004.
www.frontpagemag.com/Articles/Read/Article.asp?ID=15962

Ye'or, Bat. "Culture of Hate: A Racism Which Denies the History and Suffering of Its Victims". National Coalition for Israel.
www.internationalwallofprayer.org/A-067-Culture-of-Hate.html

Ye'or, Bat. "Eurabia and Euro-Arab Antisemitism". *FrontPageMagazine.com*, April 5, 2004.
www.frontpagemag.com/Articles/ReadArticle.asp?ID=12857

Ye'or, Bat. *Eurabia: The Euro-Arab Axis.* Cranbury, NJ: Associated University Presses, 2005.

Ye'or, Bat. "Eurabia The Road to Munich . . ." *National Review Online*, October 9, 2002.
www.nationalreview.com/comment/comment-yeor100902.asp

Ye'or, Bat. "The Euro-Arab Dialogue and the Birth of Eurabia". translated from the French. *Observatoire du monde juif,* December 2002, bulletin no. 4/5. p. 4
www.dhimmitude.org/archive.by_eurabia_122002_eng.doc

Ye'or, Bat. "Eastern Christians Torn Asunder". translated by Nidra Poller.
www.islamreview.com/articles/easternchristiansprint.htm

Ye'or, Bat. "European Fears of the Gathering Jihad". *FrontPageMagazine*, February 21, 2003.
www.islamreview.com/articles/europeanfrears.shtml

Ye'or, Bat. *Islam and Dhimmitude: Where Civilizations Collide.* Lancaster: Fairleigh Dickinson University, 2002.

Ye'or, Bat. "Islamic Encounters, Beware Historical Pitfalls". *National Review*, February 3, 2003.
www.netanyahu.org/isenbewhispi.html

Ye'or, Bat. "Jihad and Human Rights Today. An Active Ideology Incompatible with Universal Standards of Freedom and Equality."
www.islamreview.com/articles/humanrights.shtml

Young, Marlene. "The Truth About the Sharon Expulsion-of-Jews Plan". *Think-Israel*
www.think-israel.org/young.garules.html

Zeidan, David. "The Islamic Fundamentalist View of Life as a Perennial Battle". *Middle East Review of International Affairs Journal*. Vol 5, No 4, December 2001.
//meria.idc.ac.il/journal/2001/issue4/jv5n4a2.htm

Zwick, Israel. "Dismantle Refugee Camps, Not Settlements". *Think-Israel*
www.think-israel-org/zwick.gaza.html